More praise for
A PIECE OF MY HEART

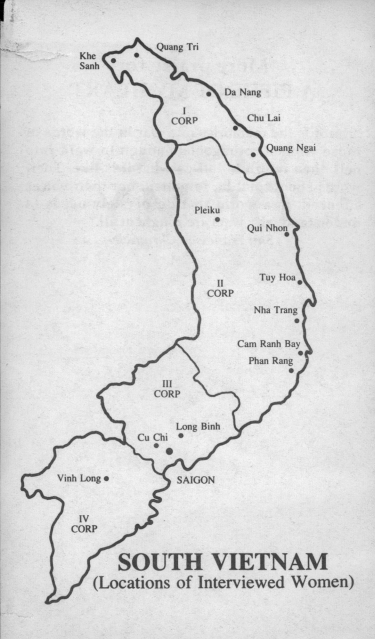

Khe
Sanh

Quang Tri

Da Nang

I
CORP

Chu Lai

Quang Ngai

Pleiku

Qui Nhon

II
CORP

Tuy Hoa

Nha Trang

Cam Ranh Bay
Phan Rang

III
CORP

Long Binh

Cu Chi

Vinh Long

SAIGON

IV
CORP

SOUTH VIETNAM
(Locations of Interviewed Women)

A PIECE OF MY HEART

THE STORIES OF TWENTY-SIX AMERICAN WOMEN WHO SERVED IN VIETNAM

Keith Walker

Foreword by Martha Raye

BALLANTINE BOOKS • NEW YORK

A Ballantine Book
Published by The Ballantine Publishing Group
Copyright © 1985 by Keith Walker

All rights reserved under International and Pan-American Copyright Conventions. Published in the United States by The Ballantine Publishing Group, a division of Random House, Inc., New York, and simultaneously in Canada by Random House of Canada Limited, Toronto.

http://www.randomhouse.com

Library of Congress Catalog Card Number: 85-19416

ISBN 0-345-33997-5

This edition published by arrangement with Presidio Press

Photograph Credits:

All chapter opening photographs by Keith Walker, with the following exceptions: p. 93 by Ann Auger, p. 133 by Sara McVicker, and p. 329 by Penni Evans.

Photographs in photo sections were provided by the women themselves unless otherwise noted.

Cover photo by John Olson and UPI/Bettman Newsphotos

Manufactured in the United States of America

First Ballantine Books Edition: May 1987

18 17 16 15 14 13 12 11

For Anne

CONTENTS

FOREWORD

MILLIONS OF WORDS HAVE BEEN PRINTED AND PUBLISHED about the Vietnam War. So why more words from me? You may think, "Old big mouth is at it again," but I do have a good reason for writing a foreword to this book. It's to help give some public recognition where it's long overdue—to the American women who served so admirably in Vietnam.

Reading these interviews brought back a flood of memories for me. I know what these women experienced (and the memories they carry with them), because I was there too. I was in that war-torn country each year from 1965 until the end of the war. I spent over two years of my life there, entertaining, nursing, visiting bases, camps, and field units all over Vietnam. I saw these dedicated women at their workplaces—the hospitals, staff offices, USO centers, Red Cross units. I saw what they did and how much they were needed.

I also understand *why* these women went to Vietnam, because it's the same thing that brought me back year after year—because American fighting men were there, and I am an American. It may sound corny to some people, but it's true. I felt privileged to be there—to be able to work with these women, to take care of our wounded soldiers, to bring a laugh to some lonely kid. The women who served in Vietnam worked phenomenally long hours under uncomfortable and dangerous conditions. The "hospitals" were often tents on the edge of combat zones. Few people realize that women were wounded in Vietnam; a few were killed. I was in many combat actions and was wounded twice.

I've often said that these American women should have been given a ticker tape parade when they returned home! But that didn't happen—they have never received any recognition. In Vietnam the troops let us know we were appreciated; we could be proud of what we were doing. Back in the U.S., everyone wanted to forget the war. Now, ten years later, people are asking what happened there. I think it's important that they know women did their share, *more* than their share, if that's possible. Our country owes them profound thanks. I'm proud to be part of this book because finally their story is being told.

Martha Raye

ACKNOWLEDGMENTS

I WOULD LIKE TO MAKE A SPECIAL ACKNOWLEDGMENT here for each of those women whose stories, for varying reasons, have not been included in this book. They create, nevertheless, a collective spirit which has a most tangible presence in these pages: Carli Numi, Marianne Jacobs, Shirley Bowington, Jane Thompson, Madelon Visintainer, Saralee McGoren, Norma Griffiths-Boris, Pat Rumpza, Placida McGowan, Pamela White, Kathy Thompson, Peggy Tuxen, Elaine Davies, and Bobbi Lee.

To the women in my immediate life, my wife Anne and daughters Julie and Christina, I must pay tribute for sharing, with such delicate balance, the roller-coaster ride of emotions that I have brought home with me throughout the past three years. And thanks are also due my mother for her belief in this book from the beginning.

I owe a huge debt to all the male Vietnam veterans who have shared their lives with me. In them, I have recognized a courage and forbearance that mark the unique qualities of a truly remarkable generation of Americans. Among them, individual credit for help with this book is due: Jeff Wilcox, Jim Newman, Jeff Ramsdell, and Richard Castro.

I am grateful to Gloria Emerson for her much needed advice regarding the early manuscript and to Joan Griffin, my editor at Presidio Press, for her vision and support during each stage of its development.

Warmest regards go to Ethel and Stephen Dunn and Susan Miller for their excellent transcription and word processing services.

How do I thank a friend like Steve Ajay who has so unselfishly shared his enthusiasm and knowledge with me?

I can simply say that he has made a major contribution to this book.

Finally, I would like to call attention to the extraordinary contribution that Lynda Van Devanter, army nurse at Pleiku and Vietnam veteran activist, has made. She has been a pioneer in securing recognition and support for those women, each and every one, who went to war in Vietnam. We all owe her a great deal.

A PIECE OF MY HEART

INTRODUCTION

I HAD BEEN INVOLVED WITH THE VIETNAM VETERANS community for several months, working on a photo essay about them, but had yet to locate a woman who was in Vietnam during the war. Then in February 1983, I was introduced to Rose Sandecki, director of the Veterans Outreach Center in Concord, California, and arranged an interview with her. For an hour and a half Rose told me of things I couldn't have imagined: how close to the war women actually were, the details of her daily routine as an emergency room nurse in Cu Chi and Da Nang, how deeply the experience had affected her life.

Then she told me of her efforts to locate other women across the country who might be experiencing the problems that she and a dozen of her peers in the Bay Area discovered they shared. They all had experienced difficulty in readjusting to life even after being back from Vietnam for as many as fourteen years.

I was stunned by what Rose told me, yet there was something beyond that, something in her eyes, an intangible, haunting presence that really drew me in—that interview was to determine what I would be doing for the following two years and would lead to the making of this book.

Rose asked me why I was interested in Vietnam veterans. I wasn't really sure myself, but in my explanation I remember speaking of a need to examine my own feelings about the war and maybe reconcile the conflicting emotions that I still carried with me. During the war I was teaching college in the San Francisco area and was constantly aware of the students' dilemma in dealing with Vietnam. The young men were facing the draft, and because I had been drafted and sent to Korea when I was their age, I had definite opinions on that subject. I was strongly against our involvement and in sympathy with the people in the anti-war movement, but having been a soldier, I couldn't abandon the people who were going over there. Their lives were on the line, whether or not our government was right in sending them there. I guess you could say, to use a contemporary phrase, I was able to separate the warriors from the war.

Twelve years later I found myself wondering about these people, waiting to hear their stories firsthand. What had it really been like for them in Vietnam? How were they doing today?

Immediately after meeting Rose, I shifted all my efforts into research on women who were in Vietnam. I learned that before 1982 the official estimates had varied from five thousand to fifty-five thousand women in-country, an inconsistency that seemed absurd. The fluctuating figures were due, in part, to the integration of the service records during those years (enlisted men and women became enlisted persons, obscuring the exact number of women). But also, the military has always been guarded in its statistics about women who enter any war zone. In 1983 the official estimates said that seventy-five hundred military women and the same number of civilian women had been in Vietnam during the war years.

I was amazed that fifteen thousand women had been in Vietnam and yet I had heard nothing about them in the aftermath of the war. I think I was typical of the majority of Americans; as the meager file of clippings I had collected indicated, there just had been very little information about the women in any of the media. Why hadn't movies been made about their war, their homecomings? Was it because there were so few of them relative to the male soldiers, or do we actually have a kind of blind spot about the subject? I did a bit of speculation.

According to military policy, women are not supposed to be in life-threatening situations in a war zone, and therefore we have never developed an image of that in our minds. We think of men in combat, and women safely in the rear echelon in offices and hospitals.

But in Vietnam there were no safe areas; so, it seems, we must have been unwilling to admit the possibility that women were indeed in dangerous situations. If we didn't think about them being there, then they were not in danger.

After a couple of months, I went back to talk to Rose. I told her I wanted to start work on a book and thought that it could help her in the work she was doing for women veterans. I said that it was about time the women's experience in Vietnam was heard; she agreed to help me get started.

Although I became very involved, very quickly, the existence of this book is still somewhat of a miracle. Because of the lack of information about women in Vietnam and the fragile threads of communication among them, they were difficult to locate. I must have written twenty-five letters that were unanswered. Another ten came back "returned to sender." A dozen phone calls turned up "wrong numbers."

When I did contact a new person, it was sometimes equally hard to persuade her to talk about her experiences over there. More than one canceled her interview after a pleasant, positive conversation on the telephone, suddenly changing her mind at the last minute. I was turned down cold by several women even after having been directed to them by a friend, and more than one was quite hostile in the process.

Then, because I had promised each person the right to read and approve her transcript before releasing it, six stories were never returned to me. I spent a year telephoning and writing these women, offering encouragement, trying to persuade them to go over the transcript and send it back. Some said they intended to do so but "never seemed to find the time." I didn't realize it at first, but most of them were having a great deal of difficulty reading those stories—going back yet again to the memories of Vietnam.

The women began to trust me as I became acquainted with them. I was referred from one to another once it became clear that I was making a book in which their stories would be allowed to stand on their own, that I wasn't going to exploit or alter the material for my own purposes, that I cared.

In a short period, I was completely involved in their "cause." As each new interview was completed, I learned another subtlety of the power that Vietnam held over them. There was a lot of emotional exchange taking place here; bonds were formed as they shared their memories with me. I found myself becoming a kind of messenger, passing information from one person to the next, relating the reactions to Vietnam that they held in common. Several remarked, "Other women have talked about having this problem?"—realizing they weren't alone in those reactions. My understanding increased along with their awareness of one another as the bits and pieces of their stories emerged.

This involvement became the heart of my motivation to continue the work. Granted, I was gathering material for a book, and it would, no doubt, be a very special book. But I was completely caught up in the process of meeting and listening to these women. It was as if I were on the other side, a part of the women's experience, rather than a writer working on a book about that experience.

I asked each of them to tell me about Vietnam (as much or as little as she was willing to recall), a little about how she got there in the first place, and then to follow up by talking about her life after coming home. For some, the memories came easily, but for others, recalling their experiences in Vietnam was a painful process. During many of the interviews there were long silences on the tapes. They are indicated in this book by a series of dots. But the dots can't possibly describe a moment when, at a dining room table late at night with tears welling in a woman's eyes, a sentence would drift away. There were times when the flow of a memory would take the person to such an unpleasant place that she would hesitate and then shift her trend of thought to avoid it. Some pauses lasted until the silence in the room became impossible to endure: during one woman's attempt to describe the scene in her hospital during the Tet offensive, there developed a pause of at least three minutes. I turned the tape recorder off.

And this was not an unusual incident. I found myself asking fewer and fewer questions; in fact, I made a serious point to interrupt only when a word or phrase was unclear. I became unwilling to influence the flow of recollection even if it meant that a degree of continuity or clarity might be sacrificed. There was a transformation taking place, a magical kind of presence reached by each woman at some point during our meeting, where past and present became one. I recognized it; it was made of the same substance that I had sensed in that first conversation with Rose.

In these stories the women speak casually of the extremes of their experience in Vietnam: Red Cross women being fired upon in helicopters on their way to fire bases and outposts or stranded in a jungle clearing with no help in sight; nurses routinely working twelve-hour shifts six days a week and often much longer during mass casualties while rocket attacks went on outside their hospitals; a Special Services worker being flown out to a safe area during the Tet offensive, her helicopter lifting off as the mortar rounds walked in across the field.

Regardless of the nature of each woman's job and the extent of the immediate danger she may have been exposed to, they all describe how they had to ''stuff'' their emotions to offset the unusual kinds of stress they constantly lived with. Whether that stress was caused by being under rocket attack, or having to deal with horribly wounded patients on a day-in, day-out basis, or losing friends, or feeling the pressures of sexual harassment, each was forced to build an emotional wall around herself in order to work at her job and keep mind and soul together.

Then for many there were the ambiguous feelings about the Vietnamese people, because the ''enemy'' was not so easily defined. And, for some, there developed a dark cloud of disillusionment: a sense of the ultimate possibility that everything they were going through—the lives lost, the suffering, a country and its people being devastated—was for nothing.

There was another kind of extreme, the elation of working at the peak of one's physical and mental abilities, knowing that despite the way the war was going, what she was doing as an individual *counted*. In the words of one emergency room nurse, it was a feeling of "knowing that I could handle anything they threw at me." Vietnam became a year-long supercharged existence completely isolated from the rest of the world. These women lived on an emotional high that, when it was over, left only one way to go. Some refer to themselves as being "adrenaline junkies" when they first came home. They were so used to functioning under extremely demanding and hectic work conditions that the everyday concerns of life in the States seemed petty. Lin McClenahan describes it well: "I couldn't get excited about the fact that the morning paper was twenty minutes late, for example."

Many women went from job to job, searching for the challenge they had known in Vietnam. Many describe the difficulties they had in establishing long-term personal relationships; they found most Americans to be shallow and self-centered, not wanting to know about the war. Several had difficulties in discussing, even with their families, their feelings about what they had been through. Almost all of them considered going back to Vietnam.

So, the women brought their ghosts back with them just as the men did. And they too have had their nightmares, flashbacks, depressions, and suicidal thoughts. (I have seen the scars on wrists carefully concealed beneath watchbands.) Back home, sadly, they have been left on their own to cope, to resolve, each in her own way, all of these conflicts. Then, once aware of the need—ten, twelve, fifteen years later—in an echo of their camaraderie in Vietnam, they take care of their own. This is a very real process, these women reaching out to one another, and one that will take years before each will have made her own peace with the Vietnam War. I get the distinct impression that none will be satisfied until they bring everybody "back home."

These are the stories of twenty-six American women who went to war. You will experience the strength they all possess—a strength I have come to know well these past two years, in meeting them, in editing their stories, and in sharing their concerns. I want to thank them for opening their hearts to me, each aware of the pain and unsettling it would cause in her life. I am proud to have earned their acceptance, and because of it, my life will always be richer.

If, through my involvement while making this book, I took a first step toward my own reconciliation of feelings about the Vietnam War, perhaps in reading it you will be allowed that same beginning.

Rose Sandecki

12TH EVAC. HOSPITAL,
CU CHI—OCT. '68 TO MAR. '69

95TH EVAC. HOSPITAL,
DA NANG—MAR. '69 TO OCT. '69

In 1979, the Veterans Administration established ninety outreach centers across the country providing readjustment counseling and other services for Vietnam-era veterans. An early motto, "Help without hassles," perfectly describes the tone of the centers: a place without all the bureaucracy and red tape of the VA, staffed by professionals, a majority of whom are Vietnam veterans themselves. The success of the centers is now being fully realized, with the number having grown to 136 (in 1984). In September of 1981, Rose Sandecki was appointed as team leader (director) of one of the centers. Besides her regular duties in this position, she has been an outspoken advocate for women veterans' needs both in and out of the system.

My uncle Frank had been in Marines during World War II, an uncle that I was very close to, my mother's youngest brother. When he came back from the Marines, at age thirty-six, he went into the Franciscan Seminary to become a priest—came back from Iwo Jima a changed man. He went through a severe depression and as a result couldn't finish the seminary. He then lived in my grandmother's house and when I was a freshman in high school, my uncle took a gun and killed himself. He died because of changes in his behavior brought on by the war. I guess you could call it PTSD from World War II, and it was a classic case of it. That is probably one of the reasons I'm doing this kind of work now, because of my personal feelings about what happened in my family as a result of war.

I was feeling somewhat restless in Buffalo. I had been in nursing about seven years, having graduated from a three-year nursing school and then gone back to school to get my BS in nursing. I had a couple of job opportunities, but none of them were that exciting to me. This was in the spring of '68, and the war was really building up. I remember watching the news every night, seeing in full, glorious color the stretchers with the young guys on them, really torn up, coming off the dustoffs. I felt I had some talents as a registered nurse, a professional nurse, and probably could offer something to those young men over there.

Going into the military was not my first choice. I wanted to go over as a civilian. Checked out agencies like AID and Tom Dooley's medical organization, and every one of those was a two-year contract, and it was working strictly with Vietnamese. That was not why I wanted to go to Vietnam.

I went down to the Navy recruiter and was told I was too old (I was twenty-six or twenty-seven). The Air Force told me I would have to spend at least one year in the States before they would train me as a flight nurse, to go over to Vietnam. I said, "I want to go as soon as I can, while I feel like it, while I've got the spirit that has moved me." Only the Army would guarantee that I could be over within a certain period of time. So much so that they had the recruiter on the phone from Buffalo to Washington, D.C., letting me talk to the individuals there with a guarantee that I would be in Vietnam within three months. And that did happen indeed.

I went to the 12th Evac Hospital at Cu Chi. My first job was a head nurse, surgical intensive care unit, recovery room. I was a captain—because I had seven years' experience in nursing and a bachelor's degree when I joined the Army. And in days of war they give rank out like candy. I had very little experience in recovery and no experience in surgical intensive care units. I had graduated from nursing school in 1960 when ICUs weren't around. They were just starting to be thought about. When I was told my assignment would be head nurse of this ward, I said, "No, I don't want that," because I'd never set foot in an ICU. I quickly learned you never say no in the Army; I had this job whether I wanted it or not.

I couldn't believe the numbers of people coming in, the numbers of beds and the kinds of injuries that I saw in front of me—I really wasn't prepared for that. This was in October of '68, it was what they called "post-Tet"—after the Tet offensive—but it was extremely busy. As head nurse, my job was basically to see to it that all patients were taken care of as efficiently and quickly and in the best care possible. The Medical Corps's motto was, and still is, I guess, "Preserve the fighting strength." The idea of working in a military hospital is to patch up the soldier so he can go back to the battle again. It was the whole theme of what was going on over there. It wouldn't be unusual when guys would come in with multiple frag wounds, be treated, go to surgery and have the tissue around the injury debrided, then be sent to Japan where they would do a DPC (delayed primary closure) of this open wound, and then sent back to duty. As long as an individual didn't lose a leg, arm, or an eye, as long as they were walking, they would go back to the boonies. So my job as head nurse was to make sure the patients were taken care of—always helping. I mean, I didn't sit behind a desk and order the junior nurses or corpsmen around. I was pitching in with the rest of them.

When I look back on it, I was naive when I walked through those doors. I learned a lot very quickly, seeing the types of casualties and the numbers of them. They were all so young. Seeing this on a daily basis twelve to fourteen hours a day, six or seven days a week, I think that I became somewhat callous and bitter. You also learned that you became almost like a commodity because you were a woman. After working twelve-hour shifts with all the blood and gore, you would change into a civilian dress to go to one of the local officers' clubs. We were chauffeured in helicopters, with the guns on the side, that would take six or seven of us up to an officers' club. You couldn't sit still, just have a drink and relax. There would be one guy after another coming up and more or less doing his number on you: "I haven't seen a round-eye in six months. Would you dance with me?" You'd say, "No, I'm tired. I just want to sit and put my feet up." They wouldn't take no for an answer and would play this guilt thing like, "God, you don't know how bad I'm feeling. Just one dance, that's all." So you would dance and drink until two or three in the morning, then at six go back to the blood and guts of the war again. The initial two or three months was getting used to the pace of the twelve to thirteen hours of work and then the three or four hours of play. And it was a pressure kind of play because if you didn't go to the officers' club there was something wrong with you. If you stayed back in your hooch by yourself or stayed and talked to a couple of the other nurses, you were accused of being a lesbian, or you would be accused of having an affair with one of the doctors. You know, you are damned if you do and damned if you don't. After a period of four or five months, I decided that I really didn't care what people said about me. If I choose not to go to these clubs and parties, I'm not going to do it . . . and I probably became somewhat of a recluse. So those are some of the changes that I went through personally in Vietnam.

The way of dealing with the sheer amount of patients, the long hours in the hospital, was by putting up a wall, the emotional numbing that we talk about. I think it built up over a period of time. Each day I went in and the more I saw, the thicker this wall became; it was sort of a skin protecting me from what was going on. Look at it from the point of view of a patient: how would you, as a patient, feel if you had this hysterical nurse that was crying and sobbing because there is someone in there that is badly maimed or is going to die? We had to be effective for the next people that were coming in. Nurses are trained to take care of other people, not look at their own feelings and what is going on with them. That is part of the medical profession.

A story from Cu Chi, another example of the sort of rude awakening to my military naiveté. I got a phone call on the ward from the chief nurse, saying, "You've got a patient there that is going to get an award. Make sure that the bed has clean sheets, the area is straightened up, and the ward looks good." Which really turned me off to begin with: Let's clean up the ward because we've got VIPs coming in. Well, the VIP happened to be the general of the 25th Infantry Division along with his aide and an entourage of about twelve people. And this patient, when he came through the recovery room the day before, had remembered me. This was his second visit to us. He had been there three months before with frag wounds, had been sent back to the jungle, and came back this time with both of his legs blown off—he was all of about twenty years old. When he was waking up from the anesthesia, he remembered me. He started kidding me about how I had made him cough and deep-breathe so he wouldn't come down with pneumonia. We were kidding around, and he said, "Don't you remember me, ma'am?" I said, "Oh, yeah." But I really didn't because there were just so many of them. . . . The entourage was coming to give him an award because he happened to be number twenty thousand to come through the 12th Evac Hospital. In 1968 there were twenty-four

Army evac hospitals in Vietnam, and he was number *twenty thousand* through *one* of twenty-four Army hospitals. We are not talking about the Air Force hospitals, the Navy hospitals . . . but twenty thousand through one hospital. So, for this distinction, the general comes in and gives him a watch. They have this little ceremony, give him a Purple Heart and the watch. I'm standing off in the corner watching all this, and as the general handed him the watch— "From the 25th Infantry Division as a token of our appreciation"—the kid more or less flings the watch back at him and says something like, "I can't accept this, sir; it's not going to help me walk." I couldn't really see the expression on the general's face, but they all left after this little incident. I went over and just put my arms around him and hugged him . . . and if I remember correctly, I started crying . . . and I think he was crying. I really admired him for that. That was one time that I let the feelings down and let somebody see what I felt. It took a lot for him to do that, and it sort of said what this war was all about to me . . . 1968.

Our chief nurse in Vietnam was a very warm, caring colonel in the Army Nurse Corps—not too many of them around, but here was one—and when we came in-country she recommended that we work six months in a "busy" area and six months in a "nonbusy" area, for "your own psychological welfare." I think it was an excellent suggestion. The six months in Cu Chi were extremely busy, extremely hard. Then I transferred up to Da Nang, which was still busy, with critical things going on, but not as hectic as Cu Chi. It wasn't in an area that was quite as dangerous as Cu Chi was . . . and it's hard to make that comparison, because the war was all around . . . but it seemed like when we were getting mortared and shelled in Da Nang, it didn't have the same impact as when we were mortared and shelled at Cu Chi. I remember once in Cu Chi they got us all up in the middle of the night and were really not sure what to do with us because we were being overrun. . . . That one was written up in *Time* magazine. Cu Chi was full of tunnels; there were Viet Cong underneath that whole city. They had hospitals underneath the ground, firing bases. . . . It turned out our military stopped them, but they were very close. They had actually cut through the perimeter and were on the compound, the base camp. That was crazy. I've never been so scared. They gathered all of us in the kitchen of our hooch. We were told to stay there and wait for the word. . . . I remember sitting around in the kitchen in our flak jackets and helmets, just bullshitting all night long. There wasn't anything else you could do. And we just went to work the next morning at 6:30.

When I was in Da Nang the closeness of death came home to me when we heard that a nurse had been killed up in Chu Lai, Sharon Lane. I remember reading about it in the *Stars and Stripes*, and the reason it had an impact on me is that I was originally scheduled to be up at Chu Lai, and that could have been me. That was in August of 1969. I remember lying to my family when I would write home that the hospitals were real safe and not to worry.

Because I had come to Da Nang as a captain, with all this experience, they made me head nurse in the emergency room—it was called emergency and admitting and pre-op. There you would get the casualties as soon as they came off the dustoffs, the air ambulances. So you would do the lifesaving measures to be done on the wounded, and you would do triage. Nurses would have to do triage because we only had so many doctors, and most of them ended up working in the operating room. Sometimes casualties couldn't even go to x-ray; they were so bad that they would take them right into the OR. There were three or four operating rooms in Da Nang, and they were always busy. Because the docs were so busy in the OR, the nurses in the emergency room had the job of doing the triage. You had to make the decision about those people who were wounded so bad that no matter how much time you would spend on them, they wouldn't live. They were called "expectants," and you would have to put them in an area behind a screen to die—these nineteen-year-old kids . . . In triaging, there were three categories to sort out: the "expectants," the "immediates" (those that required immediate attention and surgery), then there was a third category, the "walking wounded." The doctors who worked in the emergency room were called GMOs, general medical officers, and those guys were usually interns or residents with very little experience. They were learning as they were doing, just as we were. This was an evacuation hospital, which was different than other hospitals, so I can only talk about how they functioned.

When you get down to a hundred days to go before you go home, you have a calendar that you fill in, a short-timer's calendar. And you start getting a little bit crazy, thinking about going home. Then there was also the other side of the coin, where I didn't feel that the nurse that was coming in to take my place was as qualified as I was, because it took me all this time to learn what I was doing and to do it well. Every one of us has a sense of guilt of leaving the patients behind and the nurses that we worked with, the docs, the corpsmen, all the members of the team. When a good quarterback on a football team is pulled out and a replacement comes in, it's like starting all over again. So I had this feeling that it wasn't going to work as well when I left. Also there was a combination of disillusionment versus "I did a damn good job." I felt that twelve months over there was probably one of the most rewarding nursing experiences in my life, that I'll never equal that again.

It was incredible coming back a real changed person, one who was sarcastic and bitter about what was happening in America. The news was lying about the war; Kent State was going on; the feminist movement—women were burning their bras, and I was in Vietnam saving lives. . . . It was craziness; what was going on here? So my attitude changed, but I felt that my year over there wasn't wasted. I personally felt very satisfied with what I had done. When I started to question the whole involvement in Vietnam— What were we doing over there? Why were we trying to change their attitudes?—that's when I started getting into trouble. I became immersed in my work at Fitzsimmons Army Hospital in Denver, working with psychiatric patients, but I didn't question the politics because I was still in the Army—I couldn't.

When I got out of the service I was working in a hospital in Oakland, California, in intensive care, and they wouldn't let me hang a pint of blood! They made me go through an orientation course to learn CPR. That was sort of the ultimate degradation. My intelligence and experience were not even addressed properly. It was a real insult to me. I had a real "attitude problem" working in a civilian hospital. There was this need for the recreation of the push. . . . "adrenaline junkies" . . . that we are; the nurses who were in Vietnam. I really mean that. That certain rush of adrenaline, the excitement; there were all these casualties coming in that you have got to work . . . and the adrenaline starts going. So you try to perpetuate that. Nothing meant anything when I came back from Vietnam. The phrase "Don't mean nothin' " was very descriptive of the way I felt. I found it was getting in my way of jobs when I came back. Twelve to fourteen jobs in fourteen or fifteen years. You know, looking for whatever it was that I was looking for, just really unsettled, going from place to place. Never happy. Also, I refused to put down that I was in Vietnam in my applications for jobs. It didn't mean anything anyway; why bother trying to explain it to people? Vietnam was very unpopular then; you didn't want to set yourself up as being a Vietnam veteran, let alone a woman who had been there. Why cause more trouble? Learn to keep your mouth shut about it; just do your job.

After thirteen years and all those jobs in nursing, I decided to go back to school to get a master's degree in counseling. By working in counseling I'd also get a better look at myself. Just prior to that I had gone through a depression, a severe depression, so I needed to look at where I was in life, with my job and my career. Was I going to be able to maintain it? What was I doing about myself? . . . And after going through the depression and a suicide attempt, my whole life changed to do something for myself.

I had joined the Army Reserves about two years after I was discharged from the Army. One reason was financial. The pay was pretty good, and then it was one weekend a month. I also found being in the Reserves provided camaraderie with other people who had been in Vietnam, and that was important. Then, later on, especially this past couple of years, I've used the Reserve program as a way of telling people about what to expect if another crisis should occur. I try to alert them to what it is that they're going to be seeing and doing over there, which was never really told to me when I went through my officer basic training. So it's like . . . they haven't caught on to it yet. . . . I'm sure I'll get in trouble for this one of these days: telling these younger nurses that are in the units now the realities of what war and being a combat nurse is all about. It is not just wearing a pretty uniform and getting the pay for one weekend a month. There are some real serious things they have to think about. So I'm using the Reserve unit as a platform to educate those people who are part-time military.

I have about another three or four years before I retire, and I really plan to retire, but I'm also thinking that it probably won't be surprising if they ask me to leave because of the kinds of things that I am doing inside the Reserves. That is not politically correct, to be honest. "The Tightrope Walker." That could be the title of my chapter . . . and it's interesting, because I think it relates to that "adrenaline junkie" idea I was talking about. There is a certain amount of excitement, I guess, in what I am doing. I am also real excited and enthusiastic about what I am doing in the vet center and with the women vets, because my job doesn't end just being director of this vet center. My job has since become doing a lot of training across the country to other vet centers and organizations about women vets. I let them know that women are in the military, that women veterans have needs as well as men. People are starting to pick up on the fact that women were in the war and were in combat even though they didn't carry guns. So I'm an activist basically, a social activist for women in the military, especially those who were in Vietnam, because that is closest to me. And I work within the establishment, under that umbrella of the Veterans Administration and the federal government (the Army Reserves).

So there is this push-pull kind of thing. The tightrope walker—I like that.

Sometimes it feels very lonely to me, the work that I am doing. I wish there were more of me. . . . I wish there were more women working within the system who are as knowledgeable or have as much experience as I do who would be able to do this kind of work. . . . I'm responsible to the rest of my job here, and other work should go on the side: "We gave you permission to start the women's movement in the vet center system—and that's it—now go back and take care of your vet center." That's not enough for me, and again I may get into trouble because I'm not saying no to other people as far as the women's issues go. I'll do whatever needs to be done until some changes are made. That may take a long time, but I guess what I'm hoping for is that other people will become active in it and help with it. The more people who get to know about the women who were in Vietnam, the easier my job is going to be. That's why I don't hesitate when screenwriters call or somebody wants to interview me for an article in a newspaper. In one way I'm tired of being put out there and raked over the coals, but on the other hand, I know that unless I do it, it's not going to be done. The word is out, and I'm willing to talk about it if it is going to help. Not only to help women who need to come in and talk about their lives and help them to readjust from their experience, but also to make other people out there—psychologists, therapists, psychiatrists—understand that war really did a number on all of us, the women as well as the men.

Linda J. McClenahan

USARV HEADQUARTERS
COMMUNICATIONS CENTER
LONG BINH—NOV. '69 TO NOV. '70

Lin lives in San Francisco where she is a senior communications analyst for a major engineering corporation. In 1984 she was appointed by the governor to join eight males in making up a Vietnam Veterans Memorial commission tasked with raising funds and selecting a design to honor California's Vietnam veterans. She is active in local veterans affairs, a member of the Vietnam Veterans Leadership Program, Vietnam Veterans of America, and does speaking engagements at local high schools and colleges about the Vietnam experience of women.

I had a dream that I got on a bus—it was a regular Muni bus—and as I stepped inside there were no seats; there were tables. It was full of fatigues and boots and helmets; it was like a supply room. I went through line getting all my things, and all of a sudden I was standing at the back door in full fatigues. The door opens, I'm handed an M-16, I step off the bus, and I'm back in Vietnam—and I'm in the middle of a firefight, you know, combat—people are dying all around us . . . and I got hit! I got hit and fell down, and although it was a little tiny wound in front, I could feel the bullet spinning around and just ripping me up inside. I saw the helicopters coming to pick us up, and when they did, they picked up everybody but me. They just left me! And I remember yelling, "Don't leave me! I hurt too . . . . Don't leave me! I hurt too!"

THERE WERE WACs WORKING IN VARIOUS POSITIONS with the MPs, Finance, and other administrative duties around Saigon and some of the larger areas like Da Nang, but the WAC detachment in Long Binh was the only organized group of WACs in Vietnam. There were about a hundred of us there in the compound at that time. It was kind of a mini-compound within a compound. We had high fences with rolled barbwire at the top and a security guard—not for protection from the VC, but to keep us separate from the gentlemen in the late hours of the evening.

Inside the compound there were five two-story barracks and, depending on the rank, there were from one to four women in each room. Outside each of the buildings there was a bunker, which was a small green building that had a heavy corrugated-type tin roof and a lot of sandbags. There were small wooden slat benches inside that could hold about forty people uncomfortably, but we never had more than about twenty-five in there. When we would be attacked, we would run into the bunkers and sit with our helmets on, holding our canteens and gas masks. We would be in there anywhere from five minutes to several hours, depending on what was happening, and there was a lot of exchanging of cigarettes or canteens, because not everybody had water in their canteens. . . . Well, some of those nights got kind of long. As a matter of fact, one of the first times we were attacked, one of the sergeants turned to me and asked, "Have you got your canteen with you?" And I said yes. She said, "What's in it?" I said, "Water," so she says, "Great, I've got scotch. Let's mix them."

As far as the rooms were concerned, there was your basic Army cot with the inch-and-a-half mattress, a footlocker, a dresser, and a regular locker. Some of the women were able to buy small refrigerators so they could have some things close at hand. A lot of us bought those Vietnamese room dividers, the folding walls that were all intricately woven out of bamboo and painted or colored. They were very beautiful, and I regret that I didn't ship mine home. Some of the women, after they went to R&R and various other places, managed to bring back stereo systems and even small TVs. Of course, it was kind of a waste of money because you had only one TV station, Armed Forces Network. They ran the news program, some old movies, old "Combat" TV shows, and I remember seeing some Johnny Carson shows, usually two or three weeks old. We really had it pretty good, relatively speaking. The mamasans had access to a washer-drier for our clothes, and we also had one bathtub in each building, which we never used for baths, but they also used them for washing clothes. We had showers and, most of the time, hot water.

Because we didn't have our own mess hall, the 24th Evac Hospital shared theirs with us. We were right next to the hospital, and there were helicopters coming in all the time with the wounded. We got acquainted with some of the nurses, played softball with them when we could all get away.

I was twenty years old when I went to Vietnam and celebrated my twenty-first birthday there. I had come from a background of twelve years of Catholic schools and had a somewhat sheltered life—midwestern parents with midwestern values—and I don't know what I was expecting by volunteering to go, but what I encountered was unimaginable. I think I was kind of okay seeing wounded soldiers coming in, because that was the soldier's fortune, so to speak, although I guess I wasn't expecting the wounds to be quite so graphic. But I wasn't as prepared for that of the innocents, especially the children. I had a lot of trouble dealing with that.

I did a lot of drinking over there. I started to drink to cover feelings. I was one of those people who dealt with it by not dealing with it, and so a lot of my spare time was spent hitting the booze bottle and playing my guitar, anything that would make it go away for a while. . . . The CO had a trailer out in back of the orderly room, and we women built, by ourselves, our own NCO club with a bar and tables. The thing was, there was a curfew, 2200 hours (10:00 P.M.), so most of the clubs around Long Binh would close about 9:30. A lot of us weren't ready to quit that early, so we built this little club. Then we could continue on. We also had a big patio with a roof over it for the rain and a screen for movies. There were benches and tables, and we would occasionally have parties there for various reasons. I remember a big party on the twenty-fifth anniversary of the Women's Army Corps.

Every group over there that had the opportunity adopted an orphanage. About once a month we would go over and see the kids, try to take them clothes and toys and whatever we could get folks from the home front to ship to us. One time we decided to bring the kids to our compound and sent buses out for as many as could be brought back. These kids—of course, they were all victims of war, obviously—a lot of them were missing limbs; all of them had sores all over their bodies; many had infections. When you got playing with them, they actually were fairly happy. They would smile and laugh, but like a lot of the soldiers, they had very old, sad eyes. One of the reasons we brought them to the compound is that we had received a large shipment of a variety of clothes from a church back home. The idea of it was to get them into the bathtub and clean them up, get them into clean clothing, then feed them and play with them for the rest of the day. We also had a couple of the nurses and doctors come over from the 24th Evac to check them out.

When we got them to the bathroom they all went crazy over the toilets and we couldn't get them to stop flushing them. I was trying to get them washed up in the bathtub, and they were having a great time splashing each other—just kids playing in the bathtub! Then one of the other women would take them over and give them their clean clothes. Pretty soon I began to notice a couple of them were going back to the old clothes pile so they would get caught again and get to take another bath! Afterwards we passed out toys and had a big chicken barbecue with Kool-Aid and the works for them. It was a fun day—exhausting, but really a lot of fun. It was the party I remember the most; it was more preferable than going into the orphanages. They were hard to take; conditions were pretty wretched. It wasn't that the people didn't try; I mean, the nuns could only do so much. . . .

We worked twelve hours a day, six days a week, sometimes seven, depending on what was happening. Day shift was six to six. So you would get up in the morning about five, get dressed, go over to the mess hall, and eat breakfast . . . and it wasn't unusual to have helicopters coming in with the people who were wounded during the night. After breakfast it was on the bus and up to the communications center. We were in the headquarters building, which was a big, two- or three-story building. Our area was a little unusual because we were a highly secure communications area. We had no windows, and it was fairly well fortified. Inside was air-conditioned because we had a lot of electronic equipment in there. Of the sixty people who worked there, there were two women: one woman, Gail, who worked day shifts, and myself, who worked rotating shifts (thirty days on day shift and thirty days on nights).

Long Binh was the major center where messages came from all over Vietnam to be distributed. We handled a little bit of everything: troop movements, surveillance reports, even reports of agendas. I remember we had Bob Hope's agenda, Operation Hollyhock, classified at the time, of course. Then we had the casualty reports: the information would come into the area, and we would type up a message, which would go to the Department of Army, or Navy, or Marines, depending on what the person's branch of service was. It also went out to the fort nearest his home so the family could be notified. Each report would list a guy's name, serial number, next of kin, address, and a description of the wounds. I saw everything from "sprained ankle" to "pieces of remains not positively identified." I was seeing names, names, names. The nurses were saying that they had so many people come through that they never put any names with. . . . I had a whole lot of names that I had no faces for.

I was a buck sergeant when I got to Vietnam. Actually I was a real good soldier. I was in the service less than two years when I made sergeant. I had a three-year enlistment and, when I went to Vietnam, had to extend for four months so I would have a full twelve-month tour. Then I was put up for sergeant E6, and when they discovered I didn't have enough time in the service, they had to pull that out. But I was that good; I was that strac—my nickname was "Mac the Strac WAC." As a matter of fact I came back with an Army Commendation Medal. It was kind of a funny story. On the day they awarded it to me, I had the option of having it awarded at the WAC detachment or at the com center, and since I spent more time at the com center and felt real close to those guys, I wanted to have it up there. So we had a little problem when they went to pin the medal on—the captain didn't want to pin it on—so all of a sudden some of the guys started volunteering, "I'll do it. I'll pin it on."

Being the only woman on the shift, I got a lot of comments. . . . It was always sort of that fine line between flattering popularity and sexual harassment. And there were times when you really couldn't distinguish between the two. But those guys, hell, they were mostly like brothers. They were good friends. You know, that was the thing over there—I mean that's why we got invited to every party in town. The few women that were there had to fill in as mother, sister, sweetheart, confidante; you know, we filled every gap we could. And contrary to popular opinion, most of us did *not* fill the role of lover. Most of the guys didn't demand that. That's another thing: the guys that were in the more dangerous positions, the combat troops that came in from the field for their stand-downs, were always (I hate to say this) "the perfect gentlemen." They weren't going to do anything to screw up our coming back out there again! So they were always polite in the dancing, the drinking, and things like that. They wanted to talk and visit, the chance to be with a round-eye for a while. The guys who were safe, back behind the lines like we were (except there was no "behind the lines"—let me rephrase that) were the ones that tended to get a little pushy or nasty sometimes— with the exception of the guys I worked with; they knew me and worked with me every day and were very protective. So the guys out in the infantry—the 1st Cav, Americal, the 199th—those guys were always terrific; I have real fond memories of all of them.

I felt that it was the least I could do. . . . The only thing I *could* do was go to the parties. To be available to talk with the guys, and dance, and be there. I couldn't go out there and fight with them. . . . I'd be lying through my teeth if I said that I didn't have fun at most of those parties, but the point is that I went to a lot more parties than I really was up to. I didn't take a lot of time for myself, didn't stay back in the compound and read or write letters, or even sleep. I mean, if I could do it, I would go. I had to. . . .

Most of the requests came in through an official way, for instance, from the Black Cats at Phu Loi. They would send a formal request in to the captain, saying that they would land some helicopters and fly us to their party. The captain would post the notice, and as many people as could get away would go. They would have a barbecue, and they had a pool there. Now, the swimming pools in Vietnam had plastic walls. Even those that were sunk in the ground were still plastic, and none of them was more than three feet deep. They may have been Olympic-size, but never more than three feet deep. And full of bugs and various other little crawly things, but in a hundred-and-fifteen-degree heat, water was water. There was always a lot of beer.

We would dance, swim, talk, and drink beer. Then they would fly us home. We would go to parties on the Long Binh compound, to some of the units there, as well. And then there were the parties that we weren't supposed to go to, off the compound, like the 199th stand-downs.

If a woman was dating one of the guys from an infantry group and he would come in and say, "We are having a stand-down, could you get a few women together?" we would get on the truck with the supplies they were taking back to their unit; they would throw a blanket over us and sneak us off the compound. The old adage—"You work hard, you play hard." I mean those guys . . . they knew how to party, but it was like they never knew if it was going to be their last party . . . and nobody talked about the war out there. Everybody would talk about things like what they were going to do when they got home, what kind of car they were going to buy, the places they were going to visit, the job they were going to get, et cetera. Then, when you got to know some of the guys and you'd notice that they weren't there at the next party, I mean, you didn't ask, "Where is so-and-so?" You just didn't do it. You sort of knew. . . . You would hope that it was his time to go home, but . . .

I had just turned twenty-one and had met this buck sergeant with the 199th. Ski and I were becoming closer all the time. In August, he and his buddy, Rowdy, and another guy came to pick us up, and that night I was the only woman who could make it. The three of us were riding in the back, drinking Wild Turkey and joking around when Ski had to go to the bathroom. The truck stopped and he jumped down and started to jog into the bushes. He stepped on a mine. . . . He was gone. . . . All we could do was continue on and report it—someone with detectors would have to come and get him. I remember we got back in the truck, and Rowdy took a drink from the bottle, passed it to me, and quietly said, "I gotta stop making friends over here." I was filled with guilt; I was the only woman on the truck. He wouldn't have gone into the bushes if I hadn't been there. . . . I never told anyone about that . . . not anyone. For twelve years I believed it was my fault that

Ski was dead. Now I know I didn't kill Ski. . . . The war did. The war got Rowdy too, about a week later during their next outing. Except for R&R and coming home, I never left the Long Binh compound again.

When I came home everything seemed strange. All of my friends were at college or didn't want to have anything to do with me or wanted to argue with me, which was worse. My family just wanted me to put everything behind me. I had a lot of feelings that I couldn't understand. I couldn't get excited about the fact that the morning paper was twenty minutes late, for example. Everything seemed so trivial; it was amazing. So I got in my car and took a long drive around the country visiting relatives and friends. When I got back I decided, "Okay, I have survived Vietnam. I can survive this . . . turmoil." I changed jobs, I think, initially three times in the first two years, but I finally settled into a steady job, as a matter of fact with the company I'm with now. I've been here ten years.

I figured Vietnam was behind me. Periodically I'd have dreams, nightmares, and things like that, but people have those, so I thought that it wasn't anything unusual. Everything was fine until about two years ago, one of the telephone operators came by and asked if I had been in the Army, and I said yes. She said, "I've got this article from the paper about women who were in Vietnam." I told her that, in fact, I was one of them. She kind of freaked out and then handed me the article. It was written by Lynda Van Devanter. Well, I read the article, and as I was reading it I started to shake, really shake . . . and I had tears in my eyes. I couldn't handle what I was reading. I called Lynda in Washington, D.C., and talked to her for a little bit, and at that time, she didn't know that there had been enlisted women, nonnurses, in Vietnam. So I was a real off-the-wall person to her. We talked for a while, and she suggested that I call the local vet center, which I did. I went in and talked to the head of the center a couple of times and didn't feel that they really wanted me there. I mean, it was really mostly for the guys, and although the counselor and group leader did talk to me, I decided, "No, everything is all right."

Then about a year and a half ago I started having trouble with dreams coming up again, and true to form, I started drinking more to counter the dreams. I had had drinking binges all the way along, but I hadn't really related it to anything—job stress mostly. Around Christmastime I went down to see my brother, his wife and kids, and my mother. I remember very little of the trip; I was quietly drunk most of the time. I'd just sit in corners and play my guitar and drink and not be very social. Then sometime around February, I woke up in the middle of the night with another nightmare, and I sat up and all of a sudden a helicopter crashed through the roof! . . . And as I was in the process of screaming "No, no, no!" I realized there was no plaster on the bed from it coming in. I looked up, and of course it was gone. That scared me so badly I called the vet center again. They put me on with a private counselor who got me involved with an alcohol group. My theory at that point was "Are you kidding? I'm not an alcoholic. I have a little drinking problem because I'm trying to cope with these nightmares." But I stayed involved with them and have been sober since then.

About that time I got in touch with Rose Sandecki at the Concord vet center and decided to join the group of women Vietnam vets that she was forming. It has been rough since I've gotten involved again. A lot of really deep feelings have come up, a lot of anger and hurt and having to relook at something twelve years later and try to make some sense of it.

I don't know how much longer I would have survived had I not finally realized that something was going on and gotten myself to the vet center. And I don't know exactly what would have happened, but I think I was heading for a nervous breakdown or a loss of job. . . . I know that I was on the verge of—you know, there were suicidal thoughts. . . . There were homicidal thoughts.

Now that I'm able to look at things again and allow myself to feel and reexperience some of them, I feel like I've made it home. I have finally accepted the fact that things that happened in the Vietnam War were not my fault. I couldn't have done anything more than what I did to help those people that I was able to help. I couldn't have done anything to change the fact that people died . . . people that I knew and cared about and loved, and strangers too . . . and for such a long time I kept thinking that I should have been able to do more.

Georgeanne Duffy Andreason

SPECIAL SERVICES
VINH LONG—DEC. '67 TO DEC. '68

Georgeanne lives in Redmond, Washington, is married, and has "four great stepsons, two lovely daughters-in-law, and four darling stepgrandchildren."

She kept turning the tape recorder off. We would talk for a while, then I would ask a question and turn it back on—a hesitating answer, loss of trend of thought—and off it would go again. This went on for quite some time until a truce was declared. I agreed to send her the results of what we had recorded; she would rewrite the story, more comfortably alone and in her own time.

When I was in Vietnam I wrote my sister and brother almost weekly, carbon copies, and from '68 until now I hadn't read them although they had saved them in a big sack for me. In the last forty-eight hours I've gone over them, just kind of hurriedly. I did notice when I read them that at the time I was minimizing things that happened, as far as the war itself and I must have mentioned a dozen times not to worry because I was sure the reports were getting blown out of proportion. At any rate it brought back a lot of memories, a lot of things that I've suppressed and a lot of things I hadn't thought about. . . . So I'm glad I did it. It took this to do it; I'm not sure I ever would have. I don't think so. It's been fifteen years so I think I wouldn't have.

WHILE WORKING IN CALIFORNIA I READ THAT SPE-
cial Services was hiring for a club and program director to
serve in Vietnam. I had done similar work with the Red
Cross at Camp Pendleton Navy Hospital and Tripler General Hospital in Hawaii. It was probably a combination of
the challenge of serving during wartime and patriotism, as
well as wanderlust, that prompted me to pursue the job.
Eight months after my initial interview I landed in Saigon,
in December of 1967. I arrived at Tan Son Nhut airport at
3:30 A.M. with only a TIGER (phone exchange) number to
call. I was unable to reach anyone; however, two men on
my flight were aware of my dilemma and took me into
Saigon and left me at the Ambassador hotel. The humidity
and aroma of the sheets that night are something I'll never
forget.

The following day I located Special Services personnel
and received a briefing; there were only forty-six or forty-
eight of us in-country at that time. I would be activating
service clubs in the Mekong Delta. I was assigned to the
Vinh Long air field, an Army helicopter base, but would
also make numerous trips to the clubs in Soc Trang and

Can Tho. Another girl and I were the only females on the compound with twenty-five hundred men. I experienced my first helicopter ride flying from Saigon to Vinh Long. The flight was a thrill in itself, but I was also totally surprised by the beauty of the countryside in the delta. We new low enough to view the rice paddies and small hamlets. I was later to observe some of the most spectacular sunrises and sunsets I'd ever seen. It was on my first helicopter ride I was introduced to the base chaplain, "Father G" (Gianatasio). We were without a gunner that day so Father G replaced him. From then on the men referred to him as our "bless and shoot, bless and shoot" priest.

The purpose of the club was to set up a program which would serve as a diversion for the men when they were off duty. When I arrived, the club itself had not been completed. Our goal was to have a kitchen, large lounge area, music room, and library. Unfortunately the Navy plane carrying the majority of our furniture and other supplies crashed, and the grand opening was delayed. Another goal was to complete the unfinished swimming pool, but this was never accomplished. We tried to plan as many activities as possible and to bring in any outside entertainment; however, the latter was infrequent. We found ourselves spending many hours in the lounge just listening to the men "ventilate." Some days they would be particularly upset because the ARVN, our allies, displayed a lack of leadership, no initiative, and a general apathy. Other times they would just relate their "war stories": the number of "hits" their aircraft had taken that day, their triumphs, and, many times, the tragic stories of the casualties they had suffered.

Many of the men seemed to become more frightened as their tours became shorter. It was not unusual to hear about their buddies boarding a flight home from Tan Son Nhut and being mortared as they were departing. I was always happy to hear about their wives, families, children, and life back in the "real world" or anything they wanted to share. Most of them were so young, just eighteen, nineteen, or twenty. Because of the possibility they might not return after a mission, I found myself keeping a distance and not really becoming as close as one might with other friends.

The girl with whom I worked and I each had a small room in the transient quarters. Three months before I returned home, we moved into our own hooch, which had hot water and closets! The interior walls of our new quarters were made out of rocket boxes; the men were terrific at improvising. Compared to the living conditions in many parts of VN we couldn't complain; however, during the monsoon season we did have to move to a hooch in an elevated area, as ours had six to eight inches of water in it most of the time. One night we returned after work to learn a cobra had slithered in and wanted to share our quarters. It was at this time that we moved until the flooding subsided.

Just adjacent to the airfield was a Catholic convent run by ten delightful nuns from Ireland and one from Singapore. We were dependent on them to do the laundry for the base, and our transportation unit flew them to Saigon often. Everyone considered it a treat to be aboard with the "Flying Nuns." The convent had been there since the French occupation in the 1950s. They had a lovely chapel, an old brick tennis court, and a swimming pool with a helicopter rotor blade for a diving board. Despite such makeshift facilities, visiting them was like entering another, more civilized world. They welcomed me with open arms and were always so hospitable. They were very courageous ladies. My last correspondence from them was dated 12/17/73. One nun wrote: "Vinh Long is still comparatively peaceful. Cost of living has shot up sky-high. The poor, nowadays, can only afford *one* full meal a day!" I often wonder how and where they are today.

I had been in Vietnam two months when the Tet offensive occurred. We received word from General Westmoreland's office to go on red alert, in other words, to guard our perimeter heavily. At 2:45 A.M. the Viet Cong began to mortar the compound and airfield. I immediately dove under my bed, as I felt I didn't have time to get to my bunker. Within five minutes Lieutenant Colonel Thompson, the air field commander, was there to insist I go to the bunker. He saw that I was safely in my bunker and continued on to his respective bunker at the perimeter. An hour later word filtered back that he had been found in his jeep, killed by a VC suicide squad before he reached his bunker. I've wondered so many times if this tragedy would have happened had he not taken the time to look after my welfare. I truly believe he gave his life for me.

The other girl with whom I worked was in Vung Tau at the time. It was a beautiful coastal town on the South China Sea. It was known as the "in-country R&R." So the morning after Tet, I opened the club alone. It was undoubtedly one of the most memorable days of my tour. We had suffered so many casualties, but the morale continued to be high. Three days later, the temporary commanding officer came running to the club and announced I had to be evacuated because the VC were burning the town of Vinh Long and were approaching the air field. I resisted at first, as I believed I was performing a fairly important role. Regardless, he said I had to grab my toothbrush and that was all. He raced me out to the waiting Chinook, which had detoured from Saigon to get me. I later learned from the pilot in Vung Tau that because of the detour we were flying on fumes. As we flew over Vinh Long I could see out of the open end of the Chinook. The city was in flames, and they were definitely headed toward the convent and the air base. I'll never forget that sight.

The convent was badly destroyed during the battle between the suicide squads and the allied troops. While I was in Vung Tau the nuns occupied our two rooms and the children slept in the chapel. For two weeks we remained in Vung Tau. Finally they allowed us to return during the day, but at night we were still being heavily mortared so we returned to our temporary trailer in Vung Tau. Each morning we were picked up at 7:00 A.M. for the forty-five-minute flight to Vinh Long, and at dusk we would catch a plane back to Vung Tau. I can recall many nights when we would just be airborne and the VC would be "walking" the mortars across the airfield as we were lifting off.

After a couple of months it was almost back to normal; however, we did continue to close at dusk due to the sniper fire just outside the club. The music room had received a direct hit destroying the drum set. This was not too disturbing to the men living in the hooch next to the club!

On occasion we would fly to one of the nearby outposts. Because road travel was considered unsafe, we would always go by air. There were usually about ten or twelve men there with MACV. We would take them magazines, food, packages, or sometimes something from home. They were always proud to present us with a tattered VC flag they had captured.

My tour was certainly not devoid of humor. I'd been getting gray hair for several years so, of course, I planned to continue to "rinse away" the gray. But I had failed to pack enough rinse for twelve months. One fellow was going to Honolulu for his R&R, so I asked him to please pick up medium brown hair rinse. He thought auburn would be the right color, so with the combination of the Vietnam sun and the auburn rinse, I was an orange-head for the remainder of my tour. At one time I'd planned to rinse my hair in the middle of the afternoon. You should shake it lightly and then use it within half an hour. The process was interrupted by a mortar attack. When I returned three hours later, my room had a polka-dot decor due to the rinse exploding.

I was responsible for hiring some of the local Vietnamese to work at the service club. Naturally we always wanted to trust them and hoped they weren't VC. Unfortunately this wasn't always the case. A very personable young man we affectionately referred to as "Peanut" was one of the employees of the officers' club. During the day he did a conscientious job, but at night he was our enemy. One morning after a severe attack, Peanut's body was found at the perimeter of the air field. We also hired the *chu hois* (defectors) to cut the grass and do odd jobs. The majority of them seemed to be very young boys or older men. Shortly before returning home, I spent a day in court testifying against one of the mama-sans who had stolen some jewelry and lipstick from my room. The security at the gate was not always as tight as it might have been.

In the course of my year in Vietnam I vacillated from

being very pro-war—the Vietnamese cause and our involvement in it—to the point where I began to question the U.S. being there. At the close of my tour though, I was convinced we were doing the right thing and I supported it totally.

When I returned to the States I found I avoided conversations about the war, and I suppressed my memories—unpleasant as well as fond memories. Eighteen months ago I joined a group of nurses suffering from delayed stress syndrome. We discovered we had all reconciled ourselves to the war in similar ways: by pushing the memories away. During and shortly after the therapy, I still wasn't convinced it had been the best thing. However, a year and a half later, I'm positive it was very beneficial, and I would encourage anyone to seek help if he or she believes there is a need. Just recapping some of the more outstanding events has been helpful.

I returned with a much greater appreciation of America and our freedom. No longer do I take things for granted, which I was guilty of at one time. I treasure my family, friends, and of course all the opportunities this country affords us. My year was one I would never want to repeat but at the same time I will *never* regret it.

Christine McGinley Schneider

95TH EVAC. HOSPITAL, DA NANG—
JUNE '70 TO JUNE '71

Chris Schneider lives in a beautiful home near the beach in southern California. She is now a full-time housewife and the mother of a twenty-eight-month-old daughter and a nine-month-old son. While she no longer works full-time as a nurse, she occasionally assists in her husband's medical office. Chris plans to return to nursing after her children reach school age.

Chris was one of my early interviews, and I have always been thankful for that because she was so cheerful and upbeat. Her enthusiasm was of immeasurable help to me.

I WAS TWENTY-ONE YEARS OLD WHEN I WENT OVER there. I had gone through a three-year nursing program at the County Hospital in Los Angeles, and at that time there had been recruiters coming to the hospitals talking about the war, talking about the need for nurses; so that was in the back of my mind. My mom had been a Navy nurse during World War II, and I think that had a lot of impact on my decision. Then when you come out of school, you kind of feel like you want to do something to save or help the world. When I got out of school it wasn't "Should I or shouldn't I?"—I really wanted to go, but I didn't feel like I had enough experience as a nurse. So I told myself, "I'll stay here at the County Hospital and work for a year, and if I still feel this way, I'll go." I chose to work on the jail ward because they had a lot of injuries and gunshot wounds. I worked there for a year, and feeling that I still wanted to go, there wasn't any question—I was going to go.

I looked into the Red Cross and civilian organizations, and none of them was sending nurses at that time. The Navy said that I would have to stay stateside eighteen months before they would consider my request for over there. The Air Force said the same thing, but when I went to the Army they promised me that I could go over immediately, and they gave it to me in writing. So I joined the Army.

I have a large family, two sisters and three brothers. Two of my brothers were draft age at that time, but I had no idea that if I was over there, during that year at least, they would not be sent to Vietnam. There were a number of nurses that were unhappy about being there, and when I got to asking them why they went over there they said they did it so their brothers wouldn't have to serve. In my mind and heart, my hope was "If I go over and take care of these people, help these boys, and someday my brothers get drafted, maybe there will be someone who will be good to them." I had basic training in San Antonio, Texas, at Fort "Sam," went home for three or four days, then went right over. Once I made the decision, it really went quickly. As far as ever questioning what I was doing, I have to admit that I really didn't until the very last stop. We made a few stops, one in Hawaii and one in the Wake Islands, and the last stop before we got there was the Philippines. I remember hearing the final boarding call for the plane, and it was like, "Oh, my God!" I was just a normal girl; I had grown up in a real wonderful, loving family, and all of a sudden I was doing something that wasn't real normal. From the Philippines on over; I remember feeling just really alone, really isolated and scared.

I was in Long Binh for three or four days when I finally got assigned to the 95th Evac Hospital in Da Nang; it was in June of 1970. I remember going up there on a C-130, which is a transport plane. The back opens up and you all pile in the back, and it was all men except for myself and another girl. We got settled, and they wanted to know where the two VIPs were, and Mary and I were looking around because we wondered what a VIP was in Vietnam. Come to find out it was us. We weren't supposed to be in the back of the plane with the guys; we were supposed to be up front with the pilots. So we rode up front, and I remember all the way up it was like, "I can't believe this is Vietnam.'' It was so gorgeous; it was absolutely beautiful.

When I got to the 95th, the chief nurse told me I was going to be assigned to a surgical ward, and I was really disappointed because I wanted to work in the emergency room—that was kind of my thing. I asked her to please keep me in mind if they had an opening down there, and she told me that I was a second lieutenant and she had only first lieutenants and captains there. When I had signed up to go in the Army they had never mentioned rank. To me it was like, ''A nurse is a nurse.'' As it worked out, I was only on the surgical ward about three weeks. One of the nurses was leaving, and they couldn't get anyone to take her place; so the chief nurse told me that I could go down there and try it, and if it didn't work out they would move me back to the surgical ward. I never wanted to let on I was—you know . . . I was not somebody who would break into tears or run out of a thing; I keep it all inside, and that was even more of an incentive to keep how I really felt inside.

I don't know how to describe it. I had worked a year in the emergency room on the jail ward, but nothing could prepare you for the horrible things you saw. . . . You just get thrown into it. The first day they had a mass casualty, and they got as many doctors, nurses, and corpsmen as they could down there. It was just incredible; these big Chinook helicopters came in, and the corpsmen went out and got all these guys. I remember one of the nurses saying, ''You take him.'' I'll never forget him because he was my first one. Everybody was bad, but they were alive. . . . There is a wonderful line in a poem by Thomas Hardy that really gets me; the line is ''Alive enough to have strength to die.'' And that is exactly how this boy was. He was a really good-looking boy—Jimmy was his name—with blond hair, and half of his face had been blown away, and the first thing the nurse said to me was ''Cut off all of his clothes.'' They give you these huge scissors to cut off the clothes, and I was trying to comfort him. . . . He was wide awake even though half his face was gone, and he was scared. I remember cutting off all his clothes and the horror of taking one of his boots off and his foot still being in the boot. . . . I remember that nurse saying, "Draw four tubes of blood, type-cross him, and get it over to the lab right away." I remember drawing the blood, and he begged me not to leave. . . . After I drew the blood he said, "Please don't leave me." I said, "I just have to run across the hall to the lab. I promise I'll be right back." I was right back, and he had died in the time that I had left him alone. . . . And I never forgot that; I never again left anyone, because you realize that when they say that, it's like they know that they are going. . . . It's a horrible thing; I never forgot it.

So that is how I got into it. Then you don't really ever get used to it . . . and it seemed to get harder and harder. . . . I thought, "You work in it for a while, you'll get more accustomed to it and it won't be so shocking." But you never did, because every boy that came in was an individual. You knew that he had a mother and father, a girlfriend and boyfriend, and if this wasn't going on they would be at home partying in college somewhere like they should have been. For some reason I could never get that out of my mind, and that's why I think it was hard for the nurses, because you just never forgot that, you know? Then the guys wore beads or carried pictures of their girlfriends, and when you were tagging them, tagging their bodies and putting them in plastic bags, you had to itemize all the things they carried. So you always saw the wife or the girlfriend; you always had the letter that meant the most to them, and that was so hard. . . . You could never distance yourself from that.

One of the most incredible stories—this is a true story. I had gone to the Bob Hope show on Christmas, and of course I was really excited to be able to see it; I had watched it on television so many years. There weren't many girls there, of course, and they roped off the women from the guys; there were MPs standing there. All these GIs were taking our picture, and that sort of jarred my world, because you didn't go out much. My whole world was the hospital, but even when you went to the PX, people were always taking your picture. So the same thing happened here. Most of them were grunts; they brought them in from the field, and they were going right back out when the show was over. It didn't seem much longer than it takes to get your pictures developed when this guy came in just shot up really bad, and he died, but before he died he told me that he had my picture. It was the one picture that he had in his pocket—my picture from the Bob Hope show. To think that of all his worldly possessions he would carry my picture . . . and I have that picture now. He wanted me to have it. . . . He knew he was dying and I've got that . . . It was just the eeriest thing. Those are the kinds of things that make me know that my being there did make a difference to a lot of people, to a lot of guys who probably don't even know my name but will always remember that someone cared. In your own heart you know that you made a difference, and that's a good feeling to have.

Toward the end it really got harder emotionally. I was coming home in June, and I remember in April thinking I was not going to be able to handle any more; there was just too much death.

You get very close to the people that you were with, and I've never ever had the kind of bond that I felt with those people, the nurses, the corpsmen, and the doctors; it is an incredible kind of camaraderie. You experience so much together; you party together; you cried together; you had really good memories together. . . . There was just such a bond. When the day came for me to leave Cam Ranh Bay, I remember I couldn't stop crying when the C-130 took off. And I remember the pilot looked at me and asked what was wrong with me. It was just . . . I could never put it in words; it's just a feeling. Such an incredible year of your life and to be in the plane taking off and just seeing it all fading away, knowing that never again would you see that place or those people.

We flew from Japan to Fort Lewis, Washington. On our plane we brought home the first group of guys that were withdrawing from heroin, and at that point in the war there was such a tremendous problem with heroin addiction they had converted some of the hospitals into detoxification centers. The bad thing was they didn't have any drugs to treat them with on the plane, and some of them were quite sick.

As we were getting off the plane, one of the fellows fell down and hit his head, and I remember staying there with him. A head wound bleeds a lot anyway, so I had blood all over the bottom of my uniform, and by the time the ambulance came to get him, most of the people had gone ahead of me. Then I got outside after going through customs, and there were no taxis, there were no buses, and your parents weren't allowed to be there. There was nobody to welcome you home, and there was nobody to even give you transportation to SeaTac airport. I hadn't thought about that. I didn't know where SeaTac was; I didn't know if it was next door; or if I could walk, or if it was quite a distance. I was standing there all alone in this bloody uniform, and I had been on a shopping spree when we were in Japan and had bought clocks there. So I had my suitcases, these clocks, and I had Vietnam posters, and I had my boonie hat on. I looked terrible, and I was crying. About then, an older man approached me and offered to give me a ride to SeaTac airport, and ordinarily I'd never get in a car with somebody, but at the time I didn't even think about it. I remember saying, "Well, gee, thanks a lot!" and loaded in my clocks and what have you. Come to find out this man had lost a son over there. He knew what time the flights came in, and he waited there to take people to the airport. I don't know his name or anything, but I'll never forget him.

So I get to the airport, and I was waiting in line. I had bought my ticket in Japan, and all I had to do was get my boarding pass. I remember getting up to the counter and putting my suitcase on the scale, and the guy refused to let me board the plane. He told me that I could not get on the plane looking like I did. I had waited a year for this moment, and my family was down in LA waiting for me. I said, "Don't you realize I've just come back from Vietnam?" He said that made no difference, and he took my suitcase and threw it on the ground. Again, I stood there and I just cried! I couldn't believe this, and I said, "But my plane leaves in forty-five minutes," and he said that he didn't care. Fortunately the people that were behind me in line were entertainers, and they heard what happened and were just furious. They went up the line and demanded to see the public relations person. I left my luggage right there and went to a phone to call my mom and dad to tell them what had happened. My dad was really upset, and he called the airline office. The entertainers were talking to the man from public relations, and I don't know what phone call or which person made the difference, but someone came right over and carried my luggage to the plane. I was given a ticket for complimentary drinks all the way home; they sent me a note of apology and a piece of luggage.

I finally got home, and it was wonderful—my mom and dad and my brothers and sisters, my aunt and uncle—everybody was there. It was just wonderful to see them. They met me with roses, and my brothers had these torches across the front lawn and a huge sign "Welcome Home Lt. Crissy." My grandmother, who was very close to me, was waiting inside the house. Mom knew that she wasn't eating all that well at the time; she was forcing herself to eat. I remember that she kissed me and told me how she was so happy that I was home, and then she said, "You are home safely, and now I can die." It was like she had kept herself alive just so she could see me. I was home for two weeks before I had to go to Fort Carson, Colorado. She got real sick right after I left, stopped eating altogether . . . and she died by the time I got to Colorado.

I had one year left on my enlistment, and I worked at Fort Carson. They asked me where I wanted to work, and I told them the emergency room. And they told me no, I was going to pediatrics. I was really unhappy there, and I wanted desperately to go back to Vietnam. I mean, what an incredible thing! I was so happy to get out, but then when I got home and to Fort Carson, I missed the place. I missed the intensity, the people, all of it, so much. I said, "Please let me go back." But they wouldn't let me, and it's a good thing . . . they wouldn't let me go back. It turned out that the assistant chief nurse there had been over at the 95th with me, and that worked out real well because she could understand how I felt. She could identify with what I was going through even though she was a colonel and a lifetime Army person—she knew exactly. She was a

wonderful lady. Also my best friend Annie Roberts, who
had been with me over there, was coming to Fort Carson
in a month, and when she showed up that was wonderful.
We didn't even realize how much it meant to be together.
We did everything together; we'd go skiing and we'd talk
about old times. My place looked like my hooch in Vietnam; I had all my pictures and everything from Vietnam
right there. We wrote to all the people there; it was so
important to keep in contact with them. It was like you
were weaning yourself slowly. . . .

If anything, I think the whole experience, looking back
on it, was a very humbling one. You come home realizing
how lucky you are. I knew I was lucky to have the family
that I had; I think one of the main reasons that I haven't
had trouble with any of the delayed stress or whatever is
that I've always had such a supportive and loving family.
If I had been one of the people out there doing the fighting
like those kids were, I don't know if I would have volunteered. It would have been a completely different decision—I can't say. The way I was looking at it wasn't
judging whether it was right or wrong to be there, but that
there were people over there who were getting hurt and as
a nurse I could be helping them. However, I came home
feeling like most everybody else—that it was wrong to be
there, if for no other reason than to hear the guys say time
and time again that they could win, but they were told to
go only so far. To hear that over and over again and then
to see the guys come in one after another. . . . The day I
left it was just weird; I remember going into the emergency
room to say good-bye to everyone, and a Chinook helicopter was landing with mass casualties. Nothing had changed;
it was exactly the same as the day I had arrived. It was
like, "How much longer is this going to go on?"

Pat Johnson

85TH EVAC. HOSPITAL,
QUI NHON—JUNE '66 TO SEPT. '66

18TH SURGICAL HOSPITAL,
PLEIKU—SEPT. '66 TO NOV. '67

71ST EVAC. HOSPITAL,
PLEIKU—NOV. '67 TO MARCH '68

Pat grew up in Iron River, Michigan, in a family of five children. She attended nursing school in Grand Rapids at Saint Mary's and after graduation worked in the emergency room there for three years. In 1965 she became aware of the need for nurses in Vietnam and was encouraged to enlist by a coworker who had been an Army nurse in the Philippines during World War II.

Pat lives in Philadelphia, Pennsylvania, where she works as a nurse anesthetist at Graduate Hospital. She is also in the Army Reserves, serving with the 78th Maneuver Training Command, Medical Exercise Team, at Fort Dix, New Jersey.

I REMEMBER GETTING OUT OF WORK EARLY ONE MORN-
ing and going down to see the Army recruiter. I said, "I
want to go to Vietnam," and he said, "I'm sorry. You're
too young, and you have to be in the Army at least a year
before you're allowed to go over." I said, "I'll only go if
you let me go right to Vietnam. If you change your mind,
you call me." About six weeks later he called me and said,
"Pat, we've decided because of your experience in the
emergency room, you can go right to Vietnam; you just
have to do Army basic." I had to go to Detroit to have my
Army physical, and I remember a girlfriend went down
with me. This is a funny thing—they made us urinate in a
bottle, and I couldn't go; I think I was too nervous, so she
went for me. And I kept saying, "I hope you don't have a
kidney infection."

Everything was fine, and I was accepted into the Army.
They sent me these orders, you know, all this Army lingo
which I didn't understand except that I was supposed to go
to Fort Sam, which is in Texas. I remember quitting my
job, going home, and spending a month with my family.
My parents were both, I think, very worried that I was

going there, but they didn't try to stop me. After I got home I found out how worried they really were. They always wanted us to be very independent, and so they never tried to influence me not to go, and they certainly didn't let their views about Vietnam influence my going or not going.

I went to San Francisco to spend two weeks with a sister before going to Vietnam. She and her husband were really antiwar, and they were marchers and all this kind of stuff, and I rememer her husband saying some things to me about "You're going to be part of the war effort. It's a terrible war." And I tried to explain to him that as a nurse I didn't feel I was part of the war effort, that there were people being injured there. I felt very patriotic. But I remember his making me feel really bad before I went there.

I went to Qui Nhon, the 85th Evac Hospital. This was in June of '66. The chief nurse decided to assign me to a medical ward, and I had no medical experience whatsoever. I was taking care of people with malaria and having a hard time adjusting to the heat. At that time we were working twelve-hour shifts, and I was just beginning to understand what Vietnam was about. Qui Nhon was right on the coast. I remember staying in quarters that were about a quarter of a mile from the hospital—with barbed wire all over the place—and walking to work every morning. Also, I felt very self-conscious being one of so few women, and I remember not wanting to be conspicuous; I just wanted to fit into the mold and be very much part of the Army. I remember going to officers' clubs, having a beer, which is unusual for me, and feeling very wild. I remember writing long letters home because I wanted to tell my parents what this whole thing was all about. Well, I was in that hospital about a month, and I knew that I wasn't close enough to the action.

I had heard that there was a new MASH hospital coming in-country going up to Pleiku, the 18th Surgical Hospital. I'd heard all these stories about Pleiku; it was up in the highlands, close to Cambodia, and I wanted to go there. I went to the doctor who was in charge of the—I think it was the 55th Medical Group—and told him when the new hospital came I would like to be assigned to it. He said, ''You and every other nurse here.'' I said, ''Well, I really want to go. When it gets here will you at least consider me!'' So when the hospital came in-country he called me and said, ''Pat, do you really want to go?'' I said yes, so he sent me to Pleiku. There were, I think, five other nurses that had come over assigned to that hospital, and I became the sixth.

The hospital was operating out of tents; they didn't have any permanent quarters at all. We were about a half a mile off the airstrip in Pleiku; the Air Force was there ahead of us. They had a wing of the little bombers, A-1s or something, there, and their compound was about two miles away, up on a hill. About halfway between the Air Force compound and the airstrip was situated this little hospital. We were sent there to support the 4th Division, who were coming over very shortly; that was our reason for being there. There were just six nurses in the beginning, seven or eight doctors, and quite a few med-techs. We spent a lot of our time just getting organized. Then we moved over into these Quonset huts, but we didn't have any running water. We had big napalm tanks with holes cut out of them, and that's what we kept the water in. We didn't have enough bandages, we were short of IV fluids, and I remember using outdated penicillin because that's all we had. They said that would be better than nothing.

The hospital commander was a guy by the name of Senac, and the chief nurse was a woman by the name of Mary Berry. She had joined the Second World War after her husband was killed; she didn't know what to do with her life so she joined the Army. She's now living in Fayetteville, North Carolina—she's retired. I've seen her since. They really weren't used to having women there, and they didn't have any provisions for us. We had one shower with a reversible sign on the outside of it for ''Men'' or ''Women,'' and it didn't have a top on it. There was a fifty-gallon oil drum on top that had an immersion heater down in it. When I worked nights, one of my jobs in the morning was to go up there and turn this gas heater on so there would be warm water for the people in the morning.

When we first got there the helicopter pilots discovered that women were taking showers in there, and they would fly over; so they soon put a top on it for us. Our chief nurse was very aware of the fact that because there were so few women we should be very discreet in our activities. She wouldn't let us sunbathe or wear Bermuda shorts on our off-time because she felt (she was really an old-fashioned nurse) that was just too much temptation for the men.

I worked in the emergency room, myself and another nurse. We worked whenever they needed us. We were scheduled for regular shifts, but if it got busy it was not unusual to work fourteen to sixteen hours, have four or five hours off, and then go back and work those long hours again. The casualties, especially in the beginning, would come in in big groups; we called them pushes. When you were really busy, you'd get a whole lot in at once, and then you might not have anything for a couple days until they organized a sick call. They'd bring in all the malarias and the dengue fevers and other things by ambulance. Most of the other injuries would come in by chopper, dustoff choppers or, many times, other types of choppers too, whatever was available. If there was a battle where they would have some kind of landing zone already established, they would be able to bring casualties very quickly. And you would get people with big wounds who were still alive, chest wounds and that type of thing. If it took a long time to get into an LZ and get the patients to you, then many times those types of casualties would never make it to the hospital.

I'm not going to talk about the severity of the wounds and things like that. I can talk about some of the things that I felt, you know, by being a nurse there. One of the things that used to come back to me all the time while I was there is that these kids were so young. And many of them didn't want to be there. I remember having really angry feelings about the people who had gotten out of being there, because a lot of these kids in Vietnam were really young, and they were so far away from their families. They were so brave and they would come in. . . . They were really hurting, and they were really afraid. Many of them hadn't had a good home-cooked meal or even a good meal—you know, they'd been eating C-rations and stuff for such a long time—and their fatigues were so dirty. I remember one kid in particular; both of his legs had gone through a grenade thing. And I remember him saying, "I'm okay, so why don't you look at someone else?" Another thing that would just amaze me is that they would hardly ever ask for anything for pain. I'd worked in the emergency room in the States, and people come in with the smallest things just screaming out in pain and wanting something. And here are these kids with really horrendous injuries. I think they were just so happy to be alive and to be somewhere safe that they would never complain about their pain. I just remember feeling so sad for them.

I used to wonder if the families of the kids who died there knew that there were people who really cared about their kids and were doing all the extra special things that they would have done if they were there. We really tried, all of us, to do those extra special things, and looking back, I see my role probably the best as having felt a lot of compassion for these kids and trying to let them know that we really cared about them. There was a surgeon there by the name of Felix Jenkins, whom I will never forget. He had more compassion for people, I think, than any person I've ever known before or since; he just really had a feeling for people. I remember one kid coming in whom we tried very desperately to save and couldn't, and Felix figured out that his mother would be notified on Mother's Day. He turned to me and said, "Do you know, this is the kind of thing that I'm just hating about being here."

Our hospital only had sixty beds—it was a life-or-limb type place—and we kept people at the most forty-eight hours. Sometimes if we were too busy, we couldn't operate on minor shrapnel wounds and things because we just didn't have the time. We would organize med-evacs and send them to the coast, to the 85th or 67th or someplace that had more beds than we did. I remember one time we were having terrible weather; it was in monsoon time. We'd had a big push and just couldn't accommodate all these kids, so we operated on the more seriously ill, and the rest we organized to send out on a plane to the coast. We loaded them in ambulances and, I thought, had explained to them why we were sending them away, but apparently we hadn't. We took them to the airstrip and got them on the airplanes, and the weather was so bad in Qui Nhon they couldn't land, so they brought them back to us. This one kid came off, and he said, "You know, it's really funny. They're trying to entertain us by flying us around."

I remember the malaria kids coming in who were so ill. . . . Until they'd had a temperature of 104 or 105 for a couple of days, they didn't even send them out from the battalion aid stations. They would always come in feeling a little bit guilty because they didn't think they should take your time or need your attention, and they were just as sick as the other casualties.

I just want to give you one example of what I personally was aware of in the way that we tried to do the extra special things for the GIs that were there. There was one young kid that was assigned to something called Long Range Reconnaissance Patrol, and I don't know exactly what their job was—I think they're people who went out ahead of the other troops, kind of scouting and stuff. I remember being told by some of the officers who were assigned to infantry divisions that his was a really dangerous job and that the life expectancy for them was not very long. The first time he came to the hospital, he came with a broken nose, and he reminded me of my brother, who is one of the most special people to me. I took a special liking to this kid and lied to the people at the hospital; I told them that he was my step-brother. Well, he came back to the hospital many times after that with one or another little thing wrong with him, and I got all kinds of special favors for him, including staying in the enlisted quarters away from the hospital, because everyone thought he was my stepbrother. I really just loved this kid, and I don't know what ever happened to him; you know, somewhere along the way he just got lost. . . . I don't know if he was killed or what happened to him.

One of the things I think in my experience that was unique was the fact that I did stay so long. I remember going through the point when the people I had been originally with were all going home and I was staying there. I kept extending until my time had run out. I was happy to stay because I had joined the Army just to go there; I didn't want to be in the Army stateside. At that time I was still feeling very sure of myself, feeling like I was doing a very good job. By the time I came home I was really ready; I had just had enough and was extremely depressed. In retrospect I think I probably stayed too long. The Army liked you to stay, and if you would extend for six months, they would send you on R&R, for a free month anywhere in the world.

I went home because I was really homesick. I remember coming home in the middle of all that, back to Iron River and visiting with my parents. The news on TV was saying "Eight casualties were killed in Vietnam today" or "Ten casualties were killed in Vietnam today." I remember thinking what a lie it was, because I had just been there and I knew what was really going on. The other thing I found out is that people weren't really interested in what was going on. The antiwar movement was becoming very strong, and the people were just very angry. I remember feeling very angry inside; I thought, "They don't know. They don't care that people are being killed there." I realized too that I was very different than when I left there and didn't fit in with the people I'd known before. I still felt like I fit in with my family and felt very close toward them, except for my sister and brother-in-law, who had become very active in the antiwar movement. A lot of things were going on in this country that had completely slipped by me. Miniskirts had come in, and I came home wearing long skirts and feeling really sad, and these people were still talking about going to parties and dances and who they were dating; and I just felt it was so superficial. . . . I was happy to go back to Vietnam because that was where I felt secure. I went back there feeling that I didn't know what I was going to do with myself when I came home; I didn't know where I was going to fit in.

By the time I got back the war had gotten very busy. One of the things that I think to me is still amazing is the close relationships that you developed with the people you knew there. Apparently in some of the bigger hospitals there was a lot of—I don't even know what you want to call it—there was a lot of fooling around and affairs and relationships. In our hospital that didn't happen; it just did not happen. And people don't believe me. But I think one of the reasons that it didn't happen is there were only six females there, and not only that, there was no privacy. We spent all of our time together and developed really strong relationships, but they were totally platonic and supportive. People would go off to meet their wives in Hawaii, and everyone would be so happy for them to go and so happy for them to come back. We'd want to know all about their wives and their kids and what they were doing while they were away; I mean, we were really interested in their lives and in how they were going to make out when they got home.

One of the things that we did—and I don't know why we did it—but in the middle of the night, we got very bored and we got our hands on some red paint and some white paint and painted the barracks red-and-white-striped with pink polka dots. There was a little bridge that went between the helicopter pad and the hospital—well, we painted that pink. And we put up signs like the Burma Shave signs at the end of this bridge, just before the patients would be taken into the emergency room, that said, "Now that you've crossed the bridge of hope, you know you've reached the end of the rope." I remember the hospital commander coming in in the morning—we thought he would be absolutely furious—and surprisingly he never said a word; he never made us repaint it, and to this day I'm sure that building is still that color.

We didn't have a neurosurgeon or an ophthalmologist at the 18th Surg, and whenever we had someone who had a bad head injury, or they were in danger of losing an eye or something, we'd have to send them to one of the hospitals on the coast, like the 85th Evac. Most of the time the Air Force would do our evacking for us, but if it was just one person going down, then a lot of times the dustoff choppers would take him down and they'd have one of us nurses ride along to take care of him. I went very often, because I was assigned to the emergency room. I remember just how desperate I used to feel during these nights; there was really nothing in the helicopter to take care of them with in case anything should happen. We did have a suction apparatus we could work with our foot, but that was about the only thing that we could really use. I remember praying all the way down that they wouldn't die before they got there and feeling so afraid that something was going to happen—there was so little I could do. Those crazy dustoff pilots—they were really phenomenal! I think we knew them so well because there were so few of us that used to take these trips down to the coast with them. These guys, honest to God, would risk their lives all the time. They just seemed to have such an understanding, such a compassion, for the guys. I remember flying in some of the most horrible weather. The Air Force would say, ''We can't go because we can't land in this kind of weather,'' but the chopper pilots would go any time; I mean, they'd go through anything to take care of these kids. I remember one pilot in particular named John Kriner, who had three little girls, and he couldn't wait to get home from Vietnam to see his little daughters. But he was flying this crazy dustoff—a really wonderful, compassionate person.

I stayed in the 18th for about fourteen months when they decided to make the 18th Surg one of those MUST units, and they were sending it somewhere up north. So they sent the few women to the 71st Evac, which was up the hill from us in Pleiku. They had been building this hospital for a number of months, and I remember not wanting to go. I absolutely didn't want to be assigned to this big hospital, and I didn't think that they would understand what we had been through. We were used to being part of a small, elitist group and felt a lot of loyalty toward the 18th Surg. We wanted to go with them, but it was never open for discussion; we were told it was absolutely impossible.

When I got to the 71st Evac, they assigned me to the emergency room, I think because I had had so much experience. That was in November of '67. By then we were really very busy. That was shortly before Tet started. It was about that time that they started being much more careful about our going off base, and we were on something called red alert almost all the time. And that was when they started having rocket attacks. We were told—and I'm sure this is true—that they were intended for the airstrip but they would fall short and hit the hospital, and that made a lot of sense to me because I couldn't see them wasting rockets on a hospital; I couldn't believe that they would do that anyway. I remember you'd go home and just get to bed when they'd have the rocket attacks, and you'd have to go running back to the hospital with your flak vests and helmets on. I never remember being afraid during the rocket attacks; you know, I never felt like I was personally in danger. I don't know why. When I look back now, it was probably very foolish; I probably could've been injured just as well as anyone else, but I just never had the feeling that it would happen to me. Many of the nurses were like myself. You know, they seemed to be a totally unselfish group of women.

I remember the rocket attacks. If you could hear the whistle, you knew you were safe. You would hear the bang when it was shot, and if you could hear the whistle, you knew it was over your head, and then you'd hear the thud. But until you heard the whistle it was kind of a scary feeling. They used to tell us to lie really close to the walls, because apparently if you were close to the wall you wouldn't be hit by the debris. And I remember doing that, lying under a bench close to the wall when the rocket attacks would come. They always came at nighttime. . . . I worked through Tet. Tet was . . . It was . . . We all thought we were losing the war; you know, everyone was overworked and everyone was overtired. . . .

I remember my parents being very anxious to find out exactly when I would be coming home. Somebody hooked up so that we could call home on shortwave radio that would then be relayed to the telephone company. I remember saying "over" at the end of every sentence and not being able to understand very clearly what they were saying except, "When are you coming home?" I never realized until I got home how worried my parents were. I consider my father to be a deeply religious person—I mean, he certainly isn't bible-toting, but I think essentially he's a very religious person. He's the kind of Catholic who goes to church every Sunday; he never misses Mass, but he never went to communion. In the olden days Catholics didn't go to communion very often. That's the way they were trained; communion was really a sacred thing. I found out that during the two years I was in Vietnam, my father went to communion every single Sunday. I never knew that until I got back.

I went back to Iron River and stayed with my parents for about a month; it was in the middle of the winter, and Michigan's very cold. Then I went to Grand Rapids and got a job working in the emergency room. Then I moved to Philadelphia and got a job in the outpatient department at Temple University Hospital and was really happy to work there because there wasn't any trauma and it was nothing very stressful. I did that for five years and then went back to school and became an anesthetist.

After I was out for about three years, I decided that I wanted to get back into the military reserves. I looked around at Army units, but there wasn't anything that looked very interesting to me, so I went to the Air Force instead and joined the Delaware Air National Guard. That was really nice for me because, first of all, it was nothing like the Army. There wasn't anything that was very stressful; we didn't have field maneuvers or anything that brought back bad memories.

One of the things that amazed me was, there were nurses who were in the Air Guard during the Vietnam time, and I could never imagine why they never went active. I wondered what they were waiting for. Here were these nurses that were being paid all along for practicing and never doing what they were practicing for. I found that pretty incredible. And I have always felt kind of ambivalent toward them.

I remember one nurse in the Air Guard talking about Vietnam. She had gone for a couple weeks of active duty and flown some people back from Japan to the States, and she used to like to brag about that. And I was always pretty turned off by her war stories because she talked about it all the time. I remember one time she was telling me she was deadheading it back to Japan and the pilot was going to fly them into Vietnam and land there and come out again for some reason. She told me that she would've qualified then for combat pay. She was bragging about it, and I felt like vomiting. It was disgusting to me that this woman would actually want to get combat pay for just landing somewhere and then have the gall to brag about that to someone who's actually been there.

As far as having been there and what it's meant to me . . . I don't think I've ever been the same. I think before I went to Vietnam I was really a very happy-go-lucky, free-wheeling kind of person. I think I still am, but I don't think I've ever taken life as lightly as I did then. I think I've always had kind of a serious part of me that I've never shared with anyone before, not even my very closest friends. I've never really talked about the painful part of Vietnam to anyone. Mostly because I don't want to think about it myself.

Last year I was called and asked if I would be interviewed for a TV show; they wanted to interview some nurses who had been in Vietnam. And I declined to do that for a number of reasons: first of all, I don't trust reporters; I thought they would change my wording and things, and I also felt that I just didn't have anything to say that I wanted anyone else to hear. I really didn't want to share any of my experiences with anyone. They did find a nurse from Philadelphia to interview, and when I watched her on television I was embarrassed and shocked by what she had to say. She talked about making life-and-death decisions, which I felt probably was untrue. I felt she probably was never in the position to have to make a life-and-death decision, because she was there much later than I was, and I certainly was never in that position. I felt everything she said was so melodramatic, and I felt she shed a very poor light upon us, so my feelings about not talking to anyone about Vietnam were really reinforced.

At the same time, they were organizing this big to-do in Washington for the dedication of the Vietnam War memorial. They wanted a lot of us to go down, so I signed up to go and decided that I would be part of the festivities, if you will. Then when the time came, I just couldn't go. I didn't feel that I could emotionally take it. I still feel that way—I just can't go there. I'm really glad they have the memorial. I'm happy that Americans are beginning to look more favorably upon Vietnam War veterans. I hope that they'll continue to do so, I hope that this book will make people understand.

I think the Army made a drastic mistake in that they didn't do any deprogramming. We got home from Vietnam, and we were out of the Army. Never once did anyone talk to us about what was going to happen, but I don't think they knew what was going to happen to us either. I think that's why so many people like myself have never talked about it with anyone, because it was just too painful—it is too painful. It's easier to forget and to stuff it all, and until people come along and start questioning you, you try not to think about it.

I remember feeling very angry when the POWs were released from Iran—about the big deal that they made about them. I was happy for them that they had recognition but was also feeling very angry that the country couldn't rally around the Vietnam people. I also remember, when I first came home, people bragging about avoiding the Vietnam War, how they'd gotten out of it and how they were so proud of themselves. Then just recently I read a letter to the editor in the *Philadelphia Inquirer* about a guy who said today he has to make excuses about why he wasn't there. And he kind of hangs his head in shame. I feel sorry for him though too, because he didn't realize that this was something that's going to come back to haunt him. I don't want to get into whether we should have been there or we shouldn't have been there. I've never faced that problem; I've never dealt with that myself. I'm glad it's over, and I'm sorry that so many people were killed over there. And I'm sorry that all of us had to go through it. . . . I hope that the government never forgets.

I mentioned earlier about feeling very angry against the people that were demonstrating so actively during the war.

A lot of us who were in Vietnam did feel very angry because we would hear propaganda about that. And I think, in a way, it did give fuel to the enemy, that they knew there were people at home against the war, and the government had to fight this battle also. When I look back now—thank God they did it, because it did make the war end that much quicker, and they were right; it was a civil war. I'm glad I went, and I think I did a really good job while I was there. I think being there did make a difference for the GIs. I think it made a difference having nurses there, having women there. I feel sad about how I feel about . . . you know, how I feel inwardly. That's something that I will probably never deal with. I have friends who have gone to psychiatrists and stuff, but I'm just not that kind of person; I will never do that I'm sure. I think there are a lot of different ways of dealing with things. . . . I think some people talk about it to everyone that will listen. I think some people keep it all in. I think other people just forget it. . . .

Jeanne "Sam" Bokina Christie

AMERICAN RED CROSS, SRAO
NHA TRANG—FEB. '67 TO JUNE '67
DA NANG—JUNE '67 TO SEPT. '67
PHAN RANG—SEPT. '67 TO FEB. '68

Sam resides in New England, where she works as a teacher of various arts and crafts classes and a part-time designer. She also has a small company specializing in decorative wall treatments. "Most of the time I am a chauffeur, cook, and laundry maid. When not doing that, I exercise, work with two show dogs, and I am involved with a host of community and volunteer projects. Most are on the state or national level and/or the networking of the many women who served in, or are connected with, the Southeast Asia experience."

We met at the Marines Memorial Club in San Francisco. She had come with two large suitcases full of information sheets, rosters, graphs, and clippings to a reunion of Red Cross workers from across the country. I was invited to the reception that evening and had the memorable experience of being in a room with over seventy women who had all served overseas, a majority of them in Vietnam. There were so many emotional moments—the slide show alone was a heartstopper.

In 1967 I had gone into the art-ed program to pick up my teaching credentials. I was your typical destined-to-be-old-maid schoolteacher: short sleeves down to my elbows, frumpy clothes, very prim, proper collars, trying to look like a professional teacher. However, I decided that if I was going to do anything, I had to do it now. I had been offered a job in Kalamazoo, Michigan, as an art teacher but decided that I would just explore a few other avenues. I filled out all sorts of applications with the help of some people in the placement office, including the Red Cross forms. I went through several interviews, and then the Red Cross flew me down to Saint Louis, Missouri, for final interviews. When they called me back they said, "Do you want to go to Vietnam?" I didn't say yes; I didn't say I'd think about it; I said, "Yep." They said, "Are you sure?" and I said, "Yep." That was it—that's how I accepted to go to Vietnam. Called my parents and told them I was going to Vietnam. I really had no idea of where I was going; it sounded like a nice foreign country—you know, 1967 and party time. I was totally unaware, totally unaware of the war. It sounded like an interesting and exciting place to go. So my parents were very quiet; I don't remember which one of them said anything at this point. My mother probably fell in a heap on the floor, but one of them said, "If you do this, this will be the biggest decision you ever make in your life." Believe me, it definitely was.

I had to report back to Washington. They sent a list of clothing—black handbags, black shoes, you know, the appropriate uniforms—and we were there roughly two weeks. During the two weeks it was basically how to learn to tell rank on somebody's shirt-sleeve and the difference between the Army, the Navy, and the Marines. What good, proper young ladies should do, how you should act, how you behave, what you don't say, when you don't take a drink and when you do take a drink, how you drink it, what you say to off-color remarks, a little history of the Red Cross, and how to "program." That basically was the training session. We were paid employees, but most of the training was on the job; in fact, it was all the experience a person could handle! After the two-week session, everyone got a GG shot by some doctor who, we all felt, loved to give the girls their shots. The procedure was to then put us on an airplane in our little blue uniforms with our little black heels, our girdles (at that time there were no pantyhose), navy-blue raincoats, and our little Dixie Cup hats, and off we went with the troops.

There were about six or seven of us on a plane full of men. Everybody was trying to be sweet and nice, but it's a long, hard journey, and by the time we got to Vietnam it was a scary feeling—to know that this was kind of "it." We were still well taken care of, we always have been. . . . The guys were super, but the closer the plane got to Vietnam, the more frightened everyone became and the tenser the situation became. When we got to Nam it was nighttime and blackout conditions, plus all the lights on the plane had been turned out. There appeared to be no lights on the runway nor anyplace—it was just black! Everybody was dead silent. When the plane landed and came to a stop, they opened the doors, and we could see spotlights on the runways. Immediately we heard everyone shouting orders to everybody else. We just weren't accustomed to treatment like that. We were taken aside, to a billet of some sort where the group of gals spent the night. We really did not see Vietnam until the next morning at dawn. For myself, I literally opened the door of the billet and snapped my camera. There were two fellows sitting in the bunker, looking at the door as it opened, knowing probably darn well that there was a bunch of new girls there. It was 1967, and all our lives changed at that point.

My first impressions were not bad. In many ways I have a very different sense of values and way of looking at things. I didn't see the dirt that so many saw when they arrived; I didn't smell the terrible smells, though I knew they were there. I was interested in looking at the flowers and seeing the plants and different things like that. I was very interested in the people, probably because all through my college years I had been interested in people and had worked with the People to People Organization, plus foreign visitors groups, so I had a different concept of what was "strange" to our criteria. To me Vietnam was a great source of curiosity.

Our class of seven spent several days in Saigon, where the ARC trained us before sending us out to the units. An amusing story of Saigon was when I got a phone call as I was sitting in training. Here I am, half the world away from home, the phone rings, and it's for me. Now what's happened? I've been sent home already! The great fear was being sent home. Not being caught, not getting into trouble, but for the women it was an absolute disaster and disgrace to be sent home. It turned out to be a fellow from the Milwaukee chapter, because I had been from Wisconsin. He heard I was coming through in the class. He took me out in Saigon, all over town on the back of his motorcycle. We went to the zoo and so many of the places that were later blown up. It was a unique experience, one that I'll always remember fondly. That type of start into Vietnam helped my perspective on certain things and makes so much of it positive.

Training gave the honchos time to assess which girl should go to which unit. Some of the units were very safe, very stateside, and some were very rough to handle, very open and never clean. My first unit was Nha Trang, which was clean but very open. A driver took us to the flight line, where we were all separated and sent to our units. The girls picked me up at the flight line with the driver. I was informed I had to sit on the floor of the jeep with my helmet on because it was a combat zone and we might be shot at. They had this great ceremony for new girls! I spent the first night on guard duty on the steps of our hooch with a whistle to let people know that somebody was coming. Well I was naive and totally believed anything I was told. I sat out there the first night on the end of the hooch with my little helmet on, scared to death I'd have to blow the whistle. Each unit had a good time with the new kids, but that was early, that was '67. Apparently from what I understand now, things changed rapidly as the war went on. Nha Trang was a supernice unit on the 8th Field Hospital compound. We had a little hooch we shared with the nurses and some of the Red Cross field directors. There was a gal by the name of Big Mamma (I never knew her real name), Captain Marsha, who was her friend, and another nurse, Mary. I didn't know her name either, but one night, to relieve the pressure, Mary caught lizards in our hooch, and I have great photos of her chasing the lizards through the potted plants.

We all shared quarters, and apparently as the war escalated they had to move us off the hospital compound to make room for the increased load. Thus we were moved into the city of Nha Trang, to a lovely house, which was right on prostitute row. Things were quite interesting down there! On the military compound we only had a compound guard. It was fairly safe, though we looked out our window to a roll of concertina wire and the villagers. In fact I used to sit for hours, fascinated with the kids' creative endeavor at throwing a stone at a board to see how far it would skip over. When I used to watch those kids, it never dawned on me that they could kill any of us.

In Nha Trang we had a super housemaid. She took care of all of us, and I became a very good friend of hers. She would take me shopping, and I got to the point where I could shop for vegetables in the market. I, in turn, would show her how to cook American, which absolutely fascinated her. I had a fry pan and had scrounged oil and flour to make my mother's German recipe, meatballs and milk gravy. She was totally in disbelief that Americans would cook and eat the way we did. I even taught her how to make real french fries. Eventually she took me down to her house to meet her family, which was a great honor. I had a really funny feeling being this big American, which I'm really not, wandering down the streets with this tiny Vietnamese through the back rows and alleys. She took me to her house and introduced me to her husband and five children. I toured the one-room house and was shown the one bed that they all slept on, and then she fixed tea for me. All her neighbors were hanging around the window, looking and touching me, finding out firsthand what an American was like. Well, when it came time to take me home, her husband was going to give me a ride on his moped. He weighed about half my weight, so when I sat on the back of the moped, the front wheel went up in the air! We had a lot of problems trying to get me home that day. They were determined that I was not going to walk, so I don't even remember how I got home. I just remember his absolute horror at finding he couldn't go anyplace with his American guest and his moped.

Nha Trang was that type of a town at that point. There were a lot of good things happening. It was early; it was "open." There were the most magnificent French restaurants, delicious food—even though they were eventually blown up. Some were blown up while I was there. In fact, one of the bad incidents was when a young boy was going to blow up one of the clubs we were going to; we were walking toward the entrance when he came running down the street and somebody shot him. He had the grenade in his hand, which was destined for the restaurant we were going into. But in spite of that incident, it was early and it was open, so there wasn't a great sense of animosity.

Living on the row that we did, we did have ARVN guards. They would break into our house, beat up our maids, and steal our stuff. They would go through our rooms with loaded weapons at night. So if you woke up and saw them, you didn't dare move. You'd be dead. You watched your whole life be taken right out through the door. They'd take all your valuables. So you develop a little bit of bitterness about that, but when they beat up Bien and some of the other housemaids, it upset me greatly. In Nha Trang we also got to know the ROKs (the Koreans), and they were very interesting people. I even ate dog and kim chee, which is an adventure. I still eat kim chee, but only raise the dogs for pets. After I left the unit, because of the break-ins and the problems with the guards, the whole unit was moved to a different location, to another compound, but while we were in downtown Nha Trang, life was "interesting." I had built very friendly, warm feelings toward the people, toward the program, toward the military, and it was good. That basic premise led to some of the problems that I developed in the next unit I was sent to.

Usually when a unit director figured or felt that you were having problems—either being too close or too distant or just personal problems—you were moved. It kept you fresh, because in such an intense situation, you knew people so intimately well in a short period of time that they had to move you every three or four months so you did not develop a stale attitude. In some units they had to move you even more often because the situation was so intense. In others that were really very stateside, they would leave you there a long time. Nha Trang was nice because we could go out into the countryside so much, and we got into the Montagnard camps. Special Forces was there, so we did a lot of things with Special Forces, which was a unique opportunity. In Nha Trang, those who were the kickers and the Lurps were all our friends, we didn't know or, if we did know, think anything about their jobs. They were just guys, and they put their pants on the same way everybody else did, one foot at a time. Different units have different types of persons in it, and as you became acquainted with them, you felt different things toward the various groups. Each of us has our own "special" division or unit even to this day.

Most of the Red Cross units had centers or buildings that

people worked in. We always worked in pairs. There would be two girls in the center, and the rest would be out in the field. Each day, a program director would assign you where you would be going. You might have to be up at five in the morning, on a helipad, or you might be lucky and not have to be in until noon. This all depended on where you had to go and what security would be available. We always had American armed guards with us when we would be out in the field; they would either go with us or meet us when we got to a location. We were noncombatant, so we could not carry a weapon, although some of the photos we have don't go along with that. The days were long and very hard on the kidneys, so you learned very quickly how to "look for golf balls in the field" and never think much about it. It had to, and did, become second nature to have the men turn their backs while you squatted to go to the john. The men were very much gentlemen in that situation; however, a green piece of fabric does not make a great wall—nor soundproof! Let me put it another way: it was now or "until your eyeballs float," and that was it.

The job gave us the chance to work with many different units. We worked with the Navy Seals, the Navy Signal sites, the Air Force, the Marines, and the Army. Frequently we worked with the supply troops, who never got out to the field, whose boredom was a totally different type of program concept than the guys who were out in the field. With each group we would learn different programming skills and we would learn about our own abilities. The programs were designed to be one-hour-long audience-participation games, like Concentration and World Traveler. They were usually question-and-answer forms. In addition we always had a set of flashcards with us as icebreakers. That way we could get a conversation going and get the men's minds off of being in the field and being dirty or losing friends and buddies. In many cases the games were so silly that they would do nothing but make them laugh. Sometimes we would laugh so hard that they would laugh hard. It sounds a bit out of context for a war zone, but it did the trick; it gave them the lift that was needed to survive, or continue on. Many were the days when we would be lucky and get to eight units in a day—lots of work and lots of fun. To get to the units, we might travel by boat, by jeep, by trucks, by plane, or our favorite, choppers. We almost always came back on the same day. There were a few units that required overnights, but that was generally due to the security. If you went to a unit like that, the security was tighter. Regardless, the gals were always well taken care of, and the men were always careful around us and they put themselves out to protect us. Fear with our own troops never crossed our minds; the men took care of us, and we never had much time to worry about anything— that also was the way it was.

Our light blue uniforms were a curse for always being dirty and a blessing for being visible when we went out programming. There was an incident where two of the girls went out to a unit, or an LZ, and the troops had moved, but the crew that took them out was told to drop them off at such and such, where they thought someone else was going to pick them up. They let the girls out and took off. Well, the girls could not find any troops, nor much else. They had been left in the middle of a field, and thank God at that point for the little blue uniforms, because somebody flying over saw them out in the middle of the field. He called in that he had two "Delta Deltas" down there, so somebody came in and picked them up. What would the girls have done? There was no way they could communicate; they couldn't yell, "Hey, I'm lost out here." The blue "uni" was our sign. Somebody was always watching out for you. In that sense we were lucky, and yet couldn't get into much mischief either.

My next unit was Da Nang, and I must say it was where the Marines dubbed me Sam, when I lost my real name tag. Sam stayed with me for the rest of my tour. Da Nang was the Marines! It was a different type of unit, different philosophy, and different way of life. The town was a big town, in fact, a huge town—a city. We had two centers at the time, one on the flight line, which was very hot—no air conditioning, no fans, just nothing but flight line heat and lots of GIs. Whoever had that duty came back at the end of the day just fried. You were wall-to-wall people from all of the Marines coming in and going out, but they were the most tremendous group of guys. I loved the Marines; they were just super! Well, any of the units that were really close combat support or dealing with a lot of active combat were the best groups to be with. They were the dirtiest, they had the worst things happen, but they were always the most tremendous people. There was another big club up on Freedom Hill just beyond Dog Patch. Freedom Hill was quite civilized. It had a bakery, a big exchange, the USO club, and the USO shows up there too. The center we had was quite a big air-conditioned building. It was fun to be up there, but it was more fun to be out in the field. From Da Nang you would go to the LZs and the fire bases. We even got into a couple command posts because there wasn't anyplace else for us to go that was safe.

I don't remember the base or LZ, but we had gone out of Da Nang someplace, one of the hills, and there had been problems right before, so we did not program. We just sat and talked and talked and talked. There were some guys who would sit back and not talk to us; they just couldn't. Others would come over, and they'd talk about their wives or their girlfriends. It was very depressing and sad, yet so very touching, because it didn't matter who we were but just the simple fact that we were there and were "home"— America and femininity—to them. I remember when we had to leave—not wanting to go and being physically put on the chopper and told to "get the hell out of here!" Because it was getting dark, and you'd start catching incoming rounds, and they had things to do at that point. I did not want to leave them; I wanted to stay and help them. I had two younger brothers, and so many of the men reminded me of my brothers—I really felt great compassion for them. That's part of the reason I ran into problems. I got too psychologically involved; I didn't want to leave my young Marines. I wanted to protect them and make all the pain and anger go away.

In some cases it was very traumatic. We would see units during the morning hours, and by the time we got back and were put in the hospital to help by doing some programming, the same guys would be in the hospital. That just blows your mind. I mean, you've seen them two or three hours ago healthy and whole, and then you meet them with everything blown apart. It's hard to take! That's why I say there were instances that were really trying. You have to go on, just perking along, doing your thing. That's just one of the elements that you lived with. . . . You would have men who had just lost buddies or wives or girlfriends. They would bring their letters to you and ask you to read them, or they'd sit there with this lost look on their face—and we couldn't touch them and they couldn't touch us—but you just wanted to go over and put your arms around them and tell them, "It's okay." You know, you did it mentally as best you could. I will never forget some of the guys that came in from Khe Sanh, filthy, wretched, dirty, into the Da Nang center, and I remember seeing them sit there just in a total fog and daze. I found out from some of the other guys what had happened. There wasn't anything I could do for them but just be as normal as I possibly could be around them to let them decelerate, and it's a little thing, but you did what you could.

"Free time" was never really free time; we were on duty twenty-four hours a day, seven days a week. Regardless of where you went or what you did, you were always singled out—round-eye, Doughnut Dolly. . . . So in many cases you would retreat to a person you were comfortable with and/or be with a unit that you did not work with during the day. And you became that unit's protected mascot. Different people went different directions at night. We all had curfews. Regardless though, the units were hit and caught sniper fire in the houses. Again in Da Nang, we had ARVN guards. We knew when anything was going to happen because there would be no guards around. They would disappear just as fast as they could. This was in the city of Da Nang! The night that Da Nang was hit, I remember all of the gals in our unit sitting down in the laundry room because we didn't have a sandbag bunker—we were in the "city." The Marines had placed sandbags around us, and we're sitting there saying, "Any moment now, somebody's going to come in, and that's going to be it for all of us." However, we were all okay. We're all around today.

In Da Nang I spent the days with the Marines and the evenings with the Air Force. The Air Force was my retreat, my moments of sanity. They made coping with what the Marines had to do to survive tolerable. For instance, the Marine who brought me ears on a string one day. I remember being absolutely naive, a real classic. "Oh, apricots for me"—thinking, "Here I am in the war zone, and somebody got me real dried apricots, a whole package of them." And to this day I look at dried apricots, and that's exactly what I see, a string of ears. I was that naive. I was just wide open with my troops. Eventually when you established trust with the men in the field, they would take you aside and, with great pride and joy, show you the scalps and the fingers and the jars of other things. You know, I would say, "Oh, isn't that nice." The horror that we might express would just totally destroy anyone, so we were always upbeat. Our job was to be upbeat. It was never to let on, never to have anything wrong. You would go home at night and say Wooo. But during the day you didn't dare.

The Da Nang unit was very difficult for me in one way, because we got into the hospitals. Our group, SRAO, was not trained to be in the hospitals. As an example, the worst thing I had ever seen prior to Nam was when my dog was hit by a car. In the hospitals we walked right into some of the muck and mire. How the gals at the hospitals did it 365 days a year, I don't know, but heaven bless them. Hopefully, they were better prepared for it than I was. They had been trained as nurses and were more accustomed to seeing what went on in the hospitals, and they had built up their protective walls a little differently. For some of us who went into the hospitals—where we shouldn't have been—it was a hell of a rude awakening. The guys would show you their wounds with great pride, and you're standing there trying to say, "Isn't that nice" and "Gee, everything will be just fine," even to the guy who just lost two arms and a leg or had half of his face blown away. You know you're lying right through your teeth, and it just did you in, but you did it to survive and to help them survive.

I was in Da Nang from June until September, then was switched to Phan Rang Air Force Base, where I became unit and program director. I think those were, in some respects, some of the best times I had, because I made better, closer friends there than anyplace else. It was also some of the worst times in the sense I wasn't with "my troops." I wasn't out in the field and doing what needed to be done. PRG (Phan Rang) was fairly well protected. It was dull; the men were in a very antiseptic war on the base. The 101st was still on the other side of the hill and the Australians were in the center, so it was party time. There was nothing much to do except socialize and drink.

Pat, the gal I probably was the closest to the whole time I was there, was a brand new girl. I broke her in, or she broke me in—it must not have been too bad, because she went back for a second tour. You could not have long hair at the time, and Pat had long hair, which the men just adored. Of course, you can imagine what loose, long hair on a flight line looks like . . . but she would wear her hair down, and I would try and make her wear her hair up. These were critical issues at that point: hair up or down, or to wear brown shoes or black shoes, because we were all starting to wear R&R shoes, which were not authorized. However, you learned to deal with a whole different set of values of how to keep men and their morale up, because the values were not the same as with the combat troops. Everything was so easy for the men. The boredom was the worst thing that we all at PRG had to live with. As comparison, in Da Nang one day the VC came up over the hill behind the unit on Freedom Hill. We were evacuated. You didn't pick up anything; you were just thrown in a vehicle and driven out as fast as possible. In PRG you would have had six month's notice if anything was coming. We were high on a hill (we were actually sitting ducks). The area had been bought off, and the 101st still protected our perimeters. We used to sit at night and watch the ships and the rounds going in, and you'd think, "those poor bastards are down there getting killed, and here we sit on a hill watching it like a movie." It's amazing the different concepts you had of what was going on.

PRG was the end of my tour. I don't recall much—I've tuned so much of it out. I had a couple months left on my tour, but my attitude was "short." I was burned out at that point. I had been psychologically hurt and wanted to go home. I did my job, I listened to the guys, but if the girls were given a chance to get out and program, I sent them, I didn't want to go. I was better on the flight line, which was boring—just going around passing out Kool-Aid, serving time. Yeah, I really had a short-timer's attitude. The gray fog had rolled over my tired mind.

I came out during the Tet offensive; I left the unit in PRG and went to Saigon. I was one of five Doughnut Dollies who were lost during Tet. The five of us were AWOL— you know, between here and there when all the trouble began. Three were going to Thailand, I was going home, and another girl was coming back from Hong Kong. Due to all the events that took place in Tet, we were in different hotels—wherever we could find billets really. All I wanted to do was get out of the country, and of course there were no flights. I was so "short," I just wanted to go home. I didn't care how! Eventually at one of the hotels I found a friend of a friend who flew Bird Dogs. He flew me out the night the air base at Saigon was hit, and I remember seeing all the fires. Flying at night was dumb. You know, it was an unauthorized flight to start with, and I was a female, but I was determined to get out of there. He took me back as far as PRG, and it was like the "cat coming back." You know—"I thought we got rid of you once." At PRG, the men found me a ride to Cam Ranh, because that was close by. In Cam Ranh I was all set to go out, and then they found my passport had not been stamped and I was not authorized to leave the country. All I wanted to do was go home! Regardless, I had to go back to Saigon, find somebody to stamp my passport, get on a C-13O, or whatever it was, back to Cam Ranh again, and of course missed my arranged flight. I remember hitchhiking a ride by checking manifests and by going up to any plane that was going out of the country and asking if I could ride. I finally got out and went to Okinawa, and everybody was absolutely convinced I had left out of Tan Son Nhut and gone to California.

When I finally got to California and checked in, they stripped me of all the military identification and cards I had. Most of the government-related material was taken or changed. Vietnam was just a figment of my imagination when I walked out of the headquarters. My memory was about all I had, so I went to see a friend at an air base in Washington and stayed there for a while. I had a flight suit still, short hair, boots, and gloves, so we flew T-33s. Nobody knew I was a girl. The guy that I knew was great. He said, "You're ten pounds overweight at least. You better get your head together and your tail in gear!" He really kicked me in the butt, which was what I needed. That truly was a good old friend from when I had been in Nha Trang—not too many around, but Vietnam made friends like that.

It took me a few weeks before I saw my family for the first time, and then, they recall more than I do about my homecoming. I tried to get a job, and of course nobody would hire me. I was either overqualified or didn't have any experience. I also knew I was going to graduate school, since I had applied and been accepted while in Vietnam. I hadn't been working on an exorbitant salary. I mean, what I earned in salary didn't exactly cover a lot of costs, so I got an assistantship. Finally the Red Cross said, "We'll give you a job at Great Lakes Naval Hospital working in the rec department, if you'd like to come down." They were real good, knowing that I was just going to be there a short while and putting up with my antics. I was a crazy woman, totally out of control, very much misbehaving to their standards. The director made me take off the SRAO patches and put on a regular one and made me wear my uniform the right way. It nearly killed me; I was such an arrogant monster. I was accustomed to being with able-bodied men, and here I was in a hospital where they were long-term recoveries. The director had a terrible time converting me. I would go up through the wards and say, "Hi guys, let's play games." You know, the guys loved it; they thought it was super. The lady that was my supervisor was dying a thousand deaths. I thought I was the best thing that ever came through the hospital ward. . . . The guys used to call it the freshest breath of fresh air. However, I was terrible for the hospital and the formality that it functioned under. I had another good friend at Great Lakes who would sit with me on the back steps when I would break into crying sessions. I cried for my homesickness—for Vietnam, for the guys, for the high level of activity, the values I had lived by. I didn't want to face those unanswered questions of being in the war and my role in it, so I would sit and cry. This buddy sat me down and gave me great words of wisdom—"Quit trying so hard." I had been trying to repeat Vietnam. The States were not Nam, and the people here did not relate. So I started turning it all off.

A year passed, and I went to Guam, still not having resolved the feelings I had developed in Nam. Guam was another safe retreat, a safe duty station, although they did have casualties from Nam at the hospital annex. I would go over to the annex, and the hurt was still so strong, the ache so great about being back in Nam, that I found it easier to simply stay away. That was in '69. It was not until the past couple of years that I would deal with it ever again. Not until the experience of looking at slides with other friends, some men that had been to Nam, did I realize how much I had hurt, what my emotional commitments were, and how the Vietnam experience had jarred my philosophical and moral outlook on life. Events happened so fast in Vietnam that I never had time to explain them or deal with them. I had to always be on the go and always up. All of a sudden those emotions and feelings came out, and I really had a tough time recalling and dealing with them at the onset. Also, in deciding on how I was going to cope with what I had done, or said, or hadn't done or didn't say, and how it was going to affect me.

In general it's been a good experience, a positive one. I learned in the war that there wasn't a right and there wasn't a wrong. I saw very quickly from the kid who had the grenade in Nha Trang that we were not necessarily right for being there. After all, it was his homeland and territory he was defending, and I represented the intruder. Out of the whole experience I've come full-circle at this point and have discovered that there is no black or white. It's a matter of perspective and of which side you stand on when viewing life's events. For every negative there's a positive; for everything bad there is something good that will develop from the experience. Those bits of information are not always easy to see nor are they always easy to accept. Regardless, you just keep going. You don't stop forever on the things that hold you up; you learn from the events and change what needs to be done. If you never try to work through something that's tough, it really isn't a valuable lesson. Vietnam absolutely heightened my awareness level by giving me the experiences so few women have the opportunity to have.

Since that change of events and learning, my life has been terrific. It's as if my head got screwed back on with greater perception and understanding. I have the conviction and pride for the job I did and the person I was, so I can truly speak up and not be afraid of what others will think or say. It's like I have a special extra or reserve self that I can use when the going gets tough. As the expression in Nam went—"Can do!" It may sound silly, but then it's only taken me at least fifteen years to really believe it. The stumbling blocks which can make life difficult need not make one give up. Now I'm on a soapbox—what else can I say or do but to smile and admit I've learned more than money could buy, and I've learned to be positive with it.

Photo by Pat Johnson

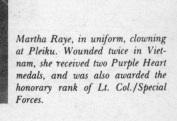

Martha Raye, in uniform, clowning at Pleiku. Wounded twice in Vietnam, she received two Purple Heart medals, and was also awarded the honorary rank of Lt. Col./Special Forces.

*Pat Johnson with children of a Montagnard village (**above**) and at 18th Surgical Hospital, Pleiku, 1966 (**right**).*

Above: Lynn McClenahan on "The Bridge over the River Don't Kwai," WAC Detachment club, Long Binh. *Below:* Guard shack, WAC Detachment entrance in Long Binh. Photo by Lynn McClenahan

*Rose Sandecki flashes the peace sign in Da Nang (**above**); Rose in front of a bunker at 12th Evac Hospital, Cu Chi (**below**).*

Right: Red Cross worker Jeanne Christie climbing the ladder of a perimeter signal tower near Da Nang in summer 1967. **Below:** Jeanne with the Marines in a base camp outside of Da Nang.

Right: "Peace on Earth"—Army nurse Chris Schneider's Christmas card, 1970. *Below:* Georgeanne Andreason and an Army Special Services co-worker wait for a helicopter at Tam Binh outpost.

Emergency room entrance, 95th Evac Hospital, Da Nang. Photo by Chris Schneider

Aerial view of 95th Evac Hospital, Da Nang. Photo by Chris Schneider

Anne Simon Auger

91ST EVAC. HOSPITAL,
CHU LAI—JULY '69 TO JULY '70

Anne lives in the Pacific Northwest, has been married for fourteen years (to a Vietnam vet), and has two daughters. She is a computer programmer and showroom manager for a manufacturer's representative. She does a great deal of volunteer work in her community using her medical background and is active in her daughters' scouting activities.

She had just come home from work with a big bag of groceries, and chased her husband and daughters out for the evening. We got acquainted in the kitchen as we ate. After that we sat on a couch in front of a large picture window. When she began talking, she put one hand over her eyes, and it stayed there during the entire ninety minutes the tape recorder ran. I remember looking out the window, not having eye contact with her, watching the effects of the sunset on a large, cloudy Pacific Northwest sky.

I REMEMBER DRIVING DOWN TO FORT SAM HOUSTON with two of the girls who had signed up with me. I can still see us flying down those freeways heading south toward Texas. We felt like we were invincible. We owned the world; we were free, independent. It was really neat.

I remember trying on our combat boots and ponchos and our uniforms; we'd never worn anything so ridiculous in our lives. And we would parade 'round and play games in them and think we were really cool . . . We learned how to march. We thought that was so funny. I remember we had field training. We were given compasses and had to go out and find our way back: we never had so much fun. We got lost twelve times to Tuesday—it didn't matter. We had a little bit of medical training in the field where they would wrap some volunteer up in bandages, put a tag on him saying what was wrong with him, and we had to take care of him. It was totally unrealistic. It was another game. We knew what to do and how to do it from the lesson, but we didn't have any idea of what we were getting ourselves into. We were given weapons training in that they showed us how to fire an M-16, but they wouldn't let us do it. Of course I didn't want to anyway—they were too noisy. They took us through a mock Vietnam village. That was a little scary when they had the punji stick trap come up, but again it was no big deal. And I don't see how the Army could have done any different. I hated them for years for not training me better for Vietnam, but I don't think it could possibly be done. I don't think you can train anybody or teach anybody to experience something that horrible without having them simply live it. . . . Anyway. We got through Fort Sam. It was a lark.

I went to Fort Devons in Massachusetts for six months. I was assigned to the orthopedic ward, and 1OO percent of my patients were Vietnam casualties. They were long-term; they had been in Japan before they came to us. I didn't even relate them to Vietnam, and it bothers me now, because they could have been suffering some of the distress that I have, and I didn't recognize it. I know some of them acted really wild and crazy, but I figured it was just because they were kids. While I was there I was dating a psychologist. He was a captain. I'll never forget when I got my orders he was the first one I showed them to, and I was excited. "I'm going to Vietnam!" I told him. He was upset because he was staying there and I was leaving; he thought the man should go. It hadn't dawned on me before that I should be anything but excited. I didn't think to question anything that was going on or to wonder what I was getting myself into. I was just out for experiences at the time, I guess.

So, I remember flying over from Travis. I was the only woman on the plane. There must have been two hundred men on the plane. But everybody was polite and friendly until we got within sight of Vietnam, and then it all just quieted down. Nobody talked; nobody said anything. Everybody had their noses glued to the window. We saw puffs of smoke. The plane took a sudden turn up, and we heard we were being fired on. That was the first time it dawned on me that my life may be in peril. Then I started thinking, "Why would they want to shoot me? I haven't done anything to them." Anyway, we took this steep, real fast dive into Long Binh, and we landed in Vietnam. I

remember talking to the nurse in charge of assigning people, and she actually gave me a choice of where I wanted
to go. The other nurses with me knew just about where
they wanted to go. They all had choices, and I had no idea
of one place from another. So I told her to send me wherever she wanted, and she still wouldn't do that. She said,
"North or south?" I said, "I don't know." I finally just
decided, "Oh hell, send me north. If I'm going to be here
I might as well get as close to the North Vietnamese as I
can," which is really irrational now, but at the time I didn't
know what I was doing. So she assigned me to the 91st
Evac.

I was assigned to intensive care and recovery, which is
like jumping straight into the fire. I had no preparation for
it. I was six months out of nursing school and had worked
in a newborn nursery until I joined the Army. It was hectic.
It was fast paced. It was depressing. I spent six months
there. Two of the incidents that really stand out from those
six months: One was when I was working recovery. I had
been there a few months, long enough to get numb and
build a few walls. This eighteen-year-old GI came into my
recovery ward. He had been through surgery. He'd been
in an APC that ran over a mine, and I think he was the
only survivor. He was just a young kid; I don't even think
he had hair on his face yet. And he came out of the anesthesia crying for his mother. I felt so helpless. I was barely
older than he was, and he's crying, "Mommy! Mommy!
Mommy!" I didn't know what to do. . . . I just held him,
and I think that's all I did. It worked, but it was a real
experience for me because I certainly wasn't maternal at
the time and hadn't thought that that would ever come up.
It got me to realize how young and how innocent and how
naive these poor kids were. And their choices had been
taken away from them.

Then the other incident. We had a sergeant, must have
been in his mid forties; he was a drinker, an alcoholic.
And he wasn't even involved first line in the war—he was
a supply sergeant or something. He came into our intensive
care unit with a bleeding ulcer. I remember spending two
hours pumping ice water into his stomach, pulling it out,

and pumping it back in. We were also pumping blood into him. He died, and he had a family back home, and I thought, "My God, it's bad enough to die over here legitimately"—the gunshot wound—but to die that way seemed like such an awful waste.

The patient that chased me off the ward . . . was a lieutenant named . . . I don't remember his last name—his first name was John. He was twenty-one. He'd gotten married just before he came to Vietnam. And he was shot in his face. He absolutely lost his entire face from ear to ear. He had no nose. He was blind. It didn't matter, I guess, because he was absolutely a vegetable. He was alive and breathing; tubes and machines were keeping him alive. . . . I just . . . I couldn't handle it. To think of how one instant had affected his life. . . . His wife's life was completely changed, his parents, his friends, me—it affected me too. And all because of one split second. I got to realizing how vulnerable everybody was. And how vulnerable I was. I took care of him for a week. They finally shipped him to Japan, and I never heard from him again. I don't know if he's dead or alive. I don't know how his wife or his family are doing. I don't know how he's doing. It seems like every patient on that ward, when they left, took a piece of me with them. They came in, we would treat them for a few hours or a few days, and then we'd send them off and never hear a word. I had this real need to see one GI who'd survived the war after an injury, because I never saw them—never heard from them again. There was one time in Vietnam when I came so close to writing to my mother and asking her to check around and see if she could find one whole eighteen-year-old. I didn't believe we could have any left. After John left I just couldn't handle it any more. We had too many bodies lying in those beds minus arms and legs, genitals, and faces, and things like that can't be put back together again.

I found I'd built up walls real effectively. I was patient and tender with the GIs. I didn't talk to them a lot because I was afraid to—afraid of losing my cool. I was very professional, but I was distant. I worry sometimes about the way I treated those GIs in intensive care (this was an insight I only got a year ago). . . . I was afraid, because I didn't feel I had done my best with them. Because of the walls I'd put up I didn't listen to them, didn't hear what they might be trying to tell me even just in gestures or whatever. I wasn't open to them because I was so closed to myself.

I got out of ICU. I couldn't handle any more. I asked to be transferred to the Vietnamese ward. Everybody had to do that—spend a rotation in the ward. This is where I found out that war doesn't just hit soldiers, that nobody is safe from war. I can still see this little boy—he was about nine months old. He had both of his legs in a cast and one arm in a cast and his entire abdomen bandaged, because he'd gotten in the way. I delivered a baby for a POW, a stillborn baby. It amazed me that life still went on even in a war. Because it seemed like everything should just stop. We had lots of medical problems too when we weren't too busy with war injuries. I had an eight-year-old girl who died of malnutrition. That's something that we only read about in our textbooks. Her mother brought her in, reluctantly, and she said we had twenty-four hours to cure her. She didn't trust us. If we couldn't cure the kid in twenty-four hours, she was taking her away. She did take her away, and the kid died the day after. To come from a background like I did, where everybody has plenty to eat, a lot of security, and to witness what these kids went through. They were older at the age of four than I was at eighteen. And I'll never forget that look on their faces, that old-man look on those young kids' faces, because they'd lived through so much. That still haunts me today.

The POWs. I took a lot of my frustrations out on them—in innocuous ways. I made one POW chew his aspirin when he wanted something for pain because I didn't think he had any right to complain while there were so many GIs injured . . . just on the next ward. One of the POWs attacked me once—tried to choke me—and I hit back at him. But I think before I even made contact with him, the two MPs were all over him. I never saw him again. We had one twelve-year-old NVA who had killed five GIs. Twelve years old! And he would brag about it to me. He would spit at me. I have never seen such hate. To see the loathing that he had in his eyes was frightening. But at almost the same time, we had a kid on the other side of the ward who was about the same age. He was a scout for the GIs, so he was on "our side." And the GIs just babied him. They thought he was the coolest kid, and he was so tough he scared me.

One of my most traumatic and long-lasting experiences happened to me while working the POW ward. An NVA was admitted with gunshot wounds he got during an ambush on a platoon of GIs. This POW was personally responsible for the deaths of six of those GIs. When he was wheeled onto my ward, something snapped. I was overwhelmed with uncontrollable feelings of hate and rage. I couldn't go near this guy because I knew, without any doubt, that if I touched him I would kill him. I was shaking from trying to keep my hands off his neck. This scared me to death, and for twelve years after I was scared of experiencing it again. I discovered I was capable of killing and of violently hating another human being. I had been raised to be a loving and giving person. As a nurse, I had vowed to help *all* who need it. As a human being I should love my brother, whoever he was. I was forced to confront a side of myself I never dreamed existed before.

After four months on the Vietnamese ward, I asked to be transferred again. So I was put on the GI medical ward. That was more depressing than the first two wards I'd been on. Mostly because the people that I had labeled as cop-outs were on that ward. The drug abusers, the alcoholics, the guys in there with malaria—because rather than go out in the field they would not take their malaria pills so they could come down with malaria. I was really very unsympathetic to them. I didn't try to understand them. After so many months of taking care of "legitimate" injuries, I couldn't handle that. I just figured, "Hell, even I can take this. Why can't you? You're supposed to be braver and stronger than I am, and somehow I'm managing."

We were shelled monthly, at least monthly. The closest call we had was when I was on the medical ward. I remember mortars were falling all around us. I had just gotten my sixty patients under their mattresses, and I dove under a bed myself, finally, and then this GI next to me says, "Hey, you forgot . . ." whatever his name was, and sure enough—he was one of our drug ODs—he was lying on top of his bed singing. I had to get out, crawl over to him, pull him out of bed, and put the mattress over him. I remember screaming at him. I was so mad at him for making me take any more chances. This happened the same day that my sister got married. In fact it was almost the same hour, and I thought, "My God, they're partying, and here I am." We had a sapper attack too when I was on that ward. That's when somebody infiltrates our perimeter. There's a certain siren that goes off. At the time, my corpsman on the ward was a conscientious objector, so he wouldn't handle any firearms. I remember I had to grab the M-16 and stand guard after I had locked the doors. I didn't even know how to fire the damn thing! I finally had to haul one of my patients—he was a lieutenant, I remember—out of bed and had him stand with me in case the gun needed to be fired. Once again, I had the preconception that women were supposed to be taken care of, and it seemed like I was doing all the taking care of.

A lot more happened; I just don't like pulling it out. . . . It's behind me now, and I think what became of me is more important anyway.

I remember on the plane home I held my breath until we were probably a thousand miles from Vietnam, because I was so afraid that something would happen and we'd have to go back. We landed at Sea Tac. I remember getting a hotel room and calling my parents, because they wanted to come out from Michigan to meet me. I ended up going back to the airport to meet them on *my* way home from Vietnam. They wanted to stay for two days in Seattle and sightsee. I can vividly see me sitting in this tour bus, looking out the window at nothing. Feeling up in the air, lost, disoriented. I was still back there. I didn't smile much. They thought I was angry. Well, they didn't know. They were trying to act like things were just the same as always—that a year hadn't gone by and that I hadn't gone anywhere. They were doing that to relax me. . . . I'm sure they were hurting too. I jumped at any noise. I looked at people walking the streets, and there wasn't even fear in their eyes. All I could think was, "If you only knew . . . you wouldn't be so damned complacent." I didn't even feel like going home. I wish I could have gone somewhere for a while—just to be by myself. I was pushed right back into everyday living, when I was still so far away from it and so disjointed that I couldn't possibly fit in. Everybody tried to ignore where I'd been. I guess some people did ask me about Vietnam, and I would say things like "It was okay." Or "Actually it was the pits." That's all I said for ten years.

I got married about six months after I got home. Rick and I had met in Japan. It was my second R&R, and I remember it was a month before I was DEROSing. All I was going to do was have a good time. I felt like I hadn't laughed in months. And I remember getting to the hotel in Osaka and people could just say "Good morning" and I'd start giggling. Everything was funny. I just laughed because I was releasing tension, I know that. But at the time I just couldn't stop laughing. I had no thoughts of commitments. And I met Rick. It was a good thing he was persistent. He's the best thing that's ever happened to me.

After we got married, we lived in Utah for four years. I put him through college. I worked in the local hospital there. I started out working newborn nursery simply because I wanted a happy job. So I worked for six months in the nursery and found I was bored. I was promoted to nursing supervisor after that, which worked out well, because I was in charge of the emergency room. I was coordinating emergency surgeries, assisting with deliveries, running the pharmacy. It was a nice challenge. But still, nobody knew I was a veteran. I had a desire to meet another veteran, but I wasn't broadcasting. I was having periods of real depression at the time—very happily married, a good job, wonderful husband, a beautiful baby—and I would consider suicide. I didn't understand why I was so depressed. I had nightmares, but I didn't attribute them to the war. It took me many, many years to even interpret those nightmares. All of a sudden one day I realized that a lot of them were centered around gooks; I couldn't see a slant-eye without getting upset. And a lot of it was centered on being misinterpreted, being misunderstood, but I didn't realize it at the time. As soon as I woke up, I tried real hard to forget them.

I've pretty much grown out of nursing. My last nursing job was at an ER in a run-down section of Richmond, California. Something happened there that was literally the straw that broke my back. It was six years after Vietnam, and one evening this fifteen-year-old black boy comes in to our ER with a two-inch laceration above his right eye from a street fight. It needed stitching, and soon. At first, he had refused to even come to ER, and after an hour of pleading, his mother finally got him in. But he absolutely, flat out didn't trust any white person touching him. I begged, pleaded, reasoned, and even threatened him, but he wouldn't let me touch him. He ended up walking out with his eye swollen shut, a gaping wound, and full of mistrust and hostility—and he was only fifteen! He took me back to Vietnam. To the hostility I felt from the POWs. To the mistrust I felt for any slant-eye—we could never be sure *who* the enemy was. I saw those young kids again, with their so old faces. And I couldn't handle it. I had one of my worst episodes of depression—it lasted for days. I still can't go back to nursing because I'm afraid of this happening again.

About nine years after I got out of Vietnam, I read an article in the paper about this guy in Oregon who'd gone berserk and shot somebody. At his trial they named his condition delayed stress syndrome. I had never heard of it before. But the article described some of the symptoms. And I kept saying, "That's me, that's me! This is exactly it. I can't believe this!" So that evening I brought the article to Rick and said, "Don't laugh, but . . ." Rick and I are very open about everything, talk about absolutely everything, but I never talked to him about my nightmares or my depressions. I didn't want to burden him, I guess, or I didn't want to talk about it. I'm not sure which. I asked, "Did you ever notice things like that about me and just not say anything?" And he said, "Yeah, exactly. I figured when you were ready to talk about it, you'd talk."

He was in Vietnam too, of course, but where he was at was relatively quiet, and he never saw combat. So anyway, I spent six months reading up on delayed stress. And it was a relief just to find out what it was that was making me do this stuff. But I still had the nightmares; I still had the depression. I'd go through periods of relative calm and serenity, and then I'd turn around and start screaming at the kids, or at Rick, or the dog. I'd ventilate that way for a while, and then we'd go back to serenity again.

I was reading the Sunday paper, and by God there was this article on women Vietnam veterans in it. First one I'd ever seen. I read that article like it was saving my life. It mentioned Lynda Van Devanter and some of the things she'd gone through, It mentioned several psychologists who were interviewed, and they talked about delayed stress in women veterans. It was like a lifeline. I thought, "I've got to talk to Lynda." So I called our local VA. They'd never heard of her, and they'd never heard of women's Vietnam veteran groups. They gave me another number to call—and I got a runaround for three or four different phone calls. So I read the article again. When I read it I knew I wanted help and that something had to be done, but God, I was scared to reach out. But I did it. I made a long-distance call to the vet center in Los Angeles somewhere, asked for the psychologist that was mentioned in the article. I told her I was trying to get ahold of someone I could talk to who was a veteran. And I made it very clear that I wanted to talk to another woman veteran. She didn't know how to help me. She said the only thing she could figure out was that I should call Vietnam Veterans of America in Washington, D.C., and see if they could locate Lynda Van Devanter. I remember sitting down before I lost all my nerve and writing a seven- or eight-page letter. I wrote down all those things that I'd been bottling up and wanting to talk about and not being able to. I didn't have to preface anything with explanations or details or justifications. I just wrote it down straight from my heart. She wrote me a real nice, supportive letter back. She sent me a whole bunch of material on other women veterans who had been interviewed, and I remember pouring over those and underlining everything that I could identify closely with. I felt literally like she was the lifeline, that I had been sinking in a sea unable to swim and she was holding the rope.

A few months later a friend of mine in Anchorage, Alaska, whose daughter was also a friend of mine down here, had read an article where Jan Ott from the Seattle vet center was interviewed. She cut it out and sent it to my friend to give to me because she thought I'd be interested. And it mentioned that there was a support group being formed. I thought, "There's nothing wrong with me. I'm functioning fine." I called Jan anyway to say I thought what she was doing was a good job. She convinced me that it was just a talk group, there was no therapy, nothing else, it didn't mean there was anything wrong with us. So I said, "Yeah, okay." I figured they needed numbers to make the group go. I sat there with my legs crossed and my arms folded, and I wasn't going to talk; I was going to listen. But they were saying the same things I was thinking. It was hard to sit there because in my head I was going, "Oh yeah. Oh yeah!" And it started coming out. It took me a long time. Some of the ladies there—maybe they'd had more practice, I don't know; maybe they're more open with themselves—but they shared really well. I would share but more superficially. Not because I didn't want to share deeper. I don't think I could have at that time. It was a slow evolving through about twelve weeks of the group. I had something more to think about every week. They'd brought out new things that I hadn't ever thought about before.

I think the turning point in the group came when I watched a certain movie on TV. *Friendly Fire.* I remember being just overwhelmed because the guy who played the part of the GI in that film looked exactly like the guy in my nightmares. He was blond; he was young; he was so innocent and so naive. He went over to Vietnam just like most of us did, thinking he was doing what he should be doing . . . and you could just see him evolve. He went from being naive and innocent through being scared and confused into being hard-nosed and cynical. Exactly the way I had gone through it. The movie was done with such perception; they really had a handle on it. I remember sitting down with my notebook and writing as I was going through this movie—thank God for commercials. I had started out describing him as I just did, and how I could relate so well to that. And then something snapped. At the end of the movie, when he was killed and brought home, another useless death, I didn't even realize what I was doing. My letters were all of a sudden three times as large. I was tearing the paper with my pen! I was writing about how angry and bitter I was. It was because those people, whoever they were, who sent us over there made us do all these terrible things, wasted so many lives, so much time and money, and so many resources, are not accountable and will never be really accountable. They've hidden behind so many other people that they will never be brought to justice. I felt really frustrated and impotent knowing that they would not be reckoned with. And I remember saying that I hope that their day of reckoning would come.

I got through the movie, and it just opened up so many things that I hadn't thought about. I realized finally where my anger and my hostility were directed. I realized how sad I was and that it would never go away. For twelve years I've wanted it to go away, to get on with life, and not have that thing hanging around my neck. I realized how badly I felt about the way I saw myself treat some of those GI patients in intensive care. How I wasn't perfect with them like I probably should have been, and how much that affected me. I realized how much each of those GIs had taken of me with them. And how much I wanted it back. Everything came all at once. I had written all this down, and I was going to share it with the group.

I remember reading what I had written because I don't think I could have said it straight out. My one hand bled from my nails biting into my palm because I was still so angry. I think that's where most of the tension and frustration and stress went that evening. I really got it out. Then, a week or two later, we had the male GIs come to our group. That was very powerful. It was really great for me to see the whole GIs. But even more important I remember Dan, this great big hunk of a guy. He was big but he was gentle, kind, caring. He started talking about how he tried to injure himself in Vietnam so he wouldn't have to go out on another firefight. And my first reaction was to tense up and say, "Oh, Goddamn you! You had to be one of those, didn't you." But Dan sat there and went through the buildup to how it got so bad he would get almost physically sick at thinking of having to go out there. To wonder where the next shot was coming from, if it was coming for him, was he going to live or die, was he going to have to kill somebody. He said he got to the point where he just couldn't take it anymore. He honestly thought that he may even have gone a little crazy for a while. He had a friend of his take the butt of his rifle and try to break his collar bone so he couldn't carry a gun. His friend did it as hard as he could, and he ended up just bruising Dan. And he said, "That guy probably saved my life, because I don't think I could have lived with myself if it had worked. I still humped and it hurt with every step, but it was almost like it was my punishment." And this big, gentle man is sitting there crying, talking about how traumatic that experience was for him. It gave me such an insight into what I had labeled as a cop-out. I saw that we all had our own ways of coping. Where I built my walls and hid behind them, that was my form of copping out. I could not judge anybody else for whatever form they took.

Since that time, when I really got everything together and spit it out to the group, things have really been okay. The nightmares are absolutely gone. The depressions are just about gone. But Lynda Van Devanter said it better than I could ever say it again: "The war does not control me anymore. I control it." I know the depressions will still come, but I can handle them because I know why they're there and that they'll go away. I know that I can't forget those experiences, but I understand why I have them and that they're a part of my life. I also know that I'm a better person, actually, for having lived them.

Probably my two biggest goals now are, I'll do my damndest to keep something like that from ever happening again, and if I can help even one other woman veteran to work it through as I have, then it's all worth it. I'm not normally an outgoing person, but I'll spill everything if I have to, if that will help just one other person. Because nobody needs to live through this. . . .

Bobbi Jo Pettit

SINGER/GUITARIST IN
THE PRETTY KITTENS
(AN ALL GIRLS BAND)—
MAY '67 TO SEPT. '67
SINGER/GUITARIST IN
THE ALLAN DALE CO.—
DEC. '70 TO JUNE '71

Bobbie now lives in the Pacific Northwest, is going to college working toward a degree in psychology/sociology. She sings and plays guitar and banjo for "casual gigs, that means every now and then for parties." She got married in the summer of 1984, "for the first time at age thirty-seven."

This interview took place in Topanga Canyon, California, in the summer of 1983.

I WENT TO VIETNAM AS PART OF AN ALL-GIRL BAND, The Pretty Kittens. We all got together at about age seventeen or eighteen in Los Angeles—that was in 1966—and in the spring of 1967 we had a manager who figured out how much it would be worth to send four American girls with miniskirts and white boots over to entertain the half million GIs that were in Vietnam. Well, he was a businessman, and it worked out real well. So he paid our fare over there not really knowing a lot about it, only that there was an agent in-country that would book us.

Our first show was at the Saigon USO club. We would do from one to three shows a day, all at different places, a different show in a different part of the country every day. Our day was filled with traveling, usually by truck, almost always military, and about one third of the time by helicopter, if it was long distance. That was it, just constantly doing shows. It was ideal because we were the same age as most of the GIs, doing American songs from home that were very current right then: "Proud Mary," you know, all the stuff that was just real American. Being round-eyed women was a real premium over there, and to speak English instead of Australian-type English made us even more valuable. That was about a five-month tour, and it absolutely changed everything for me. I mean, I had no concept of what Vietnam was when I went over there; how I managed to agree to go I don't know, but I am certainly glad that I did. None of the other girls wanted to go back. It was a real hardship tour, no question about it, but it was so adventurous. That was the thing.

From then on I wanted to go back again. I went to different agencies trying to get another all-girl band together. There weren't that many female musicians, and it was hard to get them together. It took another five years before I found the right people that really wanted to go, and that group was two men and two women. It was the same kind of thing, two or three shows every day. We'd fly up in C-130s to Da Nang, do a show, and then chopper down to Marble Mountain or someplace like that for an afternoon show, and then back to Da Nang for the night, and that's the way it would be. My suitcase was filled with everything I owned. I had one suitcase; that is all I could have for five months. We had to carry everything, so I stuffed things in guitar cases, and we had the smallest amount of equipment that we could. We'd set up on the back of flatbeds, I mean, wherever. The sound equipment by today's standards was bad—it was like going through cardboard boxes. We were in the middle of nowhere, choppers flying through, but that was okay; they didn't seem to mind that.

I remember one show during the first tour when I really realized where I was. I just didn't have the grip on what was going on there. As we were doing the show I saw blue tracer shells coming in and red going out—it was while I was singing "Proud Mary." I was watching this firefight going on out on the perimeter, and I said, "Well, wait a minute, what is this?" My brain was not connecting. . . . I was just starting to connect all the things that I was seeing, that it was normal for all these GIs to be having a great time at the show while everybody else was out there taking on their jobs. After I got over the scariness of it, you know, the weight of what was really going on, it got to be where life was at for me . . . almost as much as for the soldiers.

They were really life-in-jeopardy, but it was like we just did things not knowing whether . . . There was a thrill in not knowing totally whether you were going to get to the next stop or . . . whatever. It was the real living-in-the-moment kind of thing that was incredible. It's that excitement, that thrill, and if you could get into it as an entertainer over there, just have fun with what happened, it was fantastic.

So it was fun; it was also very hard. There were a lot of things that hurt and there was a lot of, to use a terrible word, inconvenience. There was one time when we were up the coast somewhere close to Nha Trang where we couldn't get into town and nobody could get out to bring us supplies. We were there for three days, the four of us in a room, just four eighteen-year-old kids in the middle of—I don't know how we ever made it. But anyway, we didn't have any water; it would cost a dollar to buy a small amount of ice, and they didn't leave us a lot of money. I realized, "Oh yes, we are very vulnerable here!"

But mostly it was fantastic. They treated us all really good, and the soldiers were incredible. . . . The thing that I learned about the quickest was sex. You know, I remember I hadn't thought about that before I went over there. And when I got there the subject, of course, was very heavily prevalent. That was what they were missing a lot— and there were a lot of American men over there. So I got to understand a lot of things really quick—I had to on a survival level—but they were never, even though it was an urgency for so many of them, you know . . . I never felt threatened by anybody over there. They were always on their best behavior. It was incredible; they were just so respectful. . . . It was just amazing. Since then I've done extensive work in psychology and sometimes even in my own life if I have someone to project on, you know, the movie star for teenagers or whatever. If you have a wife at home to remember, you think about her, you've got something. So I knew that they would think of things, wonder how we were sexually, be very graphic . . . all this other stuff, but I didn't care about any of that because if I gave them something that they needed, if they could use it, you know, cerebrally, to get them by, then that was fine with me.

The booking agent made most of the decisions about how we traveled when we were out of Saigon—he had a villa in Saigon. It was just not okay with the military to have us staying on the bases overnight. Boy, I remember that road from Bien Hoa back to Saigon. One night we were coming back in a truck, and there was an American chopper that came down looking at us—there weren't supposed to be any Americans on the road at that time of night—and they had a big spotlight coming down, and the guys in the truck said, "Bobbi, get out! Get out!"—'cause I had real white-blond hair, so they could see who we were—"Get out and let them see you!" As far as accommodations, we stayed in what was available. At a lot of places the officers would give us their quarters if we had to stay overnight. Some of them might even have a bathroom in them. A couple places had trailers that we could stay in, but most of the places were just a couple of beds in a room. If we were lucky there was a bathroom, but most of the time it was outdoors. At Camp Eagle, the barracks they had for entertainers was incredible. It had about a one hundred-yard perimeter fence, and the barracks was right in the middle. We couldn't go out and they couldn't come in, and that is where we slept, in that barracks with the fence around it. That was about the most overt protection, but we needed the protection there, because this is the place with the very heavy drug usage.

I must admit that I was around more officers socially than enlisted men, but it was more for practical reasons. They had the power to be able to get a jeep so we could go to dinner. They could afford a hotel and get the papers signed to say they were going out overnight. It was like that was a reality, and you couldn't get a woman into a barracks; I mean, that would be impossible. So that was the way it was.

There was a lot of difference in the two tours, from 1967 to 1971. The first time we went over we were not under the Department of Defense. We were civilians over there, and it was real rip-roaring . . . all the romantic stuff. An officer could take his chopper—just say he was going—and come down and pick you up. Things were a lot looser, a lot more wide open. There was a lot less constraint on everything. We could get a lot more things done too. We could call up people and say, "We need to get up to so and so. Could you take us over?" and they could generally do it—or we could walk into a helicopter port in our miniskirts and get our show on the road. And the energy was a lot higher too. Everybody was still in support of it; it was still "Let's get the job done." The second tour, it was like nobody wanted to be there. Nobody thought they were doing anything, you know? It was a real wind-down. We had to be under DOD then, and we were fourth-priority travel. I mean, we sat in the airport for three or four days sometimes, just trying to get to Da Nang. There was a lot of difference in things like that. . . . Yeah, the whole attitude was different; the country was the same but the momentum was a lot different.

One of the incredible memories: We were somewhere around Bien Hoa, on the other side of Bien Hoa, and they had the 100-millimeters, the big ones, and they shot them every night. They knew that, and I'm sure everybody around there knew that, but we didn't—we didn't know anything. We were doing a show for the officers; there were only about thirty of them, and they were quite subdued. The closer to the bigger cities, the less enthusiastic the audiences were. So they were watching the show, and all of a sudden one of these big guns goes off! It must not have been very far away, and the whole building . . . BOOM! . . . the whole building shook! And the bass player, a tall, skinny gal, she goes down on her knees, she's scared! She grabs on to my leg right in the middle of the show, and she's holding on to everybody—she thinks we are all going to die right then! And the officers laughed; they had a great time with that. It was like, I didn't know either, but then a couple more went by, and then we got it . . . but it was scary. I'll never forget when she was hanging on to me.

Another time, I remember we were sitting in an airport and a GI came in. He had a bush hat on with a lot of lines on it. I didn't know what that was at the time. The thing that drew me to him was that he was very singular; you could tell he was very independent, and he had an "over-and-under," an M-16 with a grenade launcher on it. I mean, he made John Wayne look like . . . John Wayne didn't look tough compared to this guy. So I talked to him for a while, and he told me he had been there for three years, didn't want to go home. His brother had been killed over there. He explained that all these lines on his hat were kills. And he was somebody that was . . . like, he was gentle. He said poetry to me right there in the airport. It was incredible. I got a letter from him when we were both back—that's the only contact I had with him—and it was a poetic letter about turning swords into plowshares, a lot of that kind of stuff. . . . But that was like what people's perceptions were on a level with. Granted that I grew up in America, in Los Angeles. You know, miniskirts and convertibles cruising the ice-cream shops . . . that was the mentality that we all went over there with. . . . That was what was so . . . well, a lot like the movie *Deer Hunter*, which I think was the common story.

The first thing I did when I got back is had five ice-cream cones made of real ice cream instead of reconstituted; that was the most important thing for me. And then I was in a place where I was wondering how people could be the same as they were when I had known them before—like, "Why aren't they doing more? Why aren't more people going over there?" I found that not many people wanted to know about it, didn't have a concept about it. When I realized that I wasn't going to get a lot of response out of them, that's when I tried to go back, you know, immediately.

There was a lot to do to get it together. The first time we went over everything was wide open and thus a lot more fun, if you will. The agent was very unscrupulous, and he told us he was going to pay us at the end of the tour. We were each going to get a thousand dollars a month—plus they paid for expenses—but at the end we didn't get paid. We had the tickets which the original manager bought. There was a slight confrontation, a gun-to-

gun kind of thing, like, "Either you leave or you don't
leave at all." And so, "Thanks, had a great time. See you
around," you know, and we left. . . . You could say that
we were ripped off, but it all depends. I thought about it,
but then I thought, "No, I wasn't." Not for what I gained
from it. . . . It was something—I mean, I was very much
alive there; it was very hard, but I was very alive.

The second band I went with, all of us were very much
the same in our heads. And we would think of things to
do, you know, when we were in a jam or something, or if
we had to sit in an airport for two or three days. We'd piss
and moan, but we knew what to do to keep interested, and
we could work off of each other. We were close enough
where if we all had to sleep in one room, we did. We had
a real good rapport, all four of us; it was a great time.

When I came home the second time my whole feeling
was different. The war was relatively over. The whole cli-
mate in America was how terrible it was over there—frag-
ging officers and all that kind of stuff. There was nothing
to go back to anymore. So I just recognized that fact. I
didn't think about it that much because it became something that I had done. Being able to have that kind of experience at that age has been incredibly valuable to me,
and I'll never be able to have that again. Even if I went to
Afghanistan or wherever there was American involvement,
it would not ever be the same. It gave me perspective on
my whole life. . . . You know, I played for the guys that
they made the movies about. I mean, I was one of them,
you know: On the beach in the middle of the war, and you
just have an hour, and bang! the world is in your eyes!

Jill Ann Mishkel

24TH EVAC. HOSPITAL,
LONG BINH—JULY '70 TO JULY '71

Jill Mishkel lives in "a small old farmhouse in an area that gives the illusion of country," near Glastonbury, Connecticut, where she divides her time among a few close friends, her dog, gardening, camping, dancing, and work. She is also very involved with local veterans' issues.

After reading the transcription of her story, she returned it to me with a letter, which contained the following paragraph:

I've been trying to write to you since shortly after you left to tell you about what the interview did to me. I have a mental picture of you traveling across the country leaving a wake of devastated women. After you left, I spent a week recovering. It all came up again. Lying awake all night and falling asleep as the sun came up. Getting to work late and getting in trouble for it. Not being able to get it out of my mind. I'd hoped for years that if I could just tell my story, write my own book or something, I could get it out—finally put it behind me, to use the cliché. It didn't work that way. . . . I'm starting to realize that Nam is part of me, not just intellectually, but emotionally . . . and I feel like I am different. . . . I want to tell everyone, make them understand. But even after [reading] eighteen pages of my story, I feel I haven't said it, that there must be another story I have forgotten that could explain it.

I GRADUATED FROM HIGH SCHOOL AT SIXTEEN. MY birthday's in July, so I went to nursing school when I was seventeen—I was pretty young. It was a three-year nursing school, a diploma school, and at that point the war was building and raging by the time I got out in 1969. For some reason I decided I was against the war. And I didn't like Nixon. I thought he was a liar. I remember telling my father that I thought he was evil.

When I got out of nursing school, I worked for almost a year in a community, suburban hospital. I started in obstetrics, but when an opening came up as a charge nurse in the emergency room on nights, I took that. I had quite a few friends, and they were all hippies, you know, the bell-bottom jeans and the headbands and long hair on the men. They were all against the war, and I was against the war. That's when I first smoked pot. But I was a good kid—I didn't ever do anything really wrong. I would never do any drugs, besides pot; I would never do LSD or any of that stuff. But basically I was bored. I finally decided that if there was a war going on and even though I was so

121

much against it, I was a nurse and I could go over there and do something useful.

I tried to get into the Air Force, and that's a little story in itself 'cause I didn't get in, and the reason they gave me was that I had bifocal amblyopia. . . . Okay, bifocal amblyopia—I think that I didn't get into the Air Force because I didn't pass the beauty contest. I had to go out and buy a dark dress with a waistband, and the recruiter came and took pictures of me standing straight, full length, side length—you know, either side—and then my face from either side. I didn't fix my hair or put any makeup on and stuff like that because I really resented the fact that they were taking these pictures. I didn't see what that had to do with it. I didn't get into the Air Force, so I figured, "Okay, screw you. I'm going to go into the Army," because I had already made my mind up that I was going to go into the service, and the Army would take anybody. I think the decision was all very idealistic, you know, the Florence Nightingale type thing.

I went into the Army in May of 1970, went to Fort Sam Houston, and soon as I got there I met a few women, one that I got pretty chummy with—that's Susan Grasky, we were in basic training together. Through her I met the helicopter pilots that were living on the floor below us. They were med-evac pilots, and they were all crazy. I mean, I think that's a prerequisite to being a helicopter pilot—you have to be a bit insane. I started going out with this man named Scottie, who was going to Vietnam; all the helicopter pilots were going to Vietnam. I think I was very much influenced by those helicopter pilots. Scottie had been underground for about six months, trying to avoid the draft and then I guess finally got tired and didn't want to leave the country, so he went into the service and somehow got to be a warrant officer and a helicopter pilot.

Anyway, all these people were going to Vietnam, and I thought that if I was going to be going there anyway, it would be much nicer to go with the people I knew. At least then I'd know somebody in-country. I went down to the place where you got your orders and told them I wanted my orders changed. They said I was too young, and I said, "Listen, I'm going to be twenty-one four days after I get there, so what difference does it make?" So they said okay. I got my orders changed, and I called my mother, and she went hysterical on the phone. Cried a lot. She really wanted me to go to Germany and couldn't understand why I wouldn't go there, meet a doctor, and get married. But I was going to go to Vietnam with people that I knew.

Went to Vietnam and went through their little orientation course which took a couple of days. I was scared, real scared, I guess really in shock. I'm sure everybody who went in-country at first was in shock. Then we were asked where we wanted to be assigned, if we had any preference. And I said no, I really didn't care except that I'd like to go where Sue Grasky went—she was Sue Lodge at the time. A few days later I found out that she and I were stationed at the same place. We were introduced to Vietnam at Bien Hoa and both assigned to the 24th Evacuation Hospital at Long Binh, which was about five miles down the road. Sue was very angry at me. She wanted to go up into the boonies, Pleiku or something, away from the big Army people and out into the real jungle to fight the war, and she blamed me for the fact that she was stationed at Long Binh. But she got over that.

I can remember when I was first there, not really talking to anybody because I don't think I knew what to say. Of course I went to work immediately when I got to the hospital. We were pretty busy at that point, and there were a lot of people that were dying. The corpsmen were the people that taught me what to do there. There were three or four corpsmen for every nurse, and everything I learned there I feel like I learned from them. I worked on the neurosurgical unit, which was two floors—well, Quonset huts—that were connected. One Quonset hut was all intensive care—type patients that were . . . "gorks," we used to call them. The other unit was mostly back injuries and minor concussions and stuff like that, people who were going back to their units. But the patients who were on the intensive care floor were "gorks," the vast majority of them . . . nice, healthy young men that were missing part of their brains or had spinal cord injuries and were never going to walk again, never move their arms or legs. I think I was still pretty much in shock; it was . . . I don't know what it was. . . . They were very young, healthy, good-looking men that could've been my brothers or my boyfriends or my husband, and they were dying.

I remember I was there for about two weeks, and somebody was leaving and they had a party; it was the first party that I had been asked to. I started to walk across the street, and some private comes up to me and says, "Didn't you hear? It's a yellow alert. You're not supposed to be out here." I got all scared 'cause I didn't even know what a yellow alert was, and it sounded drastic to me, so I went over to the party and told everybody, "Hey, we're not supposed to be here. There's a yellow alert." And they all burst into hysterics and started laughing at me 'cause I guess it was always a yellow alert. We were in the middle of Long Binh post, and from what I understand it was one of the largest Army bases in the world. We didn't even have sandbags around the buildings; we didn't have—what are those things when they dig the holes? Bunkers? We didn't have any of that stuff. We had soldiers walking around patrolling, guarding us with no bullets in their guns, but after only two weeks in-country I didn't know any of that. I was at the party for about fifteen minutes and can remember being absolutely horrified that all of these people were getting high and drunk and having a good time dancing while there were all these young guys back on the ward dying. And you know, at least one person died every day in that first two weeks I was there. I left the party and went back to my hooch and cried and thought they were all totally insensitive. Shortly thereafter I was partying and getting high and getting drunk along with the best of them.

I don't know what other nurses did over there, but we worked twelve-hour days, six days a week. And during slow time, which wasn't very often, we would have an extra half-day off. So if you weren't working, you were partying or sleeping, and that's really all we did. I started meeting corpsmen, and the corpsmen always had pot. We did a lot—well, I didn't do *a lot* of pot over there; I did it whenever I wasn't working. And with people—I didn't smoke in my room by myself, but if I was with a bunch of people or with a few people or with one person, one of the things we used to do was get high.

I have pictures of six or seven beds of people and every one of them being just not there, just vegetables. And they all died. Working on that kind of floor might have been a little bit different than working anywhere else, because you can't lose part of your brain and come back to life. Even the ones that lived didn't live much. . . . I don't know, I can remember a few things clearly, but I can't remember very much at all it seems. I can remember rows and rows and rows of beds. I can remember discussing with corpsmen and discussing with doctors whether we were going to do anymore for certain patients. I can remember doctors coming into the floor and saying, "I don't want to see that guy here tomorrow morning when I come back." That meant there was nothing more we could do to save his life; all we could do was prolong it. We had to decide where to spend our energy.

There were nineteen or twenty-one beds on the intensive care side, which were usually all full, and they were total-care patients. They were not conscious. There are two words, *decorticate* and *decerebrate*, that mean a different level of brain damage. The patients would be lying in bed, and you'd go to check their reflexes. One way was to shine a light in their eyes to get pupillary response. . . . Most of our patients didn't have pupillary response; their pupils were fixed and dilated. Another thing you would do is stimulate them, the old knee jerk. These people were way past knee jerk, so we checked deep sensation reflex, which was really a deep pain reflex. What we would do is we would pinch them and kind of chart how hard you had to pinch them to make them respond. You'd pinch the inside of their arm or the inside of their leg, a very sensitive area, and they would give the decorticate or decerebrate response, which was twisting their arms and their legs in a real stiff . . . Some of the patients were what we used to call stuporous, which meant that they weren't comatose but they weren't awake—they were kind of somewhere in never-never land. They would scream and talk and carry on, but they wouldn't make any sense at all, or they would just thrash.

One of the patients I can remember who was stuporous was umm . . . It ended up he was one of the very, very, very few men I can remember who recovered while he was in Vietnam. He had a head injury of course, probably more like a concussion patient, where he had a buildup of pressure—I don't know what it was really, a reaction to the injury. He had had surgery, but he wasn't that bad, and he was stuporous and he would lie in bed and he would scream and curse, and you'd go to do something for him and he would curse and scream and carry on. And after about two weeks of that, he woke up . . . Just about the only person I can remember who woke up, and he was perfectly normal and perfectly rational and perfectly with it. We would tell him about how he carried on while he was stuporous, and he was embarrassed and he would blush. He was a nice little guy, you know, a nice, shy, normal person. I remember him.

And I remember other people. I remember a patient who had walked into a helicopter tail rotor. Anybody who knows about the brain knows about the frontal lobe— what one of the corpsmen, and shortly after that everybody, called the "give a shit" lobe, because once you lose it you don't give a shit about anything. This guy had lost his frontal lobe, and he was like a child. He had one of the nurses write a letter to his wife—he had a wife and two kids at home—and started the letter, "Dear Honey, I did a very stupid thing," and he talked like a little boy. The whole letter sounded like it was written by a little boy, and all you could think of was now his wife had three kids, because this man would never function again.

I can remember one other patient. He came into the hospital walking and had a concussion and was there about five days. I don't even think he was ever on the intensive care side; he was going to be discharged the next day to go back to his unit. He came up to me at the desk and said, "There's something coming out of my ear." He was leaking cerebral spinal fluid out of his ear. He got worse and worse and had to go to surgery, then ended up with an infection in his head. We had infections in brains a lot; we used to irrigate them. Ever try to irrigate a brain? Make a hole and put a catheter into the skull, push saline and some type of antibiotic in with a big syringe, then let it drain out somewhere else. He ended up also with diabetes incipidus. What diabetes incipidus is, is basically you make urine—you make much too much fluid. The treatment is a drug called Pitressin, and you also had to replace all this fluid. Consequently he had a lot of IVs, two or three going at the same time. And I can remember when we were running out of spots to put intravenouses, they finally did a subclavian, which is into the vein right under the collarbone. He already had jugulars and femurals and all kinds of IVs. Dr. Meyers put it in and said to me, "Don't let him pull this out," because by this point he was pulling out his IVs— we had to keep his hands strapped. I said, "Okay, no sweat," went around to get the tape, turned back, and he had it in his hand. . . . I just—I felt like it was my fault, and I started crying, and all the doctors came running back—"He pulled out his IV again!" and where are they going to put another one? And it was just—it was a mess.

We used to go to Saigon. It wasn't that far; we were only about twenty miles away. We would work all night, and in the morning we'd go hang around the emergency room and wait for a helicopter. Or we would get somebody to give us a ride down to Bien Hoa and get a helicopter to take us to Saigon. We would spend all day walking around Saigon and come back that night. I was robbed in Saigon at Christmastime. I had my money and my ID in my breast pocket, and four little kids, maybe ten-year-old kids, came up and gathered around me and were screaming and jumping up and down and wanting money—and "gimme, gimme"—or whatever they wanted. I just pushed them all away and started walking down the street and then realized

that all the money that was in my breast pocket was gone.
So we turned around and went back, and I saw the little
girl and the little boy. I grabbed hold of the little boy and
said I wanted my money. He was screaming, "No money!"
and the little girl was hitting me with her pocketbook, this
big black patent leather pocketbook, and screaming, "No
money, no money!" I knew it was them because it had
happened a couple minutes before. Then these four black
soldiers came up, and they grabbed hold of the little boy.
Meanwhile, there was a Vietnamese policeman standing on
the other side of the street, but he didn't even come near
us. I told the four black GIs that the kids had robbed me,
and the one—oh geez—the one guy said that I wasn't a
"sister" so they let the little boy go. Then I went perfectly
hysterical, standing in the middle of the street screaming,
"I'm an American, I'm a nurse, and the next time I have
a black patient I'm not going to suction him—I'm going to
let him drown in his own secretions . . ." and crying and
screaming, and they just walked away. It was emotional. . . . The whole year was emotional.

What else happened while I was in Vietnam? What else
was Vietnam? I was popular, and that was different for me,
because I had never been popular in my life, mostly because I was so shy. It was funny, I wasn't shy in Vietnam.
I don't think I had a chance, because there were so many
men, that it seemed real easy for me to talk to guys. That's
all there was to talk to; they were all over the place. So
whereas part of me had a real good time in Vietnam because I had boyfriends and partied all the time, there was
part of me that had those patients that I had to deal
with. . . .

I left Vietnam in July of 1971. I remember being home
a couple of days, and all my girlfriends took me out to a
bar which was their hangout. They of course told everybody that I had just gotten back from Vietnam, so people
were screaming across the bar, "Hey medic!" And I don't
exactly remember what I felt except that I left after about
a half an hour and I walked home, which was about two
miles away. It was just strange. It felt like I didn't have
anything to say to these people, all having an uproarious

time screaming out "medic," asking me all kinds of questions, and I just didn't have anything to say to them. So I left and walked home.

I can remember about a day or so later I went shopping with my two sisters and being really freaked out over not feeling right, just looking around this gigantic mall with all of these people shopping and wearing all kinds of colors—the colors were driving me crazy. I could feel myself withdrawing more and more, thinking that I didn't belong there. I can remember standing at the counter at Sears and Roebuck, buying underwear, and my two sisters said, "We'll be back in a minute," and they went running off, and I stood there with the money in one hand and the underwear in the other hand, crying. This woman is standing behind the counter, and I'm just standing there crying and crying and crying.

But then I was still in the Army, and I went to Fitzsimmons in Denver, and I worked on a lower extremity orthopedic ward, which meant that like ninety percent were amputees. And that was a good experience; it really was. The guys were amazing. It was during that time I realized there were a lot of people really, really bitter about the war. We had Thai nurses, of all things, to come in and be trained, nurses from Thailand. And these guys would not want them near them. One time we had some Jesus-freak woman sneak into the hospital, come up onto the floor, and tell the patients that if they would just pray hard enough, their legs would grow back. And these guys just went bullshit.

One of my patients in Fitzsimmons was a patient that I had had in Vietnam; it was incredible. He'd had a back injury. He was walking, and I remember we didn't think he would be able to walk. The thing that he remembered the most about being a patient of ours, or mine, was that the doctor pulled out his Foley catheter without taking the balloon down. The catheter goes into the penis, and at the end is a balloon to hold it in place in the bladder. And the doctor just—I don't know, he spaced out and said, "Oh, we got to take this out" and pulled it out.

You know, that might have been the first thing that man felt below his waist for a long time. But it might have been the secret of his success—he was walking; he was doing fine!

Then I got out of the service and wanted to move somewhere that wasn't near my parents but wasn't that far away. One of the men I used to date in Vietnam was living right outside of Hartford. I had a friend in Washington and then this guy in Hartford, so I of course came to Hartford. I got a job at Hartford Hospital working on the surgical intensive care unit, where I worked for about two years. We did open-hearts and kidney transplants and a lot of real serious stuff. I think I was probably pretty good at it. I seem to be mechanically minded, and I'm good with little gadgets and machinery and stuff like that.

All the time I was there, I made no friends where I worked. Nobody wanted to hear about Vietnam; nobody wanted to even acknowledge that I had been in the service. They thought I was really weird for having been an Army nurse and been in Vietnam. I started hanging around the women's center, which was newly opened in Hartford, and I became a radical feminist. I couldn't talk to a man, I really couldn't, none. I blamed them for everything, and at that point I didn't even know what everything was. I knew the war had something to do with it, and I knew it was men who were fighting the war and men who were putting women down. I could not carry on more than two sentences with a man without getting into an argument with him. All my friends were gay; they were all lesbians. I was not, and I don't know why I wasn't, but I wasn't. I just never did. And I was working at this place where, you know, I could talk to people, but I didn't have anything in common with them. They didn't care about me, and I didn't care about them.

It got to the point where it seemed like it was Vietnam over and over again. Shortly before I quit we had a patient that had been there for a long time. It was an old man, and first he had a heart attack, then open-heart surgery, then kidney failure, and he just got worse and worse and worse. His wife would come every day, spend about an hour at the bedside crying, and then leave. I remember one morning we were making rounds; the doctors stood there at the end of his bed and said, "Well, there's nothing more we can do for Joe. Let's give him another unit of blood." And in the middle of the ward I started crying and crying, and I just couldn't understand: if there's nothing more they could do for him, why not let him die?

I just—well, I had to get out of there. There were too many people that were dying. Right around that time when I was getting ready to quit and thinking about what I was going to do, I decided I'd like to move back to Colorado. And then I met Clifford. I had gone with my roommate to a party—it was a VVAW party, that was Vietnam Veterans Against the War. It was just amazing, 'cause I walked into the room and I felt like I was back in Vietnam. There were people in one room getting high, Rolling Stones or the Doors or somebody was on real loud, and all the guys were standing in the middle of the room just vibrating to the music and talking. I felt really, really comfortable. I mean, that's what we used to do in Vietnam; we used to stand around and listen to music and vibrate, just bounce up and down with the music.

So Clifford and I started going out together, and when I wanted to move to Colorado he came with me; we went out there together. We ended up having a big fight in Colorado and he left. I freaked out and followed shortly thereafter on the bus—came back to Connecticut—and we started living together. Of course all the women that I knew at that point wouldn't have anything to do with me anymore because I was living with a man. It was really radical times, it really was.

Clifford and I were having hard times and good times and hard times and good times. Clifford was a Vietnam vet. . . . I don't know, we lived together for about six years. He's a real good man. We had our problems and good times and bad times and it just . . . We never talked about Vietnam; you know, a little bit, superficially, but we never really talked about it. I didn't want to split up. He wanted to split up, and I tried to figure out some way to prevent it, but he wouldn't talk to me at that point—cried a lot, but he wouldn't talk to me. I cried a lot. That was real hard; I fell apart there for a good year probably. I wasn't really going well at all.

After we split up I started going to the vet center with the intention of helping others: veterans that were suffering from the war, just like Clifford. The counselor tried to get me to talk about Vietnam, and I just started crying. She finally got me into a rap group with other veterans. In the rap group I remember thinking that these men just couldn't understand, and I cried a lot. When I did talk, all I can remember talking about is all the people that died. I think that probably sticks with me more than anything else in the whole war—that I saw over a hundred men die in that year. And they were all young, healthy guys. I went to that rap group, and I must have cried every week for four months. For a long time all I could get out was "They just kept on dying. They just kept on dying." Then the same thing happened last year when I went to the Vietnam Veterans Memorial dedication in Washington . . . the same thing. All I saw was just the names of all these people who were dead, and I really didn't know why, it just didn't make any sense. I don't know . . .

As far as my life, I would like to get myself into a position where I can buy a home and have a family, have a child. Having a partner to do all that with would be nice. I'm not—I mean, I'm dating, but there's nobody special in my life. I'm thirty-four years old, and if I'm going to have a kid, I can't wait forever. I really want my own home. This is a beautiful place but it's not my home. I'd like to knock this wall out and put a little greenhouse on the side. I'd like to plant some rosebushes, but I'm not going to dig up rosebushes and take them with me when I leave. And I'd like to have a kid. I'd like to have a kid. I guess the house you can put off for a long time; the kid you can't put off forever.

And what that all has to do with Vietnam, I don't know. Maybe if I didn't go to Vietnam, I'd be married and have a house in the suburbs and a two-car garage. That's what

I planned on doing before I went to Vietnam. I always assumed I'd be married; I always assumed I'd have lots of kids. And I don't have any. I'm not married; and I never have been. I don't know why Clifford and I didn't get married except that we just never did. Never got married but it certainly felt like we got divorced, you know? It certainly felt that way.

Sara McVicker

71ST EVAC. HOSPITAL,
PLEIKU—MAR. '69 TO MAR. '70

I met Sara in November 1983 in Washington, D.C., where this interview took place. She now lives in Saint Petersburg, Florida, and works as a registered nurse.

I despise the term "combat nurse," you know? I really do. It conjures up images of running around in the jungle or something like that. I wasn't out in the boonies and I came home with a lot of feelings about how easy I had it. I lived in a building, worked in a building—they weren't very grandiose and the roof leaked, but they were indeed buildings, I wasn't sleeping on the ground. We had running water, flush toilets, a swimming pool. I wouldn't set foot in it today I don't think, from my memories of it, yuk! But it was luxury then and I knew that. I saw those guys coming in out of the field grimy and dirty . . . I think it's a comparison that a lot of women veterans make—I had it easy compared to the grunts. I shouldn't be having any problems, you know—nursing is nursing.

I'M AN ARMY BRAT; I GUESS THAT'S AN IMPORTANT part of my background. I was born at Fort Benning, Georgia, really kind of grew up at Fort Bragg—lived there for seven years and when my father retired from the Army, we moved to Fayetteville, so I was still in the Fort Bragg area. I can remember being in junior high school and one of my classmates came in one day, and he was upset that his father, who was a Special Forces officer, was being sent to Vietnam. That was 1961. So I guess in a sense I knew more about Vietnam than a lot of people early on—not in any depth, but an awareness that there were Americans there and there were Americans being killed there.

I think that when I joined the Army in 1966, someplace in the back of my mind there was the thought about wanting to go to Vietnam. By the time I graduated, I'd probably changed my mind back and forth three or four times. Anyway, I finished school in June of '68 and waited to go to basic. They weren't quite sure when I would go; it would be either August or September. So I worked for a couple months at the hospital in Chapel Hill, on a pediatric unit of all things, because I hated pediatrics when I was in school, then went to basic in August, finished in late September, and went to Fort Dix, New Jersey, for my first assignment. The whole atmosphere of Fort Dix was basic training and advanced infantry training. A lot of the male officers there were back from Vietnam. On the ward I worked on there were two male nurses; one was just back from Korea, and the other one had just come back from Vietnam. When I was in basic, the second day we were there, a guy stood up on the stage and said, "If you have a three-year commitment, you can count on going to either Vietnam or Korea." And when we got to Fort Dix—there were several new nurses coming in at the same time—the CO gave us this nice little welcoming speech, said, "We're very glad to have you, and we're sorry, but you probably won't be staying here very long. Most of our new nurses get orders within six months."

I was there around four months when I got my orders for Vietnam, I guess in January. An interesting thing was I got them in the mail. I stopped at the mail room on my way to lunch and here's this envelope from the surgeon general's office, and I thought, "What is this?" So I opened it up, and there's this set of orders, and I could pretty well read the military abbreviations, so I knew I was going someplace, because it said some transportation detachment, APO San Francisco da-da-da-da. I didn't know APO numbers, so I went tearing down the hall to personnel, and the lady said, "Can I help you?" I said, "Yes. I'm going someplace," and gave her my orders. She said, "Oh, my goodness, yes you are!" I said, "Well, can you tell me where!" and she said, "Vietnam."

The guy that I was seeing had just come back from Vietnam like six or eight months before—he'd been infantry. I called all over to locate him, and that evening Ken came over to see me. I remember him talking to me, and he took off his CIB and pinned it on my blouse . . . and he said, "You're going to do okay." . . . That meant a lot to me, because I knew what a CIB meant to them, you know?

In nurses basic at that time they did not teach us anything about weapons. They showed us how to load a .45 and that was it; we didn't even handle it. I was not feeling too secure at that point so I asked Ken, "I want to learn how to shoot. How do I go about it?" He said, "When you go through the orientation, ask them." So the first day of this orientation, I walk in and there's this brand new second lieutenant standing at the doorway. "Now ma'am, you realize that you're only required to come the first day and the security briefing tomorrow afternoon." I said, "Well, if I'd like to learn how to shoot a weapon, can I do that?" He didn't know; he had to get one of the sergeants. The sergeant says, "We're not going to be doing .45s. It's going to be M-16s." I said, "Fine, anything. I just want to know how to handle a gun." The orientation was a lot of stuff about setting up perimeters, VD control, water purification, 99 percent of which did not apply to me. It's this whole big theater full of guys; I'm the only woman in the place. Most of the enlisted men who were there had been pulled back from Germany, and they were cooks and transportation people, not infantry, but the support unit people. So the next morning I get up at some ungodly hour like four in the morning—and it's freezing cold—and put on winter fatigues. I think it's the only time I ever wore them. I went over to this warehouse and learned how to field-strip an M-16. Every one of the training cadre—I think there were two or three officers and two or three sergeants there—came up to me and in one way or another asked, "Why are you here?" Finally I said, "Look around you. All these guys have handled some sort of rifle before, if not an M-16, then an M-14 in basic. And I'm taking mine down and putting it back together faster than them. These are the guys who are going to be guarding me." They took me to the firing range, and I fired expert, which was a shock—I mean, I'd never handled a gun before (and I didn't realize it until I was clearing post that they put that in my 201 file). It was funny; it cracked me up. So, you know, I think it made me feel a little less helpless about being able to protect myself if worse came to worse. I don't know what I was expecting, but after Tet of '68 you could imagine almost anything.

We got to Vietnam early in the morning. I remember when we came in over the coast it was still dark enough—

we could see tracers out the windows below us. We went all day long doing processing and stuff, and it was really hot—and here I'd dug out from a snowstorm in New Jersey. The first night, I woke up in the middle of the night and heard artillery. Well, having grown up around Fort Bragg, you hear artillery all the time; it's nothing unusual, you know. I kind of rolled back over, and then there was this realization of "This isn't just practice; they're shooting at something." You know, it was an eerie feeling: here is a familiar sound that all of a sudden means something very different.

They took the nurses in to meet with somebody within the nursing service command. They sat us down and said, "Okay, we need nurses at the following places; and if you have any preferences let us know." One of the places they needed nurses was Pleiku. I didn't know really that much about the geography of Vietnam, but I remembered Pleiku was up in the highlands, and I remember thinking, "If it's up in the mountains, it's got to be cooler than here," so I volunteered to go to Pleiku. We left the next night. They got us up in the middle of the night and we dragged all our luggage down, and there were two buses, a jeep with a mounted gun in front, and a jeep with a mounted gun in back. They said, "Everyone get on the first bus. The other one is a backup bus." We said, "What do you mean?" They said, "In case something happens on the road and the bus breaks down, that's your backup so you aren't stranded out there." So we go out and it's pitch-dark. And to this day, I do not know whether it was a real breakdown of that bus or whether this was hazing of new people, but we ended up switching buses out on the road in the middle of the night. You never saw people move so fast!

Flying into Pleiku, I could kind of see out the window, and there was all this incredibly red dirt. It reminded me of Georgia, and of course around the installations, most of the vegetation was gone. So I'm just going, "Oh, yuck," and then we pulled up in front of the hospital, and there was green grass. They were literally growing the grass to keep the dust down. And I remember thinking, "Okay, I can survive a year of this.'' It was early April 1969, spring-time, and it *was* cooler than Long Binh.

They assigned me to a medical unit. It was supposed to be an intensive care unit, but it really wasn't. All the medical units had patients equally as sick as we did; it's just that the ward was designed a little bit differently, so that we had a three-bed cubicle and some cardiac monitoring equipment there if we needed it. The patients we got were everything under the gamut of medicine—typhus, malaria, pneumonias, dysentery—you know, anything that was a medical condition. Most of the patients were GIs. We would get some Montagnards in occasionally or a Vietnamese, but I seemed to remember more Montagnards than Vietnamese.

The other thing different about the ward I worked on was that we got all the psych casualties. We did not have a psychiatrist or a psychologist; we did not have trained psych nurses; we didn't have anything as far as I'm concerned. We had a couple corpsmen who were designated as psych technicians, and I don't know what their training consisted of but it sure did not prepare them to really handle psych patients. The reason that we got them all on this ward was that the chief of medicine volunteered to take them. He had been an infantry officer before he went to medical school, so I think he had a lot better understanding of what was going on out there in the field than most of the other doctors.

The medical unit was kind of nice to work on because it wasn't nearly as hectic as the surgical units in terms of taking care of the patients. We were full most of the time, but with the turnover, they'd come in and if somebody had malaria, we'd send him down to the 6th Convalescent at Cam Ranh Bay. We didn't keep them. Some guys might be in there for just a few days. If it was something that didn't require very much time, we might keep them, but there was this constant turnover, and I remember there was always a medical chopper running in the late afternoon around 5:30 or so, where they'd check with any of the fire base dispensaries if somebody needed to come in. And you always made sure that you were pretty well caught up by then because you never knew what you were going to get.

I'd worked there five months when our chief of medicine went home. I enjoyed working with him a lot, and I thought, "It's not going to be the same after Jim leaves." I think what I said to myself is "I'm getting bored." You know, by that time I knew all the ins and outs, malaria and typhus, and we'd even had a case of plague in a Montagnard kid. I think the unspoken part that I didn't even say to myself was that I was feeling really guilty about working on a medical ward. I had friends who worked on surgical units or the post-op unit, and we had gone through a period where it seemed like the choppers were coming in constantly. I think I really felt this need to work with the wounded patients; that was what my being there was all about, you know?

So I requested a transfer to post-op and went down there right about the beginning of September. I was only there a month when this major walked in one day and said, "We're going to make you head nurse on Ward Six." That was the end of September 1969. I had been out of school, let's see, sixteen months, and they were going to make me head nurse. And I thought, "They're crazy. I don't know anything about being a head nurse," but I became a head nurse.

I don't remember much about post-op, that month I worked there; it's really kind of fuzzy. I do remember one patient, and this is funny. It was a Vietnamese patient who had chest injuries, and he had two chest tubes in. The upper one sucks off the air, and the bottom one sucks off fluid that collects in the chest cavity. So one night I had come on duty and made rounds and everybody was doing okay. . . . I went to do something with another patient, and when I finished I went back to check on this Vietnamese man. And here's this bottom chest tube lying on the bed; the tape had come loose, and it had slipped out. I just about died. I mean, to have a chest tube come out can be very, very bad. I remember slapping my hand over the hole where the chest tube had been and hollering at somebody to get me some gauze and tape to cover it up. The whole time this patient is just lying there looking at me very calmly. He's fine; he's not in any crisis because any air that went in that hole was being sucked out by the upper chest tube. So everything was okay, but you know, that's just the kind of situation that nurses got put into over there. We didn't have a whole lot of experience. Even the official Army history says 60 percent of the nurses in Vietnam had been in the military less than one year, and for most of us that meant less than one year's nursing experience when we got there. Then when you're working the kind of hours that we worked, you're tired all the time; sometimes you don't think very well. I remember calling the doctor and telling him that this guy's chest tube came out, and he said, "How's he doing?" and I said, "He's doing fine. I'm not doing so well!"

Let's see, I was head nurse on the surgical ward for about five months. We got general surgery patients, neurosurgery, orthopedics, and a real mixture. We supported 4th Division, and one of the times I remember, one of the companies from 1st, of the 14th, was just getting chewed up, unbelievably chewed up, and we were getting patient after patient after patient. I remember turning around and looking at my ward master and saying, "Is there anybody left out there?" And within the next hour, we got the answer. We started getting patients from another company. I was going, "Oh, shit, how long is this going to go on?"

Toward the end of my tour, 4th Division pulled east across the mountains to An Khe for their base camp. It was part of the Vietnamization program, getting Americans out of Vietnam, which cut down on our work load some, as far as American patients went, but we filled up with Vietnamese.

I guess the one patient that I really remember out of that period was a young black kid who had a head injury. And we had at that time, unfortunately, a real turkey of a neurosurgeon who did not want to operate on him, and that was not considered acceptable. When I think about it now, it made perfectly good sense; there probably wasn't anything he could do. But I guess the basic philosophy in our hospital was that you always tried, you always tried, even when it was bad enough where there was not much hope. We were really busy at that time, so they moved him out of post-op up to my ward, and he was unconscious . . . without very much hope. In fact, they weren't even pushing for an air-evac to send him to Japan. They just did not expect him to live. He'd been there, I don't know, several days—I can't remember how long—when we got all this mail that had been forwarded from his unit. One of the corpsmen brought it to me and said, "What do you want me to do with it?" I was going over to this guy's bed to check on him or something, and I said, "I'll just put it in his bedside stand," and I happened to look at the return addresses . . . and all of them were from people at a small black college near my hometown in North Carolina . . . and I just thought, "Shit, this guy must've been in school there." I guess my thought was, he either dropped out or goofed off and flunked out, got drafted, and here he is in Vietnam . . . and he's going to die. . . . And that really got to me. I remember just going, "This is ridiculous." Here is a kid who obviously had the smarts to get into college—it was a school that had a good reputation—and now what . . . you know, wasted . . . just wasted. So a day or two later he arrested, his heart stopped, and I remember trying to resuscitate him, and to this day I don't know why. I guess it was the thing of—you always tried, you know? You didn't want to let go, which is simply another way of saying that we had a hard time accepting that we couldn't keep everybody alive and bring everybody back. We finally stopped the resuscitation, and I remember walking out the front door of the ward; I just had to get out of there. . . . And I probably came closer to crying that day than any other time. I guess it was because it made a connection for me—you know, he was from close to home.

I ended up coming home ten days early. I got a drop—that's the terminology they use. As part of the pull-out of American troops, they were trying to get their numbers down, so they'd send people home a week, ten days or so, early. I can remember feeling very guilty about leaving early. You know, post-op was really short of nurses. I wanted out of there, but I felt bad about it; it was almost like I was deserting.

The flight home landed at McChord air base up near Seattle. I ran into the nurse that I had sat with on the flight over. It was really funny, because we had come in-country together and then gone to different hospitals and not seen or thought about each other for a year, so we sat together on the way home. The third person in the row was a guy from the Seattle area, and he very nicely said, "My mother is coming to pick me up. We'd be glad to take you to the airport." So we got chauffeured to the airport, which was also nice, because I didn't have to figure out about cabs or whatever. I got a flight out very, very quickly, called my mother, and told her I'd be in the next morning. I remember getting a little sleep on the flight to Atlanta, and it was really funny, because in Atlanta I walked into the airport and ran into a guy who had been on the flight from Vietnam. He'd gotten there via Houston, and we both had a couple hours layover. We were extremely tired but were afraid to even sit down and rest for fear of falling asleep and missing our flights. So we got something to eat and then wandered around the airport together just to keep each other awake. It was like, "Oh, my God, if I miss my flight home I'll die."

When I came home, I had sixteen months left in the Army. And I was assigned at Fort Belvoir to the female surgical ward, which was a hectic ward; it was really the busiest ward in the hospital. You know, I tell people sometimes that it wasn't until I got out of the Army that I realized not all nurses worked as hard as I did those three years that I was in the service. It was a forty-five-bed unit, and I'd work a lot of evenings with just me and sometimes one other person on. If you were lucky, you had a third person, and if you were really lucky, that third person was the equivalent of an LPN. Right after I came home I really had to go through some adjustments as far as settling back into stateside nursing. I remember getting terribly frustrated, now that I look back. Part of it was the sheer work load of that unit; it really was hectic. And I don't know how much of it was that and how much of it was stuff left over from Vietnam, or what. But I can remember blowing a couple times.

I got out of the Army in August of '71, went to graduate school and got my master's in nursing, then taught for three years in a baccalaureate nursing program, which I really enjoyed for the most part. I think I have some questions now about what my motivation was. I'm sure one of them was that I was tired of rotating shifts, but also I think that going to school was a nice way of getting away from having direct patient responsibility, and I gather from other women that a number of people have done the same sort of thing. It's like going back to school was an acceptable way of getting away from it for us. So I taught for three years and decided that I wanted to get back into a hospital and took a position that was basically an administrative position. I was not smart enough to have read the situation very well before I went in. Five months after I took the position, the director of nursing was fired and the nursing service was completely reorganized, and my job was basically reorganized out from under me. I was put into a position that carried a very nice title, but nobody knew what it meant. I did a lot of different things for about nine months, then said, "I can't stand this," went into an infection control position, and I've been in infection control ever since then. It's a nice combination of things I like.

I guess in many ways I went a long time without realizing that I had stuff left over from Vietnam. I'm one of those people who buried it pretty well. I had a pretty good denial system going in Vietnam; I got to the point where I almost ignored alerts. If it wasn't really close, like on top of us, then I just pretended it didn't matter. That was the way I dealt with it, because we had an awful lot of alerts for the first six or eight months that I was there. "If it's not close, I can't be bothered with it, because if I worry all the time, I'm just not going to be able to do anything else."

I remember the spring of 1975. I was teaching then, and I kind of kept tabs on the news—you know, about Vietnam—but it wasn't something that I concentrated on. The first few weeks I was home, I was glued to the evening news to see what was going on, and after that I got away from it. But that spring, in that final offensive, I think I knew that was the beginning of the end when it started. In March, I remember sitting in the living room, watching the news, and they said the South Vietnamese had pulled out of Pleiku and Kontum provinces—no fight, they just flat pulled out. I couldn't believe it. I took it so personally, it was like that was *my* province and they gave it up without a fight. They just left . . . and it devastated me; it was like the whole thing was for nothing. The South Vietnamese didn't even put up a fight after all the blood we shed on that territory, and I think that's when I really pushed it away, for a good while.

I don't know what started the whole process of getting it out and getting me to work on it. I very clearly remember a period when I would watch "M.A.S.H." regularly. In fact, I was watching reruns as well as the current ones, and I would sit there and cry, and it really didn't matter what the story was about; it would just trigger it. Then in 1979 I went to work for the VA, and I guess that's when I started becoming really consciously aware of some of the things that were going on with Vietnam veterans, as well as some of the attitudes toward them. I met a woman who was our psychiatric clinical specialist at work, and she knew I was a woman vet. We had talked and kind of skirted around some things, and then she asked me if I would be willing to talk for an in-service class about Vietnam veterans she was doing on the psych unit. She wanted three of us to talk about what Vietnam had been like, so that the staff would get some perspective. I agreed and I'm not sure why, but I agreed. I remember being incredibly nervous that morning. One person finked out on us, he had second thoughts. I remember thinking, "I wish I'd had second thoughts." And I remember standing up and I practically had to hang on to something. That is probably one of the most difficult things I have ever done, because not only was I talking to strangers in a sense, but I was talking to people that I worked with, and there's always this wondering, this feeling of "How are people going to perceive what you're saying? Are they going to think you're another wacko Vietnam veteran?'' I think that's when Joan, this clinical specialist, realized that I had a lot of stuff going on and that I had not talked about Vietnam before to anybody really, nobody. She knew I was interested, because I had at that point been doing a lot of reading about Vietnam: history, some of the novels, some of the personal recollections that people had written. I had a lot of jumbled feelings; I didn't know how I felt about the war. I've always tried to handle things in a logical way. I guess I had this feeling that if I learned more about the war, how we got involved and what went on, then I would be able to figure out how I felt about it. Well, that didn't work very well, because you can't really handle it logically; you're talking about feelings, not logic.

Shortly thereafter, she came in one day and handed me an article that was an interview with Lynda Van Devanter and said, ''I think you ought to get in touch with her.'' I had seen it in the paper and read it, and I finally looked at Joan and said, ''I know this woman. I served with her.'' I eventually did get in touch with her. It took me close to a month to get around to writing her a letter. I would not call her—I couldn't deal with that—so I finally wrote her a letter. It was really funny, because Joan had talked to Lynda in the interim and had passed on the message, saying, ''She got your letter, and she's going to get a letter into the mail to you. It's practically on its way.'' Well, it didn't come and it didn't come, and when it finally appeared I realized that it had been misaddressed. Ohio had become translated into California, and a couple numbers were transposed in the zip code. I can't believe I got it. Someone in a post office out in California went to a lot of trouble to get that letter to me. Because the envelope had the VVA logo on it, I've always wondered if it was a Vietnam veteran. That letter got me started coming out of the woodwork really. I guess it was in the fall of '82, a little over a year ago now, that I met Lynda and another nurse that we served with at a conference on post-traumatic stress that was done out in Ohio. We talked practically nonstop for three days—I mean, really.

I have found that talking with other women, particularly

when it's somebody you knew over there, really makes a connection. It's been very good. It brings out a lot of stuff and helps with filling in some of the gaps in memories. And it puts it back into perspective. Somebody said one time, "I'm glad you said that because I've always wondered if I imagined that." There are so many things out there that thirteen years later you're really not sure what's real anymore. You wonder, "Did that really happen to me? Am I making this up? Am I exaggerating things?" I'm sure there are some faulty memories—the brain is not infallible—but it helps to have some validation, and particularly validation of your feelings.

I had a real rough time when the Marines were killed in Lebanon. I got up that Sunday morning, bounced out of bed. Sunday's my morning when I fix a nice, leisurely breakfast, sit down, and read the paper, and I like to watch Charles Kuralt's program—he's generally not dire news or anything; he handles lighter subjects. So I'm fixing breakfast and I turned on the television, and they were talking about Beirut. I was lost that day. I got absolutely nothing done. I just wandered around from room to room. I'd pick up the paper and read a little bit and put it back down because I couldn't concentrate. . . . And then the invasion of Grenada. I guess I had the feeling that it really doesn't matter how I feel, because it's not going to make any difference. Then as the week went on, I think some of the reactions in the newspaper made me feel better about it simply because there was such an outpouring of support for the military people who were there. And even though I think some of it was an emotional response, I'm glad to see it, because no matter how people feel about it, they aren't blaming it on the peons who are out there doing the fighting. If they've got policy differences, they're directing it someplace else. Instead of what they did to us.

I don't know that we've learned anything from Vietnam, maybe some basic things, like learning that PTSD is real, but as far as looking at foreign policy and military intervention, I don't know. I remember when I was in Vietnam, in the fall of '69, there was a big moratorium back in the States, a protest against the war, and some of the people at the hospital decided they would fast to protest the war. I remember thinking, ''I cannot do that. I cannot look my patients in the eye after what they have been through and tell them that this was all for nothing.'' I don't know what I'd tell them today. I'd like to think that something positive came out of it, but I don't know what.

Maureen "Mo" Nerli

USO, TAN SON NHUT—JUNE '69 TO DEC. '70

Maureen was in Vietnam as associate director of the Tan Son Nhut USO Club. She went to Thailand for eighteen months from 1971 to 1972, as associate director of the Utapao Air Base USO club. Then in 1972 she was in Korea with Army Special Services for another eighteen-month tour—an overseas career spanning five years, which seems even more impressive considering her rather modest request of the USO show director in 1968: "Can I just go over there and help out—you know, go out in the field and sing a song or something?"

Maureen currently resides in the San Francisco Bay Area. She works as an independent TV and film producer and is writing a book about her life in Vietnam with the USO.

WHEN I FIRST MADE UP MY MIND TO GO OVER TO
Nam, I was musical director for KFRC radio station in San
Francisco. I was also a volunteer hostess at the USO airport
lounge, dealing with the Vietnam vets as they were going
over or coming home from Vietnam. I always wanted to
be part of this war. I wanted to help. I just wanted to be
able to show the men that I saw every day coming in and
out of the USO that somebody really cared.

At that time I knew the head of the USO shows, Jimmy
Sheldon, and I asked him, "Jimmy, can I just go over there
and help out—you know, go out in the field and sing a
song or something?" He said, "Mo, you haven't really
done much in that phase of it. I'd like to send you, but I
can't really do it." I was heartbroken, but I said to myself,
"I'm going over there. Somehow, some way, Maureen is
getting over to Vietnam. She's going to see this war firsthand." I was working with a gal who was doing PR for
the USO lounge, and she said, "Write to the main office,
and I'll call them and put in a good word for you." So I
called instead, and they said, "Wonderful. We'll mail you
a ticket and you can come to the East Coast for an inter-

view.'' I flew back there and was interviewed. The man I talked to said, "Well, yes, but of course you know the only spot open is Vietnam." And I said, "Oh, yeah? Terrific!" He said, "When?" and I said, "When? When what?" "When do you want to go to Vietnam?" Then it finally hit me. I went into total shock, and I said, "Oh, my God, can I think it over?" I thought to myself, "Mo, you might as well do the things you've always thought that you might want to do, because when you go overseas you may never come home again." So I sang with a local band, modeled—did all those things.

Finally the time came about, and I called HQ, as we used to call it, and said, "I'm ready." I committed myself to the USO, packed my bags and, before I knew it, was at Camp Lejeune, North Carolina, training at the Jacksonville USO club there. Marine grunts from the base would come into the club and I'd be making shakes and sundaes for them, and I just fell in love with every single one of them. You know, with those big eyes and their shaven heads and their starched green fatigues, they were so cute. I was there about two weeks when Mr. Sheehan, the club director, said, "Mo, you are ready? It's time for you to go." That wasn't before I had a patchwork of shots: cholera, plague, my God, I was a pincushion from all of the shots! I came home and the first thing I did was make out my will. Now that really kind of joggled me. I was told to make out my will. That done, I packed my one suitcase and said good-bye to my mother and my brother and his wife. I kept looking out the window, saying, "Those hills, my wonderful hometown, I wonder if I am ever going to see them again?" And then I was over there; I was in Vietnam!

We arrived at Tan Son Nhut air base on June 9, 1969. It was a hot, sticky day, and I'll never forget it. I thought my body was just going to explode. Everybody was screaming around me, and I thought, "My God, what is wrong with all of these people?" Then I realized that they were just speaking their own language. This was Vietnamese?! I felt like a totally lost sheep. Finally this American man walked up to me, a rather tall, pudgy fellow, and he said, "Hi there, I'm Dick, from the USO. Did you have a nice flight?'' I told him that I was really quite upset because there was a man sitting next to me on the plane, who was coming back from R&R, and he said, ''Well, lady, you're never going to make it. I'm telling you there are VC out on that landing field, and the plane is going to land and you are going to be shot at, and I guarantee you are not going to make it one day in-country.'' Here I am getting off the plane remembering his words and hearing all these people screaming, and the hot weather . . .

The first day I was in shock and very tired, jet lag and all that. The USO had a penthouse suite on Nguyen Hue, and every new person in-country would live there for a day or two until he or she got his or her club assignment. It was amazing—no one told me anything about gun fire on the streets at nighttime, curfews. . . . This was Saigon. The next morning I woke up refreshed and decided to take a tour. I ate breakfast at a Basque restaurant on Nguyen Hue, walked around to Tu Do Street, and was greeted on one corner by a man urinating on the left side of an Army jeep. I thought, ''What am I getting myself into?'' I mean, this is basic, Lord, this is basic humanity!

The USO had about twenty-five clubs in Vietnam. I was assigned as associate director of the Tan Son Nhut USO near the air base. It was a big club, a four-story building, basically white with red-and-white awnings. We had pool and Ping-Pong tables, overseas telephones, a barber shop, and gift shop. We served between five hundred and eight hundred shakes, hot dogs, and hamburgers every day. We had fifty Vietnamese on our staff, three assigned GIs, one Chinese program assistant, one director, and three associate directors. The GIs came from all over Vietnam—Tan Son Nhut, Long Binh, Da Nang—you name it. If a GI needed money or a loan till payday, we'd call the gals at the 3d Field Hospital American Red Cross office. I can only praise the work those gals did.

The Vietnamese on our staff were very hardworking people. They would come to work very early in the morning and make the rolls and clean up the club. They were always smiling and whistling. They were all very dear people. They worked very hard for us. When I left there, I was worried sick about them. What was going to happen to them? They had kids. They had to buy food and pay bills. They were like us; it's just that it was *their* country that was being torn up. To this very day, when I think back, I miss them. One of the GIs that worked for us, Moose, was a really big guy. He would help us round up the food at the Army depot, plus he would be there to lift things for us and to calm down a GI that was, you know, whatever. So we had primarily all Vietnamese on our staff, and we were completely selfsupporting; we actually ran our whole club that way. Well, we did. . . . This is where scrounging came in. And it was funny because I never thought that I could do this. One day my boss called me into the office and said, "Mo, I need about eighty feet of telephone wire." And I said, "What do you need it for?" He said, "Well, don't ask me. Just get it. I'll give you at the maximum one hour." Here I am on the phone, calling all these guys over at MACV and the TSN air base, "Hi, this is Mo, from TSN USO. Do you happen to have any phone wire?" "Mo, what do you want that for?" I said, "Just don't ask me. I need it. Can you get it for me right now?" And they were over just like that. It was terrific! It was like we were all working together; everybody was helping. But you know, a gal's voice on the phone really helped.

Those Vietnamese, they were really dear. We had two gals that worked for us in the office. One was Miss Phu; the other was Mrs. Qui. Now, Miss Phu was like a typical American; she wore miniskirts and talked like we all did. And then Mrs. Qui, she was a dainty little lady, who talked very softly, and she always wore her *ao dai*, the native gown. When you would see her wearing this, walking down the street, she would just glide. She was so beautiful. Qui always wore her hair pulled back. She was very polite and never raised her voice. Whereas Miss Phu was just the opposite in her miniskirts; she had acquired a lot of our ways. They were such a contrast.

Then we had certain special days. We used to program events and try to have them done so that we would cater to every group—Mexican Day, Irish Day, Southern Day— and we would work on these for months, planning food and entertainment, putting out our PR. I can remember, we had an *Oktoberfest* with German food cooked by a Vietnamese cook. . . . It was funny, he was making German spuds and sauerkraut and all that stuff. The Vietnamese had never seen this type of food before, and they were saying, "Miss Mo, what I do with this?" I'd say, "Just put a little of this and a little of that in there." And they would laugh. We had a thousand GIs show up for that, and they weren't only the enlisted men; many of the officers came too. It was funny, because the staff went to the Saigon marketplace and gathered chicken feathers, and we used brown paper bags and made Alpine hats. To see all these officers and enlisted men sitting at the tables with rubber bands around their necks with these hats on—it was hilarious!

We were asked, day after day, to go out to a fire base, or a camp. When we did, we would talk to the guys and sing for them, maybe do a show or something, serve food. We usually went out by chopper, but we went by jeep too. One time we flew up to a little place called Song Mao. The captain arranged for us to fly with an Aussie crew in that strange plane—I think it was called a Caribou—that took off straight up and landed straight down. When we went there I had to bring a rock band—the drums and guitar player and the singer, the whole bit. The captain told me, "You can't set foot on this base unless you've got a show." We were asked to do this time after time.

During Christmastime we all worked for a week straight—we really did, hardly any rest at all—bringing gifts out to the guys in the field, going to the hospitals and giving gifts out to the men on each ward, talking to them. I can remember one hospital visit we made at Tan Son Nhut air base medical facility. Some stateside company gave us the money to set up phone lines to the States so we could go on each ward and ask if a GI would like to call home. The emotionalism of having these GIs call home . . . I mean it was . . . "Mom, is that . . . Mom, it's me, Mom!" The other gal and myself stood there with tears rolling down our faces. It was a very emotional thing, and yet we were doing something, and I am really pleased to say that I was part of what little bit was done by all the

men and women who were there with the USO. I think
there is one point that I must make here: everybody that
worked for the USO was a volunteer; nobody said, ''You
must go.'' We wanted to go over there, and in wanting to
go over, we made the very best of it. We put our hearts
and souls into it, believe me. Oh, I don't mean to say it
was all work—we had our own lives; we had friends and
parties and dated, went on R&Rs. We didn't work twenty-
four hours every day, but many times it seemed like it.
The USO, I think, really did a whole lot of good. Well, of
course in every war there is always the USO—''Your home
away from home''; it's on every letterhead.

The one day I'll never forget as long as I live: I was in
the office writing the monthly report, and I noticed two GIs
outside the office door. I beckoned for them to come in.
And this one young man—Oh God, he was so cute and he
was so shy, and you could tell he was ashamed of what he
had done. I had a feeling that I knew already what he'd
done. The other fellow kept pushing him and saying, ''Go
on, man, talk to her. Get in there!'' So he came in, and he
stood in front of my desk and said, ''Ma'am.'' And I said,
''Hi. Can I help you?'' He said, ''Well, ma'am . . . and
his buddy opens the door—''For God's sake, will you tell
her!'' . . . The whole thing was hysterical! So he sat down
and finally said, ''Well, ma'am, you know, I was down
the alleyway. . . . I said, ''Don't tell me, you were in Mrs.
Whatever's little house?'' And he said, ''How did you
know? Yeah, I was there.'' And I said, ''And you got
ripped off, right?'' He started to relax a little, and he said,
''Yeah, and she took three hundred dollars of my money
while I was asleep.'' Well, we were supposed to call the
MPs and file a report. When this situation occurred—basically this was going on everyday, but it was taboo, you
know. He said, ''Oh, please don't, ma'am, please don't.''
And I said, ''You're putting me on the spot. I've got to do
this because this is SOP.'' So I called the MPs and I was
talking to them outside the office. I said, ''Hey, go easy
on the guy.'' They said, ''Well . . .'' And I said, ''Just
give him one more chance. Don't throw him in jail for
this, for God's sake. . . . This poor guy has been in the

field for three months. This is his first R&R, and he had three hundred bucks in his pocket and was ripped off by this little gal down the alleyway." So he said, "Well, okay for this time." So I called my friends at the American Red Cross at 3d Field Hospital, and they arranged for him to get a three–hundred–dollar loan, and he went on his R&R. I never saw him again, but I still think of that time when he walked in that office and I saw the blond head of hair and his green outfit and smelled that Vietnam earth and I just . . . I thought to myself, "Honest to God, the people back home don't know what they are really missing. This is first-class life here; this is what's goin' on!"

When I left for Vietnam I was extremely shy and quiet. I would blush at the drop of a hat. After eighteen months there, I was totally changed. I mean, for the first time in my life when I got mad, I said "damn" and "hell". . . . You sort of loosen up; you realize it doesn't matter. I was born and reared in the Bay Area, went to Catholic schools my whole life—aside from Stanford, where I took a post-grad course in radio and TV, and after being in that field for all those years you would think that I would have loosened up, but it took Vietnam. My eighteen months there went extremely fast, and when I left I felt that I was losing my best friend. My whole life had just really changed, and I didn't want to leave it. I didn't want to leave all that I had been through; I didn't want to leave all of the very close friends; I didn't want to leave the Asians that worked for me.

When I came home, I was more afraid here than when I was over there. People that I thought were my close friends said, "You commie, what in the hell were you doing over there?" I had all of these people cutting me down because I felt that I should serve my country. It was painful, and I've never gotten over that, never. And I know how our GIs felt when they came home, because we got the same treatment, that same "I don't want to hear about it, forget it, don't talk to me about it!" How many times I just wanted to say something back to them and had to hold back. So many times I just wanted to scream or wanted to rent a corner on First and Market and put my soapbox down and stand on it and say, "I was in Vietnam! Now Goddammit, you've got to hear me!" It was this complete total silence; people just could not face it. I think maybe this is one of the reasons why after I had been home about two months I accepted an assignment from the USO to a club in Thailand. I thought, "Oh boy, this is going to be terrific." And before I knew it, I was on my way back overseas to Utapao, Thailand. This time I was dealing with the Air Force. Again it was a very big USO club. We were open twenty-four hours a day. The club was always busy; we served food constantly. We had USO show troupes doing shows; we even did our own shows using GIs who wrote music and sang. We had a very full day's work. At that club there was the director, three associate directors, and about seventy Thai civilians on our staff.

Utapao was primarily a B-52 base, and it was going twenty-four hours a day. It was a large base. I don't know how many men were there, but I know there were many. About five miles to our left was the U.S. Army base of Samae San, and then you would drive north and there was another little camp. There were more Air Force camps scattered all around. The bombers . . . they would take off three at a time. It would shake the whole place; they would wake you up if you were asleep. I got to the point where I just dreaded hearing them—not so much for the sake of them being noisy, but for the sake of what actually happened when they dropped their bombs. That is what triggered something in me; I thought of all those poor people who would be just blown up and shattered, and I thought of the many, many lives being torn by this. I got to the point that I resented every single plane that took off. . . . It was as if a fear was just beginning to creep up inside me. I couldn't rest there.

I had more turmoil there than I did my whole eighteen months in Nam. I didn't feel I was really doing my part there, whereas I did in Vietnam. It was an experience, but it wasn't the same. The grunts coming in out of the field, smelling that Vietnam dirt smell—I can still smell it to this very day. There's a certain aroma that every GI had when he came in from the field. It was like an earthy smell; it was war smell, paint smell, a green smell—it had all these different things to it . . . something else. Utapao was different. I mean, the men there didn't really see any war. . . . All they did was get the B-52 planes ready for takeoff. It wasn't as heavy on them. In Nam, with the GIs in from the field, maybe they had been out there for two or three months and had seen their best buddy blown away. They were totally—they were . . . Oh, golly, it's hard to explain. I know what it is that I have seen, and yet I can't speak for them. . . . Whereas for the men that were at Utapao, it was just like getting up at eight o'clock in the morning, being to work at nine, doing your work, and then coming home. They didn't experience the emotionalism of it all . . . of being down on the field, hearing gunfire, feeling it, hearing the screams, and seeing your buddies in pain. It was different.

When you are up there and you are flying how many thousand feet in the sky and all you do is push a button and the bombs drop—and believe me, I'm not saying that they weren't doing their part. . . . I had a major of a B-52 crew tell me that what they were doing was the only thing that counted; their part of the war was what was actually winning the war. The GIs were down there, but so what? And my anger was aroused. I told him such egotistical thinking was sickening. He never spoke to me again, nor I to him. There were many B-52 planes shot down; I'm positive about that. But still I don't think as many lives were lost as on the ground.

I will say this however, that I have the absolute greatest respect for the U-2 pilots. They didn't say too much, but the ones that I talked to said that they were up there for nine hours at a time, taking photographs of what was going on around Vietnam, who was moving where, and who was taking what with them. So that was tough duty, and I think a majority of the MIAs were from that group, because they were the ones that were shot down. They were all alone up there; they didn't have any support.

I can only say that when I came home the second time, a voice kept saying to me, "You must go over there again." I felt very, very lost here. I knew Asia, because being over there we could travel extensively, and I thought, "Well, maybe I should go over again." The USO was going through an internal change so I joined the Department of Army Special Services. Within a matter of months I was cleared and sent overseas, this time to Korea. Again, it was totally different. The war was winding down. I was beginning to wind down from Nam too. And now I was beginning to feel that maybe home is where I should really be. So I was in Korea from one end of it to the other—I was at Ascom, Pyeon Tek, Chunchon. It was an eighteen-month tour. I decided I really had had it; if I was to smell another piece of dried fish hanging on a wall somewhere or see another bowl of rice, I might scream.

After having served overseas and seen so many, many things, my life has really changed. It's the things that seem important to people here, like a new car, a fancy house, an Yves Saint Laurent suit, or whatever. I mean, that's marvelous, but you actually learn that those things just don't make you you, nor do they make you happy. What really matters is caring. Caring for your loved ones and having close friends and making a friendship grow, because when it is all said and done, you don't have much else. I feel that as a person I have totally changed. I can't stand to see unfairness, after seeing so much of it overseas. It just galls me, and I get up in arms and my face gets red and my heart pounds. I just can't stand to see people used or taken. I mean, Vietnam has really done that to me. It has made me accept the fact that if you are going to do anything in this life that is worthwhile, you have got to push for it; you've got to fight for it. I feel that maybe that change was really good; maybe this is what I was mentally looking for, a sense of something, a sense of growth, that I couldn't find here. I think being in this wonderful land— believe me, I'm not saying that it isn't wonderful, but it's too easy. . . . I saw women over in Vietnam carrying heavy bricks when the men were seated along the road laughing! These women worked hard. It was an awesome sight . . . something that my eyes will always see. I will never forget Vietnam. . . . It is always there, and until the day that I am six feet under, Vietnam will always be there: the sights, the sounds, the smells, the happy times and the bad times. . . . It is as real now as it was when I was there.

Grace Barolet O'Brien

85TH EVAC. HOSPITAL,
QUI NHON—JAN. '66 TO JAN. '67
67TH EVAC. HOSPITAL,
QUI NHON—FEB. '67 TO AUG. '67

Grace is currently coordinator of Improved Pregnancy Outcome and Adolescent Pregnancy Programs in Saint Mary's County, Maryland Health Department.

She is divorced from a Vietnam veteran, the mother of two sons, Jim and Kevin, loves outdoors, camping, backpacking, and travel. She is active with local outreach to Vietnam vets and also works as a National Park volunteer at the Vietnam memorial in Washington, D.C.

I HAD THOUGHT ABOUT BEING A NURSE FOR AS LONG as I can remember. There were a lot of different nursing schools that I wanted to attend, but being the oldest in a family of eight children, I really didn't know if I could afford to go anywhere out of state. I decided to go to the junior college that was near our home for two years and commute as a day student. My studies were all geared toward getting a nursing degree.

When I finished the two years at junior college, I wasn't really sure how I would get the money to complete my education. One day my brother said, "Grace, I think I found the way for you." He was reading an Army magazine about helicopters, and there was something in it about the Army student nurse program.

I went to Fort Meade for an interview with the Army nurse recruiter, and during that interview she showed me pictures of herself as a combat nurse in Korea. I remember feeling really high over those pictures. She explained the program to me and how they would pay for my education and books. After graduation I would owe three years of service to the Army. That was my only hang-up. Three years seemed like a long time.

In July of 1963 I went into the Army Nurse Corps program. Coming from a patriotic family, I think my dad was delighted that I had chosen the Army and that I was going to do something to serve my country. I spent two years at the University of Maryland in Baltimore, until I graduated in June 1965. In September I finally got the telegram indicating when I should proceed to Fort Sam Houston for officers basic training. I was quite excited about being able to leave Saint Mary's County and go someplace really different.

We spent about six weeks at Fort Sam, and while we were there, talk of Vietnam was in the air. Everybody was saying, "I wonder how long it's going to be before we go there." I got really caught up in thinking how interesting military nursing was going to be and how I'd get such good experience.

I got orders to go to Walter Reed Hospital in Washington, D.C. and I don't know how long I was there when I decided to volunteer for Vietnam. I'd kind of had it in the back of my mind, so several weeks after I got to Walter Reed, I went over and told them that I wanted to volunteer to go to Vietnam. I only stayed at Walter Reed from late October of '65 until early January '66. During that time I worked on two wards which were orthopedic wards. I don't remember the actual patient size, but they were pretty big. That to me was a terrible shock. I had been used to taking care of a maximum of about four patients in nursing school. To all of a sudden be on a ward and know that eventually you were going to be responsible for all these patients was kind of scary. I remember looking at these guys and thinking, "My God, most of these guys came back from Vietnam."

During that period of time I really got to care for the guys. I don't remember them talking a lot about Vietnam, but they would mention the unit they'd been with. One guy, a sergeant, had been in Ia Drang Valley. I remember him very distinctly because he had a high amputation of both legs. He had stepped on a land mine. When his legs were unwrapped, it was the first time that I had seen what an amputation looked like. I remember very vividly thinking, "My God, how is this guy going to get by in life?" His morale was great, however. Most of the guys had excellent morale. They seemed really happy to be home. I had always been a pretty quiet person, but I learned to lighten up quite a bit because they loved to harass the nurses. I had a lot of laughs with them. When I worked night shift, they'd sit up and talk with me. Several of them were very concerned about the fact that I had volunteered for Vietnam. They really didn't want me to go. They didn't want to see any nurses going over there and possibly getting hurt.

I got my orders and was supposed to leave sometime around the middle of January 1966. One of my roommates and I were assigned to 85th Evac Hospital, and my other roommate was going to Nha Trang. We found out that we were going to be flying out on the same date, so we agreed that we would all meet in San Francisco and then go up to Travis Air Force Base together. When we got to Travis we went to the officers' club to wait for our flight. There was another gal there in dress greens. We asked her if there was any chance she was going to Vietnam, and she said, "Yeah!" So it ended up there were four of us nurses going on the same flight. A couple of guys who were in the club found out we were going to Nam so we all cliqued together. One of the guys was a captain and was a real comic. The other was a major who had already served a tour in Vietnam and was going back over for a second. We all sat toward the front of the plane for the trip. The guys in the back must've thought we were a bunch of absolute nuts. I had taken my ukulele with me, and the captain decided to entertain the troops. We had also taken a bottle of champagne with us and popped the cork when we lifted off. It was like a circus. It was such a long flight, but I never did sleep. We landed in Saigon. After we got off the plane, I remember someone saying, "Any of you that are nurses come with me." We had to say good-bye to all the guys at that point. We didn't know whether we were going to see them again and that bothered me a lot. We nurses were to report to the chief nurse and she would give us instructions about when we were going to our destinations. When we got there, all I really wanted to do was sleep, because I was so tired. We were told we could sleep for a while. Several hours later we were woken up and told to go to the "O" club to eat. We went with the chief nurse to the club, and I heard a comment like, "I think we have about one hundred nurses in-country now." I don't honestly know how many nurses were there at the time, but we were there in the earlier part of the war. She told us that the next day we would be taking a flight north. Charlene and I were going to Qui Nhon; we would drop Cheryl off in Nha Trang on the way up.

When we arrived at the 85th Evac, we met the woman who was the chief nurse. She was a very small, slight white-haired lady who looked like a grandmother. She seemed so nice. She told us, "Take the next seventy-two hours if you can. Try to get some sleep and get settled in because we are expecting mass casualties. We're going to need you then." We didn't really know what that meant, but we thought we'd take advantage of the sleep.

Initially we lived in a beautiful three-story villa which was right on the water in Qui Nhon. Nurses were assigned to the top floor, the men were on the bottom two floors. All were officers in the building. It was a Vietnamese villa that had been turned into a MACV compound and was located a mile or so from the hospital. We nurses were going to stay there until they could get some other facilities for us. The rooms were a decent size, but because we had our gear, we were kind of sandwiched into them. I got a top bunk and shared the room with three other nurses. I think one of the first things that struck me was the heat and humidity. I couldn't get over how wet the sheets were. I didn't think I would ever get used to wet sheets!

The staff that was there at the time had gone over together as a unit. They had actually landed on the beach and established the hospital in August of '65. They were pretty experienced by the time we got there. When we arrived in January, they were working in Quonset huts but had initially lived and worked in tents.

When the mass casualties came in, they suggested that we tag along with one of the more experienced nurses. I was told to go to pre-op that first night. They had triaged the patients and had taken the ones who were to be operated on immediately into the OR. I went into the Quonset hut and felt overwhelmed seeing all those guys either on stretchers or the small metal beds. My first recollection was of old, funky green fatigues that had mud all over them and those brown gauze bandages that were all bloody. I remember feeling almost in shock. I didn't know what to do and said something like, "Well, what should we do?" I was told to help take vital signs. I wasn't very fast at it; I hadn't been used to doing it before. The corpsmen had done it for us in the States. Then I was asked to start IVs but couldn't because I hadn't been trained. Later, I was assigned to a young soldier who was on a stretcher. They told me that he was really bad off. He had a head wound. He was unconscious, and I was supposed to take his blood pressure. They told me he would probably die, and all I could think of was, "What in the world am I taking his blood pressure for?" I didn't want to accept the fact he was going to die. That night I came back to our villa and cried, because it just overwhelmed me. Somehow I got through that first night though.

I was assigned to Wards 4 and 5, orthopedic wards, and 6 and 7, which were general surgery wards. There were several nurses on each ward, but they needed someone who could fill in as a float and help out where they needed the most help. I worked a lot more orthopedics initially. I felt more comfortable with orthopedics because I had worked ortho on Ward 35 at Walter Reed. Gradually, somewhere between shifting among the four different wards and rotating through the shifts, I started feeling more comfortable.

I remember feeling really thrilled when I was finally able to start IVs. For me it was a real sense of accomplishment. The guys were eighteen, nineteen, twenty years of age and very healthy. Their veins just popped right out. I heard that later on in the war they had intracaths and butterflies, but we didn't have anything like that. If anybody had connections back here in the States, they wrote and asked for intracaths and butterfly needles to be sent, but generally we started IVs with eighteen-gauge needles. And we didn't have nice Foley bags for the guys who had to have catheters. We used bottles that had been emptied of either sterile water or sterile saline for drainage. The bottles were put on the floor with a piece of tape on them so you could measure how much urine was in there. The tubing would just drain into that bottle. That was one way we improvised.

If there were casualties coming in on the helicopter and we were crowded, I'd either send a runner up to ER to find out what was coming in, or one of the corpsmen would cover and I'd go myself. Sometimes the doctors came running down to the wards and would say to us, "Who can we move out of here? We've got so many coming in—we need to make room for them." We nurses would go around and say, "So-and-so is stabilized. I think he can be air-evacked." We had a great deal of responsibility in caring for the patients. I eventually ended up working on the surgical floors all the time. The overflow from ICU would come over to us, and I used to always think, "God, are they going to be really hairy cases? Am I going to be able to do a good enough job?"

I remember one lieutenant who had a bad belly wound. He really hurt an awful lot. It was very difficult for him to get out of bed. Once I got very aggravated with him and told him that he better get out of that bed or he was never going to get better. He was very angry with me. Days, or weeks later, whatever it was, he was up and walking around and doing well. His last evening on the ward, he asked me if he could walk me out to the bus that took us back to our quarters. I'll never forget him giving me a big hug and saying, "I'm so glad you got mad at me and made me get out of that bed. I'm really grateful, because I don't think I would've ever gotten out of it."

I really tried to spend time getting to know the guys and listening to them. I remember feeling that they had been hurt so much out in the field, I didn't want to hurt them any more. I found myself saying things like, "Now, I don't want to hurt you, so let me know if it hurts and I'll stop."

One of my very favorite patients was a guy named Danny, who was from California. He was with the 101st Airborne. He'd been wounded three different times. The first couple of times his wounds weren't too bad, but the third time, he got a belly wound. I didn't even know he was at the hospital until one of the Red Cross gals came down to my ward and told me that he was asking for me in the emergency room. I went tearing up to emergency to see him. I was afraid to find out how bad he was. . . . I knew I had to be strong when I saw him. He looked like absolute hell. He wanted to come to my ward. I said, "Danny, you can't right now. They want to operate, and you'll probably have to go to ICU, but I'll be there to see you." He was just waking up when I got to recovery room . . . talking about how much he hurt. It didn't seem right. . . . He was only nineteen years old!

Danny ended up staying in ICU for a while. He eventually did come over to my ward. In the period of time he was there, he told me how concerned he was of going back out in the field after he recuperated. He was afraid he wouldn't make it out alive next time. I told a doctor who worked with us and who had operated on Danny, "You can't send him back out there. This is the third time. If he really thinks he's going to get killed, he probably will." Meanwhile, I asked Danny if he wanted me to write a letter to his mother. I told her how we'd been taking care of him, that he was doing okay and let her know that we cared. Danny did end up being air-evacked stateside. His mom wrote me a thank-you letter and told me he had made it home safely. I still have that letter.

I went on R&R to Hong Kong right around the end of October 1966. When I came back, the ward had ten VC POWs, and one of them was a woman. I was really angry. I thought, "God, I didn't come here to take care of POWs; I want to take care of our guys." There were rumors not long after that about converting our ward into a POW ward.

Eventually they did convert it, and several of us wanted to transfer off the ward but couldn't.

When I was back at Fort Sam I had met a guy and really liked him right away. We dated during that period of time. I beat him over to Nam. He came over with another unit in August 1966. We started seeing each other after that. His colonel would sometimes send him on messages down to Qui Nhon, and when I got a day off, I would try to hitch a ride on a Huey or a Chinook and head up to his unit so I could see him. It was getting closer and closer to my time to DEROS back to the States. I had put in for Fort Ord and really wanted to go back to California and have a chance to serve there. I was tired of taking care of POWs, and if it looked like I couldn't get off that ward, then heck, I might as well go stateside. But it was getting harder and harder, knowing that I was going to have to leave my guy— wondering what was going to happen to us. We had started talking marriage at that point.

I thought about extending for six months and that maybe I could transfer to the 2d Surg Hospital, which was north of us. But I was not able to transfer to the 2d Surg. I did not have an OR MOS, and they needed nurses who had double MOSs. My option was the 67th Evac hospital right there in Qui Nhon. They had established themselves in a permanent building right on the airstrip, which made it easier to bring casualties in and then to air-evac them out. What I didn't know was that my fella had gone to personnel to find out if there was any way he could be transferred to one of the hospitals in Qui Nhon. Neither one of us knew what the other one was doing! He couldn't transfer to Qui Nhon, and I couldn't get up to the 2d Surg.

I came home to Saint Mary's County for my thirty-day leave before the six-month extension. My folks were really glad to see me back. I don't remember telling them how serious I was about my boyfriend, but I think they suspected, because when I told them I was going to extend, they weren't surprised. During that thirty days I spent the time at home just kind of regrouping. I remember listening to the news and reading the papers and thinking, ''My

God, it looks like there is a lot going on over there in the area. Gee, I should really be back there.''

When I got back, I reported to the 67th Evac and was assigned to the intensive care unit. The 67th was a big, beautiful building. It seemed lighter; it was roomier and had better equipment. The ICU itself had thirty-three beds on it. The patients we got were in pretty bad shape. As I look back on it now, I just think I was almost like a robot, although I certainly wasn't unfeeling. I really cared about how the patients felt, but I think my skills were just kind of lickety-split by then.

Oftentimes I'd go on the ward in Nam a half an hour or so early to help the shift that was going off. You'd work your twelve hours and then stay there for about another half an hour to one hour to help the shift coming on. I found twelve-hour shifts really tiring, especially if I worked night shift, because I couldn't sleep well during the day. If they stretched it out and you had to work seven or eight days in a row, I would always be a basket case by the time I was finished. It would be so hot in the daytime that when I tried to sleep, I couldn't sleep for very long. I would feel panicky that if I couldn't get enough sleep I wouldn't be able to function well enough. Even if I took a sleeping pill, I couldn't sleep more than three or four hours. I sometimes wonder how I did it. There were a few of us nurses who used to go down to the beach when it wasn't off limits. Several of the life-guards built a little hooch for us right on the beach. We'd get wet and then come in, lie on an Army cot, and try to sleep. I would use that as my escape. When the day was finished, I'd come back up, put my fatigues back on, and go back in for more duty.

While I was in Nam, my brother had gone in the Army. He was the one who had suggested the Army for me. He came over to Nam three months before I was due to DE-ROS back for good. We weren't allowed to have passes to Saigon, but I told the XO, "My brother is flying helicopters. I'm scared stiff he'll go down and I won't ever get to see him again. . . . I've got to be able to see him." The XO worked it out so that I could get a pass. My brother was assigned to the Big Red One. They were located in Phu Loi at that time. I flew to Saigon on pass and then, somewhere along the line, through different hops, ended up getting to a waiting area that was basically just four poles and some corrugated fiberglass. My brother flew in, I got into the helicopter with him, and he flew me out to his unit. They were having a party that day. The guys thought it was great that my brother and I were in-country together. We had a couple days there. It was really good to be able to see him, but I remember wondering how the rest of the year was going to go for him and if he'd come home safely.

Right before I was due to come home, I found myself having very mixed feelings about leaving. I wanted to stay, but I wanted to come home. Because I was going to be getting married, I thought, "Well, you know, we're going to make a new life back in the States, and it's going to be great." I only have vague recollections about going around to some of the wards and saying good-bye to some people that last morning. I later got a picture that was taken on the airstrip. Apparently one of the patients had gone out there and taken a picture of me. He had said to one of my nurse friends, "That's the happiest captain I've ever seen." He sent me the picture later, and my expression was definitely a happy one—I was going home on the Freedom Bird!

I was assigned to Walter Reed after Nam. I had high expectations of being able to get on an orthopedic floor. The one thing that Nam did for me was that I felt like I could walk on water. I honestly felt like I was the greatest nurse in the world and could do absolutely anything. It was upsetting when they assigned me to a neurosurgical floor. The patients that we had on the ward were mostly guys from Nam. The front part of the ward had guys with gunshot wounds to the head. The guys in the back were guys who were either paraplegics or quadriplegics.

One of the things I noticed about some of the guys who were back from Nam was a real difference once they got back around their families again. When they were in the hospitals over there, they seemed to be very grateful to be out of the field, to see an American woman who was a nurse, a round-eye, as they called us. When they got back, some of them got very demanding. I felt kind of angry about that. We were trying to give the best care we could. What I didn't understand was, they had a lot to deal with at that time, being back, adjusting to the fact that they had disabilities.

I was officially discharged out of the Army in March of '68. I didn't stay in touch with many of the people I had known at Walter Reed; it was like I just wanted to push away that part of my life. I got really caught up with being a new mom and a wife. My husband was talking about wanting to go into Special Forces and figured he would go back to Vietnam for another tour. It was hard for me that whole year that he was over there. I felt that my son and I should be there and found myself thinking about the places that he would be and what it was like . . . and somehow that I should be there. I think I tried to recapture what I had in Vietnam during that year and realized I couldn't just stay home and take care of a baby all the year.

I heard about the shock-trauma unit in Baltimore and thought, "Good, it's going to be somewhat like Vietnam." So I went to work there. It was exciting because the patients were air-evacked in on the helicopter, and I really felt like I could be that dynamite nurse again. I worked there from November to the following July. As I think back on it now, it wasn't the same.

Over the years I had a number of jobs on medical-surgical floors and also worked recovery room. Initially there was a real challenge, but after a while I kind of got bummed out; it just didn't seem the same anymore. In '74 I decided to go back into the Army. I went back as a public health nurse and was in the Army for a couple of years. It was an interesting experience, but very different being a stateside nurse, not helping during a war.

My marriage during all those years had a lot of difficulties. Some people I have met recently have alluded to the fact that because we were both Nam vets it was a double whammy. I don't know whether it was or not. In 1980 our marriage was definitely going downhill, and despite marriage counseling, the marriage did end in divorce.

I had never spent much time thinking about Vietnam all those years except on a real superficial level. I thought about different people that I'd known there, wondered what had happened to them, but just passed it out of my mind, never really thinking about what type of an impact Vietnam had made on my life. In 1982 I heard about the Vietnam memorial being built and found out there was going to be a dedication and welcome-home parade for the Vietnam vets. I thought, "By God, I'm going to be there." I decided that I would go to D.C. on Veterans Day because I really wanted to see the memorial. The first time I saw it, I just . . . I just stood there frozen. I couldn't believe how big it was and that all those lines that I was seeing at a distance were names. The impact of how many lives had been lost just hit me. I felt a lump in my throat and thought I would cry. I was by myself because I didn't know anyone. I felt terribly alone.

Two days later, when they had the parade, I went up there early in the morning and looked for the plaques with the state names on them. I saw "Maryland," went up, and asked the guys, "Are you here for the parade?" And they said, "Yeah." I said, "Well, I was an Army nurse over there." They cheered and said, "Oh, we got another nurse!" Then they grabbed this other nurse, named Charlotte, introduced us, and we hugged. We hadn't known each other in Nam, but it sure seemed like we did. It was so exciting to meet another Army nurse.

When we were getting ready to line up for the parade down Constitution Avenue, we linked arms and did our best to keep in step while waving our flags. That has to rank as one of the highlights of my life. Seeing all those people all along the street, cheering us on, welcoming us home, and saying "Thanks" made me cry. I felt so appreciated for what I had done and felt proud to have served my country in Vietnam.

Since that November, I've gone frequently to the Wall. I've met so many vets and heard so many different stories. . . . I never knew so much about what the guys went through or realized the problems some of them have had over all these years. I had distanced myself from all that. Since then I have done some reading, looked through pictures, and talked with people. Charlotte and I have gotten together several times. I even got more involved. . . . I felt it was important for people to understand more about what Vietnam was to all of us.

This past summer, I became a National Park volunteer just so I could help people find names on the Wall, learn a little bit about the Wall, and even answer questions about what it was like to be a nurse in Vietnam.

I'm so glad to see Vietnam vets rallying together. People need to understand what an awful war Vietnam was and how it made such an impact on us. The vets have had such a tough time because of what was going on in the country at the time and because of the reception they got when they came back. I really feel strongly about us all pulling together again. The dedication was definitely a healing time for many of us.

Vietnam was for me, then and now, a powerful growth experience. I'm glad I served.

Karen "Kay" Johnson Burnette and Donna B. Cull Peck

24TH EVAC. HOSPITAL,
LONG BINH—OCT. '68 TO OCT. '69

After corresponding by letter, I arranged to meet Kay Burnette in Washington, D.C., in November of 1983. When I arrived, I was pleasantly surprised to find that she was having a reunion with an old friend of hers, Donna Peck. They had met in nursing school in Pennsylvania, gone into the Army together, and then to the same hospital in Vietnam. They hadn't seen one another in twelve years. It was their idea to do a dual interview, relating their lives as one story: they were, after all, interwoven continuously from the time they had met in Erie, Pennsylvania, 1967.

Kay currently lives in Knoxville, Tennessee. She works as an RN team leader in a private home health agency. She is active in women's and equal rights issues, and serves on the Veterans Administration Advisory Committee on Women Veterans and is a member of TVVLP (Tennessee Vietnam Veterans Leadership Program). She has been married to a Vietnam veteran for twelve years and has an eight-year-old son and a six-year-old daughter.

Donna lives in Westminster, Massachusetts. She is a "Christian homemaker," married also to a man she met while in Vietnam. They have three children.

Kay: I WAS BORN IN '46, AND I WAS IN HIGH SCHOOL from '60 to '64. This was still a very sheltered time, and I can remember my guidance counselor saying, "What do you want to be, a nurse, a teacher, or a secretary?" I came from a small town and pretty much took the man's word. I picked nursing.

Probably my first step away from home was to go to nursing school. It was sixty miles away, in Erie, Pennsylvania. I was homesick maybe for a week, and then I found I really did all right away from home. It took me a while to make some friends. I realized then that I probably would never live in my hometown. I felt very free, but still sheltered and protected from most things. Nursing school was a lot of fun; it was an all-girl environment. We were right across the street from the hospital. There were no men around and a few scattered colleges, and we made a lot of our own fun—we did some crazy, stupid things. Nursing school was hard at the time we went. It was a three-year diploma program, and you worked all summer; you worked shifts. We got a month off in the summer and two weeks at Christmas, and that was it. It was an excellent training program as far as practical experience goes. We did some real antics while we were in nursing school, and Donna was the head of most of them. I don't guess I was Donna's good friend until the last year; I had my own separate little group. But I enjoyed nursing school and did well. I had no doubt about this being the career for me at the time.

Donna: I was born and raised in Erie, Pennsylvania, but when I was about five years old we moved to probably one of the first suburbs. It was really out in the woods, but there were, like, sixty-six kids on our street, and we had our own little town right there. I think we grew up kind of slow. I can remember playing with dolls until I was about thirteen. We went to junior high, and everybody's boogying at the soda shop, and we didn't understand what was going on. They were worried about what they were wearing the next day, and we just wore clothes. I had a brother three years younger than I, a mom, and a dad. I looked at Kay's family sort of as the Waltons or something for a while when I first met her. Mine, I don't know. . . . We didn't really go anywhere all the while I grew up. I was kind of determined that I wasn't going to rot in Erie; I was going to go see something and be somebody and do something.

I knew a lot of kids that flunked out of nursing school. It was the hardest thing I've ever gone through, before or since. I knew my mother was making toys to put me through, and I knew I had to stop fooling around and really put my nose to the grindstone. When we got to Hamot it was just like a nunnery—you had so many rules. But after about a month there, I realized they were trying to teach us self-discipline, which I'd never had. Since the fourth grade, they wrote on my report card, "lacks self-control." In high school I was a cheerleader and I had a lot of boyfriends, and especially one, but I gained thirty pounds in the first month of nursing school, I really did. I was a compulsive overeater.

Then I got this instructor who reminded me of Lucille Ball. She had red hair all teased up—Mrs. Trokey—and she made me do stuff. She said, "You don't have a choice about it. You go in and you do it." And I did it and I got confidence in myself. We had to give shots and I was a wreck during the practice. I couldn't do any treatment that caused pain to somebody. So, there's this old man laying there, about 90 pounds, and I gave him a shot of penicillin in his rear end and the guy came out of coma, I swear, and said, "Oh my God!" I was so upset. But I learned, and I did it, and that girl got me through. And I realized you can learn things, you can get over things, you just have to plow through.

When it came time to join the Army, they sent this recruiter. I didn't want to stay in Erie because I had seen all these nurses staying in Erie year after year just rotting away, so I decided, "Well, I'll join the Army with everybody else." I couldn't join. They said, "You have to lose weight first." I remember Phil took all my Easter candy, and we were doing calisthenics in the hallway. But I knew I was different from all these girls; eating was like a drug to me. I just couldn't stop. The recruiter came back the next year, and she said, "Why didn't you sign up?" I said, "I haven't lost the weight. I guess I'm just not going to be able to go. But you know, it gets me kind of mad, because I can run just as fast as them on the floor, and I'm just as good a nurse even though I am overweight." She said, "Oh, we can get you a waiver. I didn't know that's what was stopping you." I can remember my father was very upset. He had been in World War II, and when I said I was going in the Army, he was not too pleased. My mother always—"Well, whatever you kids want, whatever will make you happy."

Kay: This is really funny—there were five of us that joined together; it was like a security thing, I think, five people that didn't have any ties. My parents were the same way. My dad was the one that wished I wouldn't join; he was the conservative one. My mother was like yours, except she went to the recruiter and asked him, "Will my daughter have to go to Vietnam?" and he said, "Noooo, the nurses volunteer for Vietnam, and we have so many people that want to go." They didn't have any idea how many nurses they were going to need, and they were trying to get everybody they could in the Army. You know, they held it over our heads, one hundred dollars a month—when you're not making a salary. I went right out and bought a car. Finally we could bum around Erie like everybody else.

Donna: Phil bought a Cougar.

Kay: We had no knowledge of what the military meant.

Donna: None whatsoever!

Kay: We just knew that we wanted to travel. We didn't want to stick around, that was it. It was so naive at the time. We were not into the college scene; we were not into the demonstrations; we were isolated. I can honestly say I knew nothing about Vietnam except there was a war there.

Donna: My girlfriend Phil, Muriel Phillips, and I drove to Texas. Now, I'd hardly ever been out of Pennsylvania, and I was amazed that we could actually read a map and get to Texas—we were so proud of ourselves. We decided we were going to take horseback riding lessons and we were going to go to the gulf and go to Mexico. We were going to do something every weekend of the six weeks down there. . . .

Well anyway, we had a lot of fun. We spent all day in classes, and we learned about the uniform, and we learned about fraternization, like we were officers, and they said, "You can't date anyone that's not an officer." I can remember saying, "I don't agree with that." And I did end up marrying my corpsman, who wasn't an officer. I've really shaped up though. I'm more obeying of the rules now.

Kay: Fort Sam was a picnic, and we were not prepared for any future situations. They had classes where we took goats and did a tracheotomy, but how realistic is that really? I mean, you know, this is a goat, a dead goat.

Donna: No, it was living.

Kay: Oh, that's right, they were alive, weren't they? The worst thing they made us do was march. Fort Sam has a quadrangle and they'd make us march every morning around Fort Sam.

Donna: With a band.

Kay: Yeah with a band, and *all* the officers and the guys would get up in the buildings around us and just roar.

Donna: You know what? I loved that marching secretly,

I loved that marching to the music every day. I thought it was fun.

Kay: But you know we partied.

Donna: We never drank, and finally somebody said, "You guys from the Pennsylvania nursing school, you're getting so cliquey, you won't join in with us." So we said, "Well, all right, we'll go to the officers' club." But why should we go? We didn't want to drink. Well, I remember I didn't know what to drink. I looked at somebody's drink that looked good—it was a Singapore Sling, and it was so good. So I ordered three of them, and I could hardly stand up to leave. But we started dancing and having the greatest time. We had a good time there. I hated to leave Fort Sam a lot. I'm the type that doesn't like to try new things that much, and I was still scared to death to start nursing. So when we put on our dream sheet what we wanted, I put on Madigan, you put on Madigan, and so did Phil. Poor Phil got sent to Fort Campbell, Kentucky, and you and I got Madigan. I was never so happy in all my born days.

Kay: Well, let's see, we went up to Madigan Hospital at Fort Lewis, Washington. It would've been the end of March, 1968. I got assigned to a medical ward. It was a very difficult time for me too, because I was not a leader. I was very thorough, I was very conscientious, but it took me a long time to get my leadership qualities together, and I really didn't deal with any of the returning Vietnam vets or anything. We both loved Washington. It was a beautiful place. We were really having a good time until that terrible day. Five months later they called us into the office and sent our whole class out of Fort Sam. . . . They wouldn't even say Vietnam. They said Southeast Asia, but they would not put on the official orders "Vietnam." It wasn't until we got to the airport after leave that they said, "Destination: Bien Hoa." When we got to the reception center, there was everybody we knew from Fort Sam.

Donna: There were those four platoons—how many were in each one? It must have been over a hundred of us.

Kay: I can't remember figures, but I have the list. And not only did Donna and I end up in the same place but several other people we knew from our basic training ended up at the 24th Evac. That was a real shock, and me with a little surgical and a little medical experience going to Vietnam. I thought of some pretty drastic things. I'm not saying I didn't want to serve my country—and this was another part of my obedient phase—I wouldn't have dreamed of doing anything else. I joined the Army of my own free will. They told me to go to Vietnam—"I'm going to Vietnam," you know? But my dad was . . . I remember him crying when I left. I thought, "This is more serious than I think it is!"

Donna: My parents had come to the state of Washington to visit. While they were there I found out I was going to Vietnam, and they both just turned dead white. I had to justify it; I thought of not going. Not because I was afraid or didn't want to serve my country, but I wasn't all that sure of the war. I thought, "The only reason I can go with a clear conscience is that half of these guys are like us: obedient. They wouldn't have thought of saying no, and they were getting wounded and probably didn't want to be there either." I don't know, that's how I kind of justified it. I just went. I was real glad I was going with Kay, but I was scared.

On the other hand, when I got to Madigan, I worked under a head nurse that was the best head nurse I've ever had. Her name was Sara Lee Blum McGoren, and she taught me a lot. I worked on a seventy-bed orthopedic ward, and we'd get air-evacs in from Vietnam. I'd never done treatments like that, but I learned an awful lot before I went over there, how to care for real bad wounds. I was very, very naive, and I remember walking on the ward just a wreck, my first job there, pushing this big med cart, and somebody putting on the record player "Light My Fire" by Jose Feliciano. I turned red. I just died. I was so embarrassed, but they were just joking and after a while you got to know them. But oh, geez . . . Most of them were back from Vietnam, and they'd call you "Butterbar Lieutenant" and all this stuff. And these ward sergeants that have been in twenty years and you were over them in rank, but they knew what they were doing and you didn't. It was so awful, that way of learning. When I got my orders I was glad I was going with Kay. And when we finally got to Bien Hoa I remember they said a piece of tread had come off the plane, so we had about two to three hours to think about how we were going to land without treads on the wheel.

Kay: You looked down, and there was the Fire Department.

Donna: Fire Department with foams! We just hung on to the seat, and we landed all right, but I thought we were going to have to get out of the plane and run for cover like Roy Rogers or something. We got out and nobody seemed that all upset.

Kay: It was October of '68. We went to some kind of replacement battalion.

Donna: Ninety-third, 193rd, I don't know.

Kay: Then we got our assignments, and we just couldn't believe it—the same hospital. I sometimes think that's the only way I made it through the year. You made friends, but I don't know, people came in and out all the time, and you might have made a friend for two months that left, and she might have been the only real friend you made, or he. So there we are—we go there together and we leave together; even though we worked different places and had different experiences, we still had each other to fall back on. We had some things happen to us during the year that we needed support with. I really think that made a big difference.

I got my assignment the first day and found out I was going to be working on the surgical ward, post-op. They'd not been cleaned up, but they'd been stitched up and then taken to my ward. I walked in and they showed me around. It was amputations and tracheotomies and burn cases, chest tubes. They also had Vietnamese on the ward, Koreans, and any women that were injured. I mean, if you want a hodge-podge of illnesses—we had any overflow from the other wards. I went back to my room and thought, "What is the least traumatic thing I can do to myself to get out of this?" I'm serious! I was never so scared. I went the next day to the ward for the first time, and the nurse says, "Well, you need to start an IV." I had never started an IV, never. We went to nursing school at a time when a lot of transition was going on; nurses didn't do certain things.

Now they do an awful lot, but we didn't start IVs at all at the hospital. She said, "I'm sorry, I can't show you because there's twenty men watching you and you've got to gain their confidence." So she takes me in a corner and tells me how to start an IV, and I go over and use this guy as a guinea pig. . . . There was some real trauma the first few days. I lived through that first week, but I think that I must've matured and aged because I felt—and this is something I felt later—that I wasn't prepared to go to Vietnam. That's one thing I think they need to change if they're going to send you into that type of situation—you need some real honest-to-gosh training.

Long Binh was a huge place. The 24th Evac was somewhere in the middle, nowhere near the perimeter. Actual danger was not what was on our minds. My concern the whole year was my nursing ability: how I was caring for the patients—that was an overwhelming concern. All the other things that happened were really secondary. I think that I went over there as—I don't want to say a poor nurse, but untried, and having a kind of an insecure personality didn't help. I had a wonderful head nurse, Captain Holley, and if she did anything, she helped me. She'd just put me in situations and say, "You can do it." Most of the time we were busy all night long; we'd get somebody in from the ER once or twice a night at least. And the doctors were three hooches away—if you needed them you could get them there; that was an advantage. Then at five in the morning I would turn on the radio to the country music station. Those poor guys would have liked to have killed us, but you had to start baths at five if you wanted to get done by seven. And that was my favorite time. I loved those guys—they were mostly just so grateful to have clean sheets, to get a shower. They'd be in the shower twenty minutes. You'd have to open the door and say, "Get out! The doctor is here. You've got to get out of the shower." You know, these were the minor wounds, the frags and so on; they were going to go back out, and they just wanted every bit of cleanness and good food, that and socialization, they could get. That was really nice. A lot of the other was hard.

I kept a diary, and some of it was just personal feelings

and experiences, but some of it I wrote down about patients, and I'm glad I did because a lot of them blurred together. We had a fair number die on our ward. I'm not sure what happens; I think you have to get hard to handle it because I was twenty-one and twenty-two, and the guys I was taking care of were my age or younger for the most part. I remember one especially, whose name I'm going to look up today on the Wall. He was eighteen but he looked fifteen, and rumor was that he had lied about his age to get into the Marines anyhow. He had black, curly hair, and I don't have the first idea what was wrong with him, but we knew from the minute we got him that he wasn't going to make it. And he just slowly died. His bed was right in front of the nursing station. He died, like, a week before his nineteenth birthday. I can remember him vividly (and a burn case that we worked on forever and ever and ever). And always knowing—you know, changing these rotten, filthy dressings—he wasn't going to make it. He eventually died. Sometimes it wasn't the ones that died that bothered me as much as the ones that had to go back. That's come over the number of years, I guess, but those that died, at least they were gone. There are some of them that are still living through hell.

The other patient I remember distinctly was a red-haired guy with skin pale like mine and freckles and a shock of red hair. He was a paraplegic. He couldn't move from the waist down, and he was on what's called a stryker frame. What he kept saying was, "I can't wait to get home to see my wife." And she was sixteen, still in high school. That's when I first started realizing what this war was all about— it was only a couple months after I'd been there. All of a sudden I said, "This is not worth it. I know that kid's wife, when he gets back, is going to say, 'Am I going to live with a paraplegic?' " Maybe I wasn't right, but I just had a feeling that a lot of them went home to heartbreak.

I just got bitter and I did something I kind of hate to admit—I turned it onto the Vietnamese. They were smaller than I was, the first people I'd ever met like that. But I did something that was very much against their culture—the temptation was to pat them on the head. And that was a no-no. For the first time in my life I think I was prejudiced.

I think I turned a lot of my frustration and anger to the Vietnamese. I didn't realize this until later. I put them down in my mind, and I didn't really trust a lot of them because we'd have a lot of stories about little kids with booby traps. It took me several years to realize that we've kind of been indoctrinated into that, but that was something kind of hard to live with, the fact that I could be prejudiced.

Donna: I met my husband about two weeks after I got there. He was a corpsman that came to my ward. I thought he looked like an old boyfriend of Kay's, and I said, "You've got to come down and meet this guy." I'd just broken up with somebody before we went over. . . . We'd meet somebody and get engaged and break it off at the next duty station—it was just unreal. We were always in turmoil over our personal life, I guess. I can remember we played hard. About four months after, I decided that I wanted to change wards, but I was scared to death because I'm always scared when I go to a new situation. I saw Kay's ward and thought, "I can't take that." I knew I couldn't. I thought I could take the maxillofacial ward; we had two wards of head wounds and then maxillofacial, face wounds. After working there about a month, I knew the routine and I felt very comfortable with it, and not many people died on our floor. I was glad of that because I would've felt it was my fault—if I did something wrong or something like that. And what you said, Kay, your main concern being, would your nursing care be good enough—that's the way I felt. Always, I hoped that I wouldn't make a mistake.

I can remember Christmas there. It was the first Christmas I was ever away from home, and I was so sad. It was hot, and I was used to being in Pennsylvania, where it was cold. I can remember school kids sent cookies and letters and stuff to the wards. They sent candy and decorations and we decorated. But when it came right down to the line, Christmas was a hard time to be there. I can remember this one thing, we went caroling to the wards. We went to this ward where there were amputations, and this guy had both legs amputated and one arm. I went up next to him and I'm singing carols, and tears were running down his face, and tears were running down my face. . . . That was really a sad, sad moment. I think I was glad when Christmas was finally over.

I think most people reacted like Kay with the Vietnamese. A lot of nurses felt like that, but somehow I didn't. I really loved them. I can remember seeing the way the mothers loved their babies, and the papa-sans would come and lie down and curl up at the end of the bed and dote over their babies, and I said, "They're the same as we are; they're no different than we are." And we trained Vietnamese nurses that were so smart and bright and hard working. I really loved them.

The saddest thing I saw had nothing to do with a GI—and in a way I feel guilty about that—but it was a mother who took a rocket in her face, and she had a cross section of her face missing. She was pregnant at the time, and she also had an eighteen-month-old. She didn't complain or anything. But one night she was just kind of complaining and complaining, and I checked her dressings and everything. Finally I looked under the covers, and she had had a miscarriage, like about a five-month-old fetus. I said, "Johnny" (my corpsman), "Johnny, come here." We called the doctor, and he said, "Well, what in the hell am I going to do about it?" He was probably tired from working. He said, "Just put it in a basin or something." I just felt like I was on sacred ground there, and I felt so bad for that woman, and little tears rolled down her face. That wasn't the saddest thing. She missed her little eighteen-month-old so they arranged for her to come and see her mother. But the woman was disfigured—had a bandage all over her—and when the baby saw her mother, it just screamed in fright and had to be taken away. I thought, "That has to be suffering beyond all."

The patients were so good; they had to do a lot for themselves. In stateside hospitals, patients could be babied—you'd arrange their Kleenex; you'd have their little spit bag next to them, you'd arrange everything. But we could really do less than that. On our ward, they'd usually come in with a pressure dressing that had to be on for three days to stop bleeding and everything. Sometimes their whole mandible would be gone, or part of it, or neck wounds and just massive swelling and noses gone, blinded. . . . So you'd have the kid's ID card, and they'd take the dressing off, and that kid was nowhere near his ID picture. Their jaws were wired together, so you had to teach them to feed themselves. We said, "If you take care of your suture lines and you put peroxide and then bacitracin, you're going to have less scarring, so it's very important that you do this three times a day." You're trying to be very matter-of-fact, but you know you're going to have to go to the mirror with them that first time and they're going to look in that mirror and see such a disfigured face. And I'd say to them, "I know you feel bad when you look in this mirror—this is an awful shock to you—but this is the first step in many steps." And I'd tell them that eventually they're going to take pieces of bones of other parts and place it for a jaw and that this is really the worst it's going to be. And I didn't know if I was telling them the truth or not. I just said it, and I hoped it was the truth.

I think for the first time ever in nursing, I felt comfortable in that kind of a ward. I felt like I was a warm person, that I could really meet their psychological needs, but I can remember feeling frustrated—I don't know if I should even bring this up.

Kay: What's it about?

Donna: Doctors that I didn't feel were competent, like on that ward next to you. And I don't think I'll mention names.

Kay: I wouldn't mention names, but I'd bring it up.

Donna: I can remember feeling very helpless because that ward always had a lot more infection, and many did die because . . . I felt, poor medical attention.

Kay: It wasn't perfect.

Donna: It wasn't. Your ward had crackerjack doctors. My ward did too, but that ward had that one guy.

Kay: We were still in a military situation even though we didn't have to salute very often—you know, you get out of a lot of that when you're medical. But still, you wouldn't dare go to the colonel—or we didn't—and say, "This doctor doesn't know what he's doing." They either knew it and ignored it or you took care of it yourself. There were a few doctors who drank far too much, and you wondered, when they were called in the middle of the night, what kind of job they did. But I don't want to overemphasize that because there were excellent ones too.

Donna: That was a minority.

Kay: But it was not a perfect situation by any means. I have a couple flashback feelings—like, I think that was probably the loneliest year I ever spent, even though I had a lot of—I guess you'd call them surface relationships. I was a minority among a million men. We had a lot of men coming along then to eat in our mess hall—generals' aides, helicopter pilots, and so on. Of course, there was nowhere to go. You didn't go dating. You just got to know people and went to these little hooch parties. I think it bothered me that I couldn't really establish a relationship. It seemed like every relationship—I wanted it to be the one. At the time I felt guilty about that, but now I feel that was probably my way of coping. You know, you just wanted to have a relationship to have some happiness and security on your off hours. And sometimes your feelings and your actions were like they had no consequence. I mean, you might've done some things I would never have done here. I'm not saying they're terrible things, but they are things I wouldn't have done at home. It's just—it was an unreal place. Fortunately we had some figures of stability at times, some real good leaders and a chaplain that was very dear. Donna and I both had fair singing voices, and we sang in a choir. There were some good times, but there were some real lonely times. And I didn't see Donna a lot; for a while we worked different shifts, and then she had an important boyfriend and that took a lot away.

I want to talk about when Pat Nixon came. My version may not be the same as Donna's but this is what I remember. President Nixon came, and he flew someplace safe to visit. I voted for him too, but that was right after I got there and I never made that mistake again. Anyhow, Pat Nixon came. We prepared for a week for her visit. We had our ward scrubbed; we had our patients fixed up as best you can—what can you do with the patients? We did everything. We were so proud; we were straight that day—we were perfect. The Red Cross were the only ones that got to talk to her. We were like lepers; they put up ropes, and we had to stand behind the ropes. Here's what they showed her: the medical ward, the one Donna used to be on . . .

Donna: No dressings could be shown.

Kay: If I remember right they faked some dressings on those guys.

Donna: No, they were not allowed to show her a dressing because it might turn her stomach.

Kay: So she saw guys—and I'm sorry—but some of them had VD; this is what they showed her: VD, malaria . . .

Donna: That could smile and wave.

Kay: That's what she saw when she came, and all that did was just add to your frustration. We couldn't even say hello to her. And we have dear friends in the Red Cross, but that day they were not our dear . . . They showed her around; they socialized with her. I know it would've meant so much to our patients if she had come in and been compassionate and spoken to them. I don't know whether it was her choice; it probably wasn't.

Donna: It wasn't.

Kay: I'm sure she's a nice person, but that was an incident that I'll just never forget.

I have to tell about my corpsmen. You were not allowed to fraternize, but of course you worked with them more than anybody else. During the day you might work with a couple nurses and a couple corpsmen, but at night it was you and a corpsman. And you just got so close to those guys. I can remember a couple of mine, especially J. D. and Dotson, would've done anything for you or for the patients. You could put so much trust in them. But you never went to their club, and they never went to ours. What I miss is being able to know where they are and how they're doing. Hoping that they're getting some of this feedback about what good jobs they did and hoping they got something out of it. I'd like to call them up now and say, "Boy, I think of you guys a lot." Like I said, we weren't allowed to fraternize, and Donna found that out in a hurry. But she, being rebellious, went right on ahead anyhow. I would've never done it!

Donna: There were consequences. Around January I started dating this corpsman, which is really hard to hide when you live on a city block. We hit it off pretty good and we fell in love, and I don't know—who knew if it was going to last or not—you just didn't know. I spent most of my time with him. I just didn't care and he didn't either, but I was afraid he was going to be sent to the field as punishment if it got found out. At the end of the year everybody, unless you were a real screw-up, got an Army Commendation Medal. I don't know of a nurse that didn't get one. I'd been told meanwhile by three nurses, "You're not to fraternize, you're not to fraternize." And I just didn't stop. But they had the ability to say who got the medal and who didn't. We went to this chapel, and I was standing up there with Kay and two other people. They passed out three medals and gave me a certificate of achievement. I was so humiliated because that sort of said, "You didn't do very well," but it was because of Tom. I can remember throwing that certificate of achievement in the trash on my way out. That night all the doctors came over and said, "I don't know why that happened. I hope you don't think we did that. You're a good nurse; you're one of the best on the ward." I was real angry about it, but I can remember from then on—I took Tom's hand; we walked out together holding hands. I said, "What would I rather have, a medal on my chest or Tom?"

In June I got sent to neuro ward—that's the head injuries. I couldn't take that on a steady diet; it just wasn't me. I hated to be pulled down there. I was changing IVs, changing trachs, and just doing the best I could, knowing the routine of the floor, when somebody said, "Colonel Ledbetter wants you in her office," and I thought, "Uh-oh, they found out about Tom and I. I'm in deep sneakers here." I walk in and there's a Red Cross worker and a chaplain. They all have this awful look on their face. "Do you have a brother, David Cull, in Germany?" I said yes, and they said, "We're sorry, but he's been killed in a car accident." I remember I put my hands up and said, "No, sir, he is not, because he just couldn't be." . . . Within about two hours they had me on my way. My suitcase was packed, I'm on this plane, and I had these earphones, and

. . . sometimes I'd forget about it, and then I'd hear "I believe for every drop of rain that falls a flower blooms" or something like that, and I'd cry. When I got off the plane my cousin Deak was there. We just held each other and cried our eyes out. I can remember finally there was a funeral. There was an airline strike and his body was held up, and I felt so twitchy to be at home. We had company and I hated it. I just felt like, "Oh, please, go away." You know, I just felt panicky almost. My mother needed all this, and I kept saying to her, "I wish they wouldn't keep coming." So I made the decision. I missed Tom so much and I wanted to go back, and I said, "Ma, I'm going back." I didn't have to; I could've waited.

The day the man landed on the moon was Tom's birthday, July 20, and I wanted to be back real bad on his birthday. My mother is a wonderful woman; she never throws guilt at me, ever, and she said, "Well, if that's what you want, then you go for it." But she didn't tell me until like five years later, "When your plane took off I hit the rail and I said, 'God, if you take her I'll never speak to you again.'" You know, I didn't know what a sacrifice . . . Now I think how I hurt her and my dad to go back after they had lost one kid. But I just had to do it. I flew to San Francisco on my own, to Travis Air Force Base. They said, "There's no plane out of here tonight, only a cargo plane, and it only has like six seats along the side." I said, "Oh, please, let me go back on that cargo plane!" They said, "Well, there's no plumbing for a woman." I said, "I'm not fussy. Please let me go!" It was the best plane ride I've ever had. It was dark, cold, and there were pillows and blankets, and you could lie down on these long seats, and I slept and slept and slept.

I got into Saigon—it must have been in the morning on July 20. But I had to get to Long Binh, and I had no idea how to get there. I hitchhiked. I mean, I think of this now—I wouldn't hitchhike today if my life depended on it. Tom was on his ward sitting with his hands on his knees, and I remember walking up and I just stood there, and he said, "Donnabelle, you're back." And I was so glad to see him. It was the day the men walked on the moon, and I didn't care about the men on the moon; I just was so glad to be back to see him. I was glad to see you, Kay, you know, because I couldn't talk about this with anybody at home. I could tell Kay about it because she knew my brother and she knew my family, and it made sense for me to talk to her and Tom, but it just didn't make sense at home to talk.

Kay: The last thing I want to say about Vietnam is I think that's the closest I ever came to being an alcoholic, and that's something that's really gone against my grain too, because I believe you can solve problems without an artificial substance. But anyway, the point is, we drank because of the cheapness and the availability and nothing else to do. From going from an occasional drink, I must've drank two, three, four drinks a night when I was off duty. I was a little 105-pound person, and I can remember some terrible nights! Unfortunately I think there were an awful lot of people, even from our hospital, that went home with drug and alcohol problems—some patients who, for their pain, sought medicine and got it for so long that they became dependent.

Well, anyhow, I wasn't sure about going home. I was very indifferent. I didn't have any idea where I wanted to be, where I wanted to go. I had asked for three choices of assignments in the States to finish my tour and got none of them. I went to South Carolina. Donna and I would be separated because she was going somewhere else, and of course she and Tom had planned to get married, so I had real ambivalence. Went to South Carolina, and I got a really good little ward. I was the head nurse there. It was a small ward and not mostly people that had come back from overseas. I remember a couple people that blew their feet off to keep from going overseas. I did a good job there; I really enjoyed it. I had some nice people to work with. I felt very much within my realm; things were going well. I even considered staying in the Army. I think the main reason I didn't is that I was kind of tired of people telling me what I was going to do with my time.

I'd kind of gotten used to South Carolina and the warm weather, and I just stayed and worked in a local hospital. It was my first civilian job. People had this image of a career-type, strict military person, which I was not at all.

They expected me to be some kind of a supernurse or something. I feel where I grew in Vietnam was inside. It wasn't so much what I did on the outside; it was inside stuff. So I put it away, I just put it away. And I haven't talked about it for years. I met my husband Craig about a couple months after he got back from Vietnam. He was infantry and saw a lot of things that I never could understand. We talked some but we didn't talk a lot about Vietnam. We just hit it off immediately and developed a very serious relationship. After he got out of the Army, he started back to graduate school, we got married. He went into the counseling field, which was really good for him. He's regained some of his feelings and worked out a lot of his feelings about Vietnam that way and is a very compassionate, kind person.

We moved a lot, settled down finally, had two children. I have no contact with anybody in the service at this time, except Donna. My life has really gone very well; I can't complain. I've always wanted a home. I had to think about whether I wanted a family. It took us a while to make that decision, but now we couldn't think of it any other way—children are wonderful. I never really had any association with other women veterans, and I never dwelled on it with anybody. Craig and I talked some, but I didn't understand totally what he'd been through and he didn't understand what I'd been through totally, and there were no books out at the time. Craig got in the vet center business a couple years ago. This is the strangest thing to me—even when he was in the vet center and it was recognized that women could come to the center too, I only went to eat lunch or to talk to the other guys there. They were great; the staff was wonderful. I never, though, accepted the fact that I was a woman veteran and it was something to be proud of.

So I never really became a woman veteran until I came up to Washington, D.C., last November for the memorial dedication. I think I had a catharsis when I saw the Wall; just so many things came over me. All those names—I just felt overwhelmed. There were a few of them that I knew. Just so much happened there. I looked around and saw veterans holding up gold-star mothers so that they could touch their sons' names, and that's all they have left. I love the memorial. To me, it's got a million changing qualities; it can be warm or cold depending on the time of day. You've got something there you can touch and feel, and you can make a transfer and take it home. You can find anybody's name you want to because it's so easy to do. It reflects shadows of people in it and the monuments and the trees and other living things in it. To me, it's perfect.

I got home and I got involved in the vet center to a degree. It's not where I work, but I became much more active and interested, and more interested in the male vets. I spoke to one of the groups there. It was real hard for me because male combat veteran groups at the vet centers are not always the most friendly. I was afraid I was going into hostile territory, but I had to tell them what had happened to me in Washington. You know, when you have a cause, it makes a difference. They were extremely receptive, most of them. And we tried to form a women's group, but there was only one other woman, an in-country vet, and it's been hard to get together. We've been on TV a couple of times, trying to promote it, and there's a lot more to be done. The vet centers, they're great but some of them have got to learn to be able to receive the women properly.

Although I feel my life is really going smoothly, there are some hang-ups. One thing I find is that when I was in the hospital, I had to be on a real busy ward; I couldn't take the slow pace. Though I never liked the emergency stuff, not even in Vietnam—I could not have worked in the emergency room. I'm so glad that there are people who could do it, but that is not me. I think the nurses that worked there are probably the ones that are having some real problems dealing. They saw so many people die. They had to make life-and-death decisions, things that you don't do here. You know there is such a thing as PTSD; people that don't believe it are not sensitive to the Vietnam experience. And that does happen to some nurses too. But I've been real fortunate. I don't think that that has happened to me.

The chance for the GI Bill came, and I didn't use it toward nursing. I used it for general arts and sciences, the

AA degree. Then, instead of going into nursing or public health, I tried to go into computers, and at the time when I finished up, we had small children and I never did finish. I felt sorry that I hadn't done that, and I didn't realize why, why I was doing everything but nursing. I could have a master's degree by now. I realize that I was trying to get out of the field. Now I'm in home-health care. It's got a good schedule for my family. I like the teaching that goes on with it, and it's working out fine for me; I don't have any qualms. Maybe someday I'll further my education otherwise. I realize now that my Vietnam experience did change me. I think it made me more sensitive to life, more understanding of people's problems. I have more understanding of my initial prejudice against the Vietnamese. Now I think that I work even harder not to be prejudiced against anybody, and I'm working more and more into being sensitive to people's feelings. I think I've got a lot of growing to do yet. It just wasn't a bad experience for me, and it's not been negative at all.

Another thing that helped me come out as a person and helped me relive some of my Vietnam experiences was my father's death from cancer two years ago. We were extremely close; we're very much alike. He was a very kind, sensitive person. Even though I didn't see him much in the last few years before he died, because of distance, we continued to stay close. At his death, a lot of things came together. It seemed like I cried for the first time in a long time, and I talked about things that were important to me, and I began to realize how important relationships are and how you need to develop them and not be afraid to speak things out that are in your mind. Even now it's hard for me to talk about him because he was so special to me and to my children. He had so much influence on my life that I just hope he knows what he did for me.

Donna: I can remember the week before we left Vietnam, knowing that I was going to be married within a few weeks. As I look back on it now, I really went into it very naively, spending less than a year with a person that I only knew in a war situation. Kay and I went to see her brother in the Philippines on the way home, and I was real glad that we had that break, instead of going right to the States. I remember I was glad I had a vacation with Kay, and I was really dreading leaving her because I just couldn't picture life without her. . . . You were always there, you know . . .

When I went to Massachusetts I was really lonely. I think I had an awful lot of low self-esteem. I had the weight problem. I thought, when we got home and Tom started looking at all these girls, that if he had his choice, he probably wouldn't have picked me. It just wasn't a real happy year, I'll tell you. It was up and down and insecure. We've had some hard times, the two of us, had two separations, but we just really do love each other and we're committed to the marriage, and I think it's better for all the turmoil that we've been through. We have three children that I wouldn't trade the world for.

I went to school for two years on the GI bill until I got pregnant. I took all art courses and just loved it. I was just so happy doing that. I never wanted to take another nursing course again. Plus I felt, "Why should I take these nursing courses? I'm a three-year grad—why should I take all these courses over again just to get a degree? I don't even want it." I still feel that way.

Kay: Me too. I'd never get my degree in nursing.

Donna: I, like Kay, put Vietnam behind me. I went to school and they were demonstrating, and I remember demonstrating too, because by that time I wanted us out of there. Yet I felt embarrassed to say that I was a Vietnam veteran at the same time. I felt kind of like I wanted to hide that fact. By the time I went over to Vietnam, I had been like a backsliding Christian—probably backslided even more over there. Through different things that happened in my life, I guess, I had a spiritual awakening, and I'm really thankful to God that He just puts me in the right place at the right time. I've been getting a lot of help. For instance, with my compulsive overeating, I'm at Overeaters Anonymous now, and I'm really happy. I'm full of gratitude today. I have a husband that I love, and I have three kids that I love. I'm thankful I'm not working. I'm thankful I'm never bored. I'm thankful that I have a lot of good friends.

I've been in Massachusetts now fourteen years, and I'm not like an oak tree, but a little willow. I never want to travel again, and I don't ever want to move. I want to stay right in our red gambrel house on Newcomb Road. I'm real happy to have roots.

I don't regret going to Vietnam; I regret that so many people got hurt there and that there was a war. I don't know still whether it was the right or wrong thing to do, but I think it was the right thing that I went over there because, like Kay said, we wouldn't have thought of saying no. There were so many young boys that wouldn't have thought of saying no. They had the courage to do it, and I'm glad I did too. I'm not political in VA things; I don't go to any support groups or any meetings. I don't think I will when I go back home either.

Kay: I think that's typical of a lot of women vets that we don't hear about—they've adjusted and had support and they just get on with their life.

Donna: Sometimes—and this is prejudice on my side—but I think sometimes people are—oh, I don't know, you know, almost glorying. . . . I realize that you have to face your problem of the past and go through it to the other side, but sometimes it looks like people are taking an awful long time to get to the other side. And that's prejudice on my side, because I haven't even really heard anybody's story and I haven't lived what they went through either. My prayer for all the veterans that were in Vietnam is that they can face everything that happened and if they feel they've done something that deserves forgiveness, ask for it, be cleansed altogether from it. Live today and see the sunsets and see the foliage and see their children and their wife and not waste twenty years moaning and groaning over Vietnam. It's over. And I pray that they can resolve it and get on with today, because that's all we have. That's all we have. I am thankful for this opportunity that Kay and I have had to get together after about twelve years, and you know, the love we share as sisters is one of the most—it will never go away.

Left: Intensive Care/ Recovery Room staff of 91st Evac Hospital, Chu Lai, Christmas 1969, Anne Auger is kneeling at left. Below: USO Club associate director Maureen Nerli (center) with children during her weekly visit to the Immaculate Conception Orphanage, Tan Son Nhut.

*Maureen Nerli (**center**) serving coffee on the wards of the 3d Field Hospital, Tan Son Nhut.*

Army nurse Grace O'Brien with her brother Frank Barolet in Phu Loi (1st Infantry Division) in 1967.

Vietnamese woman doing laundry outside the latrine, 71st Evac, Pleiku. Photo by Sara McVicker

Ward Six, 71st Evac, Pleiku—Sara McVicker's ward.

Right: Army nurse Kay Burnett off duty. *Below:* Kay and her friend Donna Peck on a med-evac, 1969.

Left: Bobbi Pettit (center) returning home with members of her band, "The Pretty Kittens," August 1967. Photo by Tom Shaw, Long Beach, CA, *Independent* *Below: Donna Peck on the Maxillo-Facial Unit, 24th Evac Hospital, Long Binh, 1969.* U.S. Army photo

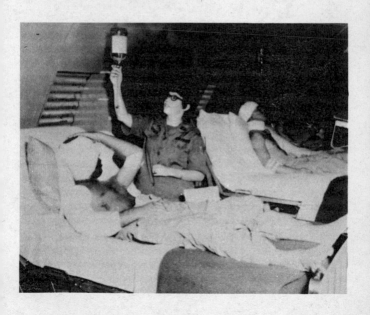

Sandra Collingwood

INTERNATIONAL VOLUNTARY SERVICES AND CATHOLIC RELIEF SERVICES—1967 TO 1969

Sandra went to Vietnam to work with the Vietnamese people. In 1967 she joined the International Voluntary Services organization, which had been in Vietnam several years providing people as teachers, agricultural advisors, and community service workers. She was taught the language while living with a Vietnamese family and worked in Saigon, Ba Ngoi (a small village near Cam Rahn Bay), and Qui Nhon. After the Tet offensive, Sandra left IVS and went to work with Catholic Relief Services as a community development team member.

Sandra now resides in the Bay Area. She is employed as a medical social worker in a rehabilitation center of a hospital, working with spinal cord–injured patients who are paraplegic and quadriplegic.

DURING MY LAST WEEK OF COLLEGE, RIGHT BEFORE
finals, I happened to see a poster for the Peace Corps.
There was an exam down at the post office that I didn't
have to study for, and I thought I might as well take that
as well as the other exams that I had to take. The Peace
Corps at that time was about a year and a half to two years
old. This was in 1963.

I really didn't think anything more of it until neighbors
started telling me the FBI was coming around asking about
me, which is what Peace Corps does—they do an investi-
gation of you. I thought maybe I better tell my parents what
was going on! I had decided that I wanted to go to South
America. They assigned me to Peru. I worked there for
two years as a community development volunteer. It was
a wonderfully positive learning experience for me, and
that's not to say I didn't struggle a lot, because it was my
first exposure to living and working within another culture.
I was the typical naive liberal arts graduate who went there
to help "those people." I learned more from them than I
was ever able to offer them myself. It really opened me up
a lot to what was out in the world. It made me aware of

213

how limited we were in the States to the whole learning process of other cultures.

When I returned to the States, I went into reverse culture shock; it was mind-blowing to me to come back. I would try to talk to people about what my experience was like, and they really weren't interested. I was back about a year and a half, during which time I realized I wanted more exposure to other cultures and decided I wanted the exposure of an Asian culture. I didn't want to always be comparing Peru to the States, or a Latin culture to ours. I found out about IVS (International Voluntary Services) and inquired with them about where they were in Asia and what it was like within their organization. I liked the idea of working with an international organization, although most of the volunteers were American. There were some volunteers from other countries, not quite as international as I would have liked it, but at least the concept seemed to be there. They were going to send me to Laos. A few weeks before I was to begin training, they wrote and asked me if I would go to Vietnam instead. Vietnam I had vaguely heard about through a friend of mine I had worked with in Peru, but my political awareness wasn't really there at the time. I took about a week to decide whether or not I'd go to Vietnam, then agreed to do it. I feel fortunate that I did, because at the time I arrived in Vietnam I was told the war was more severe in Laos than it was in Vietnam, although that was very hushed. During this period I found out that when the American military men were killed in Laos, their bodies were brought back to Vietnam, and they claimed they died in Vietnam. That all came out later.

As in the Peace Corps, we had training in the Vietnamese culture, here in the States first, and then in the Philippines, where we learned about the Asian farming culture. We actually planted rice in the mud paddies and experienced what it was like to work with the water buffalo, which was the Vietnamese farm equipment, like our tractors. To get behind a water buffalo in the mud and plow was quite an incredible experience for me. It made me appreciate what was involved with farming in Vietnam. Later, while working in Vietnam, I saw that lack of respect or consideration by many American military toward the Vietnamese farmer. Some of the American military men would come back from their day's assignment in the troop trucks and throw a grenade into the farmer's field and laugh while watching the farmer jump. Sometimes they accidentally killed the water buffalo, which for that farmer would be very devastating. Coming from the Vietnamese perspective, with the struggles they were going through economically to survive, this activity done "for fun" created an even greater hardship for that family. The tendency of a lot of the American military men, with the exposure and training they had regarding the Vietnamese, was to not trust any Vietnamese. Often I found that they did not, or could not, see them as human beings. So, intellectually, I can see where that kind of action would happen. When one person did not see someone else as a human being, it didn't seem to matter what that person did to a "nonhuman." Coming from my perspective, it was really a harsh thing to see, because in reality it always matters how any living being relates to another.

My training as a community development volunteer started in the late summer of '67. IVS was going through some turmoil at that time. The director and several other IVS people had reached a point where they felt that IVS should not be in Vietnam. So while we were in the Philippines we didn't know if we were going to go to Vietnam or not. We did go over, and I was there for approximately two years. I came back to the States in May of '69.

My first three months in Vietnam I was in training. I lived with a Vietnamese family. There were twelve or thirteen of us in the training group. I was the only woman. The family that we lived with was really great. It's where we learned to use chopsticks, got exposed to the Vietnamese food and, of course, the culture. None of us spoke Vietnamese. The family spoke no English. Their sixteen-year-old daughter adopted me and would take me around to her friends within the community, introducing me to them and taking me to the market. While we were living with them we got our language training. We had three Vietnamese teachers, two men and a woman. The woman, who was very young, ended up sharing a room with me. She came from a very traditional North Vietnamese family. I thought I was making her nervous or uncomfortable, because she would always sit up as soon as I came in the room. I talked about it to one of the other language teachers and was informed that because she was younger than I, she was showing respect for her elders. Here I was thinking just the opposite, that I was making her feel uncomfortable! So those little pieces of information I gathered firsthand.

I had an experience while I was in training that I would be confronted with on a regular basis while I was there. I was walking home from a visit with the sixteen-year-old Vietnamese girl's friends; she and I were walking back together. There was a jeep that came by with two military men in it, suddenly slamming on their brakes. One man jumped out, having seen me, an American woman. He started yelling and jumping up and down. He looked like a monkey, going through all of these gyrations, hooting and hollering and oohing and aahing. It was an incredible scene for me. Of course the Vietnamese girl was dumbfounded; she didn't know how to respond to it either, and she was embarrassed. I just ignored him and we continued walking on, and he finally got in the jeep with the other guy and took off. But that kind of interaction or exchange was very detrimental for us women and our work with the Vietnamese people. To the Vietnamese people, for me to have that kind of contact with the American military hinted of my being a prostitute, because that's how they saw many of them relating to Vietnamese women.

There was one small community that had several IVS women working in it that had been overwhelmed by American military. The base that was there was almost larger than the Vietnamese community itself. There were so many similar incidents in that town that the IVS women could not be effective in their work there. Later if I saw a convoy coming I would go into a store, or somewhere where I would not be seen, because if they saw me they would blow their airhorns; they'd go through their catcalls, making noises or whatever. To me that was harassment. I was there doing the work that I wanted to be doing with the

Vietnamese and this was an interference. Plus, I felt lack of respect for me as a person. They were judging me as a round-eye woman there, rather than as a person. So I started developing antagonism toward American military soon after I got there. I ended up not differentiating between who was a volunteer American military man and who was a draftee. If they wore khaki green, then I remained at a distance. I know some of the difficulties that they went through, whether they were volunteers or draftees. Many felt that they were doing the right thing as far as fighting for their country. Then after being in Vietnam for a while and seeing what was going on, some would tell me "I don't believe in this war." Yet they had no choice but to stay or to go AWOL, either decision being traumatic.

There were other incidents that I saw happening, for instance the black market that was going on. Some military men who might be located in a particular town for a while would go to the local orphanages and they would bring in C-rations and so forth for the children. Some of the orphanages, or really, the people who ran them, were in it for their own profit. Instead of giving these items to the children they would sell them on the black market and keep the money for their own benefit. I walked into one room of an orphanage one time, and all the way up to the ceiling were these rations. Not all orphanages did this, but the military men usually did not take the time to find out which ones they should donate to.

When I finished training, all three of the projects that had been set up for me had fallen through, so I had to find my own work. One of the jobs that I found was working with a Vietnamese nun, who was working with the local men's prison. They had a wing with about three hundred boys in it who were so-called juvenile delinquents. There was no other facility available for them. I started assisting her initially in her work with the boys. The idea was to set up activities and develop some kind of skills for them while they were in there, so they'd have something when they left. Some of them had stolen a military man's watch or something and had been caught at it. Others had no place to live and stole food to survive. That's why I say "so-called juvenile delinquents'': a lot of them were just street boys.

I also worked with a Buddhist nun, who was trying to get an orphanage started while she was in a monastery. There were children who had just started habitating the place when they found out that she and the nuns were there. She created a shelter for them when I started working with her. This was all in Saigon. The other job I had was working as a liaison between a Vietnamese youth group and either the Vietnamese or American administration in Saigon. They were not registered with the government, which was required of all youth groups. The Vietnamese government had some fears of youth being, you know, organized and antigovernment. This was a loosely formed group of youth who were trying to work with refugees, in some of the refugee camps and with one of the orphanages. They were very community-conscious and wanted to assist in whatever way that they could, and I was more than willing to work with them. When there were doors that could not be opened or would not be opened for them if they went directly to local offices, I would be the intermediary. I also would sit down with them and show them ways in which they could approach government officials where they would be more apt to have doors opened for them. I was using my community development experience from Peru and teaching it to them so that they could do their own form of development with their country-people. That was really great; I enjoyed working with them a lot.

I walked into some things very naively when I was in Vietnam. I saw so many things that were going on and felt that I could not even write home to family and friends to tell them because they would think I was going crazy: sitting down at a lunch with several people including two men who were with the CIA who were talking about what kind of activities they were going to have in a village they were going to that night—who it was they were going to kill and whether or not they were going to display the heads and so forth—this is over lunch! I'm sitting there and saying, ''I'm not believing this conversation.'' That type of experience was fairly commonplace. I mean, maybe not to that extreme, but that kind of mentality, that lack of respect for another human being. I feel it gets so compounded in a war situation. That is how I became very strongly opposed to the war. I was accused by others of being a communist because I was opposing the war. And I'm saying, "I'm a what?" Because I oppose people killing each other, you know? It was incredible to me.

I don't know of any Vietnamese person that I had contact with that was not directly affected by the war, either by the loss of a parent, a sibling, some relative somewhere—if not in the immediate family, in the extended family. When one of the young men would be drafted, it was often referred to as their death day.

There were a lot of politics that were going on in Saigon so some projects would be started and then dropped for various reasons. I found it very difficult to work there and thought that I really wanted to work in a smaller town. I did my own research and was going to be working in a small fishing village. I got the approval of the Vietnamese province chief, the American advisor, and talked to the volunteers that were there. I had set up exactly what it was I was going to be doing and had decided to come back to Saigon to spend Tet with my Vietnamese friends. I had been invited to several Tet dinners. That's the biggest time of year, the most important time of year for the Vietnamese, so I had come back to that area to stay for the week and was living in my old house.

I had been living with a Vietnamese woman in the Chinese section of Saigon, which was called Cho Long. The landlord and landlady were very caring for me. My Vietnamese roommate would normally eat in town before coming home after work. I chose to come home, and they fixed my meals for me. The custom was, they would set the food by the door, knock on the door, and I'd come. They wouldn't be there but my food would be. Then when I finished eating I would put the utensils out by the door, close it, and within five minutes, just as I'm sitting down to do some of the work that I had laid out to do that evening, there would be a knock at the door and they would come in. They would stay with me conversing until my roommate got home. This happened night after night. What I learned was that it was proper for me to eat alone but it was not considerate of them to leave me alone after eating, so they would stay with me until my roommate got home. I learned to wait awhile before I put my tray outside so I could get that work done.

The night of Tet, my roommate and I had both decided that we were going to stay elsewhere. There were all these festivities going on, and she had decided she wanted to stay with her relatives after the dinner. I was going to go to my Vietnamese friends' home for Tet dinner and stay at the IVS house because it would be hard to find a way home. The ironies of decision making. That night Cho Long was surrounded by the Viet Cong. She would have been in a lot of trouble for having me, an American, as her roommate, and who knows, I might have been taken captive at that time (just as three IVS volunteers were, in Hue). Right after the Tet offensive we were on twenty-four-hour curfew. We were not allowed out of the building. When we ran out of food, we had to go one by one to the building across the street, to the cafeteria, to get our food. We could not go in a group in case someone decided to shoot at us. It was a pretty chaotic time. Some of the volunteers had been brought in from outlying areas. They had found their way to Saigon and were trying to locate us, hitching rides with American military. I remember one woman hitching a ride with two MPs to where we had been evacuated. They would not bring the jeep to the building. She had to walk a couple of blocks because we were in what was called the "red area," because it was not considered safe. So they gave her her suitcase, and she had to walk those two blocks to the building. We were on our own in a number of ways.

While we were there, the American military had rocketed a four-block area right next to us. The people in that particular area were very much pro-American. What happened is that a handful of guerrillas, or Viet Cong as they're more commonly known, entered this area, moving from building to building sniping at American military vehicles that came through. The Americans then rocketed each building the snipers fired from, and we were told later the Viet Cong managed to get out. This guerrilla warfare technique was very effective, because the whole area was burned down; the residents lost their houses, their belongings, and they became very anti-American overnight. What better way to have the Vietnamese become anti-American. I'm there in the building, watching this whole area burn down and listening to the scramble. I want to go help the residents get out so that they could save what they could, so that no lives would be lost, but I knew that being an American there was no way I could go and help; I would have been killed. That kind of helpless feeling happened a lot for me the whole time I was there.

After the Tet offensive, the fishing village I was transferring to was seriously damaged; half the town had been destroyed, including my house. I was asked by the volunteer who was up there, the Vietnamese province chief, and the American advisor to come help them. Letters were written by them to the IVS requesting my services. But the new director did not want me to go. I would have been the only woman there who was not Vietnamese. They had evacuated the wife of the missionary worker, and there was a woman on the Chinese medical team who also had been evacuated, so they were concerned about having me up there. I strongly opposed this concern. My help was needed, I knew that area, and I felt I could be helpful. This is something that was a common theme that ran through the whole time I was there . . . that I would not be able to go to an area because I was a woman or an American.

I decided to try to find another organization I could work with in Vietnam and be more free to do the work I wanted to do. Part of my decision to remain in Vietnam was to try to be as effective as I could in doing community development work. I wanted to give it a full try. My idealism was still very strong then, feeling very much that I wanted to make the attempt to perhaps counteract a lot of the negative things I saw happening by the American government. So, a friend from IVS and I did quite a search as far as finding another agency we could possibly work for and found that Catholic Relief Services had just recently gotten a government contract. Catholic Relief Services had, up to that point, been strictly dealing with commodities with the Vietnamese people in giving them food, clothing, and money. They had a contract to form community development teams, which were to consist of a team administrator, two social workers, and two nurses. The concept of it was, I felt, very good. There were six of us from IVS who decided to remain in the country and transfer to Catholic Relief Services.

One of the first things we discovered is that they had no training program for new CRS staff coming to Vietnam regarding the Vietnamese language and culture. So I asked a couple of my Vietnamese friends if they would be willing to work with me if I could convince the CRS administration to do a training program. The kind of exposure the new staff were getting was from American military—"Why aren't you carrying guns?" or "You shouldn't go to that area of town because it's too dangerous," coming more from a fear aspect of the Vietnamese—yet CRS staff were supposed to be working hand in hand with them. I think that as many good intentions that were going on with several of the civilian organizations that were there, good intentions were not enough. You can destroy a lot of potential effectiveness in working with people by not understanding their culture and expecting to do all your work through an interpreter. I feel the CRS organization could have been so much more effective by being more willing to understand and learn from their host country.

I ended up working in a small town just outside of Cam Ranh Bay. One of the other people on the CD team I was with was from the Philippines. He had been in IVS also; and we had negotiated with a Vietnamese family for the five of us to rent their house. We had made all the arrangements, only to be told by CRS administration that we could not live in a Vietnamese home, we had to live on a military compound. They were interested in trying to take care of us to make sure no injuries happened to us, but at the same time really not understanding what a community development team was there for. Any of the Vietnamese who wanted to come visit us had to be interrogated, even to come onto the compound, which started to do something to me also. How could my Vietnamese friends be put through that every time they wanted to see me? So again, the common theme of fear surfaced.

In the small village outside of Cam Ranh Bay, we were to work with a refugee camp that was being built. They were relocating an entire village from further north to this area: people who were agrarian, who were now to be exposed to the industrial life. That was not in the tradition of Vietnamese culture, where respect for the ancestor is so rich. The expectation was that they and their ancestors' spirits remained on that particular land forever. We were supposed to help them settle and then to develop some kind of training system to help them adjust to being in an industrial society now. But it wasn't a Vietnamese industrial society, it was the American military base industry, again creating that kind of dependency on the American system.

Then I was asked to go, with another CRS worker, further north to Qui Nhon to start a community development project in that town. He and I were to set up the project, since I knew the language and culture and had quite a bit of experience in Vietnam. The rest of the team members were very new to Vietnam; most of them were nuns, nurses. After I moved to Qui Nhon there were several ground attacks. One was next door to our house. It was at that time I decided I was going to leave Vietnam. I felt that if anything was going to be done as far as ending the war, it was not going to be done in Vietnam; it was going to be done by convincing our government at home that we needed to pull out of Vietnam. I had by that time reached a very strong opinion that none of us foreigners should be there, whether we were carrying guns or not. I went through a whole process my last three months there, trying to figure out how I was going to emotionally adjust to going back, knowing the reverse culture shock I had gone through when I came back from Peru.

My parents at that time were living in Florida. I decided that I would take two months to travel across the country and visit people who I felt could give me a positive experience in being back, knowing I needed that. I also decided that I would go to grad school. So, that's what I did. I traveled for two months visiting friends. A couple people who saw me right after I got back have since told me they didn't know if I was going to make it or not.

I could not talk about Vietnam when I came back, there was no way. I went through an irrational hatred of khaki green, an irrational hatred of anything military. I was not objective at all; I could not be objective at that point. Then when I got to grad school, I immediately got exposed to a fellow student who had just come back from Vietnam, who had been there in the military. It was good for me right at that time, because I had such an irrational hatred for anything military that it couldn't benefit anybody, including myself. We ended up becoming friends; I was one of the few people he could talk to about what had happened. He was definitely not considered a hero by other students. He would go on these drunk binges, just having the full realization of what he had done there—you know, what he had been exposed to, the killing that had happened and so forth. It was really good for me to see what he was going through emotionally, because then I was able to start seeing that people who had been in the military in Vietnam were also human beings, and that I wouldn't continue doing what I had accused others of doing, which was being inhuman to another human being. So we were able to work some things out through each other just by that exposure, which was a reluctant one for me, but one I'm really glad that I allowed to happen.

While I was on campus I started being asked to talk to different groups about Vietnam. I agreed to do so reluctantly—only because I have a fear of speaking before either large or small groups of people—but because I felt it was so terribly important to develop an awareness in the American people about the total devastation of war and how many lives were being ruined, I felt an obligation to do it. I was not on a campaign to give these lectures, but if people came to me I agreed to speak to their groups. It just started happening on a regular basis. Then I found that the dean had been giving my name out because, as he told me later, I was not talking just from a political perspective, I was talking from a human perspective as far as what was happening to all the people involved, in particular the Vietnamese and their country. So I just started a whole lecture series.

I decided to come out to California after grad school and continued to give some talks when I came out here. The last I gave was at Hayward State College. I discovered that there was a man in the class who was a Vietnam vet. I was coming from my perspective as far as what I had seen over there and some of the human misery and so forth. I happened to mention about the American military men feeling that they could do some good helping at the orphanages by giving them C-rations or other such commodities. What I was trying to point out was lack of awareness on the soldiers' parts, thinking that they're doing something that is helpful and yet in the long run not necessarily. He got very upset because it turned out, as I let him talk more, he had been one of those men, he had been bringing in those items to an orphanage. I decided on the spot not to challenge him, and I let him talk that through. He had been there. He had seen some of the destruction. And this was the one part of his life while he was there that he felt he was doing some good. I could not deny him that. If that was what was helping to hold him together, I could not deny him that. The students started getting very upset with me for not challenging him. After it was over they started attacking me for how I had handled it. It was at that point I decided I was giving no more lectures. I was starting to be able to see how the military men were having their own emotional struggles as far as adjusting to being back and trying to deal with what had happened while they were in Vietnam, and their part in it. I did not want to stand in the way of that process because I knew we were talking about survival. . . . We're talking about emotional survival, including my own. As irrational as some of my feelings were, I also could see that human aspect of it too. I may not have agreed with his reason for being there, but I could see the suffering that he was going through. Also it was reaching a point where I realized that I was constantly reliving what had happened while I was in Vietnam each time I gave a lecture. I was not adjusting, giving myself an opportunity to be here and try to get on with my life. I decided I needed to stop opening up all of those wounds. I needed to just back off, and someone else could take over and do that part of it.

It was only three years ago when I really started allowing myself to start dealing with what had happened when I was in Vietnam. I think that I have worked through some of the emotional scars. I say scars because I think they will always be there for me. What I need to learn to do is to accept those scars as they are and go on with my life. For many years, what I did was to deny that those scars were there, try however I could to pretend that they did not exist. It was directly affecting my relationships with other people, whether they were lovers or friends or relatives. At different times I became a social isolate, then I went to the extreme of desperately needing to be around others. To where now, I'm just riding it as I can, working through things as they come up. About three years ago I started taking workshops from Cheri Huber, who's a Zen-Buddhist monk. Through my exposure to that philosophy, learning to deal with personal growth through that kind of perspective, I have been able to allow myself to be more vulnerable again, especially in what happened to me in Vietnam, and to deal with it more directly.

Some people can have a kind of basic understanding of the things that I am dealing with; they can relate it to an experience they've had. However, I need to talk to people who went through similar experiences. I do feel that the civilian women who were in Vietnam working with the Vietnamese are really an invisible group of people. I have fortunately kept contact with some of the people I had been over there with. Some of my processing has been able to be done through meeting with them, having discussions with them, and each of us helping the other to try to piece things together.

Dot Weller

AMERICAN FRIENDS SERVICE
COMMITTEE
REHABILITATION CENTER,
QUANG NGAI—
JULY '67 TO OCT. '71

Dot currently works as a physical therapist for a home health agency in Santa Clara County, California, treating patients in their own homes or convalescent hospitals.

My interview with Dot Weller never took place. A day or two before our scheduled appointment, she telephoned me, and in the difficult and emotional conversation that ensued I learned I that she was unable to go through with our interview.

I wrote to her, apologizing for having caused her to be upset, and explained how I was beginning to feel guilty for stirring up memories that possibly should be left alone.

Several weeks later I received the following letter.

Dear Keith Walker:

I owe you several apologies, my friend. One, for having subjected you to one of my weak moments and imposing a certain amount of guilt on you for problems that are strictly my own. Secondly, for not having written sooner and proffered some kind of explanation for my bizarre behavior.

I came home from Vietnam in 1971. That was twelve years ago, Keith. You would think I could have sorted things out by this time. I certainly expect that of myself, but I guess the "abcess" still drains in me. Once before— oh, I guess about three or four years ago—I was visited by an ex-ABC correspondent who wanted to write a book about women in Vietnam. He had called and asked permission aforehand, which I gave to him thinking that surely I was able to discuss these things now, and I felt it was a good idea to bring this aspect of the war to the attention of the public. However, when he arrived and we sat down to talk, I just fell apart after a short period and could not continue. Fortunately for him, I had kept a daily diary during the four years in Vietnam and gave him that to work from. He has now decided to try to edit my diary and get that published. This I have consented to as he plans to structure it so as to bring out the plight of the common people in Vietnam and how the long years of war affected them. Out of all the books that have been written on the subject, this aspect has not been emphasized as far as I know. And this is the aspect that bothers me the most—what happened to the people? The women, the children, the old people.

I was with a voluntary Quaker relief group, the American Friends Service Committee. In many ways, my experiences were similar to the military woman's. But in most ways, my experiences were very different. And I came home with some different problems. I have not experienced any lack of recognition or rejection, none that bothered me at any rate. The Quaker's position was to be there to help the Vietnamese civilian to cope with the injuries suffered at the hands of all participants in the war. We built a rehabilitation center and then taught the local civilians in our own various professions (e.g., physical therapy, nursing, surgery, prosthetics, etc.). When the team finally pulled out, approximately six months after the fall of Saigon, they were able to run the center on their own and are still doing so to the best of my knowledge. We were absolutely neutral in regards to the political situation and vowed to treat anyone who came to our center as long as they were civilians. The longer we were there, however, the more our sympathies were with the NLF and, of course, with the innocent civilians. We came to hate what the United States was doing to this country. During the four and a half years that I was there, from 80 to 95 percent of the war-injured that came through our doors were injured by the U.S. or South Vietnamese troops.

We were unwilling witnesses to atrocities so horrible that no one at home would ever believe us when we tried to relate the stories. And these atrocities, Keith, were committed by *all* sides in that complicated war. What stuck in my memory is that this type of inhumane behavior is what war does to the minds of men. All men! Not just the so-called VC but the Koreans, the Americans, the South Vietnamese, the CIA—all men.

I think I am wandering somewhat, but we were talking about rejection from the people of America. Of course, I felt the sting of backlash from people who had supported the government's position in Vietnam. For two years after I returned I continued to work for AFSC as a lecturer and fund-raising person and made speaking tours all over the western United States. In those audiences were many people who violently disagreed with the things I was saying, who swore and called me a "commie," among other names. In essence saying that their loved ones had died in vain. Yet I received loving support and approbation but from the "other side." Those who felt as we had about the American involvement in the war. I would think it would have been the same (in reverse, of course) for the military women. The rejection and anger they ran into undoubtedly came from the lunatic fringe of the antiwar ranks. Believe me, the majority of those of us who were against the American involvement in Vietnam held no animosity against the U.S. military as individuals. They were doing what they felt they had to do on what they felt was right. How can that be wrong? Part of what tore me to shreds over there was witnessing what was happening to our American military friends. Yes, we had many of them. We saw them turning to drugs or mindless savagery to try to justify what they were being asked to do day after day. We saw them struggling to be courageous in the face of a war that they didn't understand and in the face of widespread criticism from many nations of the world. Everybody suffered in that war, Keith, *everybody.*

I'll tell you some of the things that did and still do bother me. First of all, the nightmares don't stop. They *never* stop! During the course of the day, some sound, a smell, a phrase heard—all can trigger flashbacks. Chills running down the spine. Sudden tears which dismay and confuse whoever might be around to witness them. Nightsweats. Helicopters overhead can reduce me to a quivering mass. I have not been good about maintaining contacts with my friends that I was in Vietnam with. Why? Because seeing them or receiving letters from them brings back too many memories. When I first came home, I tried to talk about the things I had seen, the lessons I had learned, the problems I was having. But unless one has been through that experience with you, they simply cannot understand. And this is not their fault. They have no basis for comparison. As I talked, I saw that they didn't believe many things I said. I was making them very uncomfortable. They would hush me and say, "Don't talk about it now. It will go away." They would change the subject. "Don't be morbid," they would say. They were uncomfortable with my tears and moods. I finally came to realize that if I wanted to have friends or comfortable relationships with my family, I had to submerge it all. Try to forget it. I have found that if any of my friends (made after returning from Vietnam) are exposed to these feelings, the relationship is compromised to some degree. So I have been working very hard at keeping the lid on "Pandora's box."

I guess one of the reasons that I agreed to having my diary published was that I really understand that if I stand any chance at all of putting my Vietnam experience to rest, I have to talk it out. Maybe forcing myself to go through this re-hashing of the years there will help. But I can't do it face to face with another person, Keith. I just can't. A mess, huh! I'd be a psychiatrist's pot of gold!

At any rate, do your thing. It is worthwhile. Don't feel any guilt about stirring up painful memories. This happens anyway. With your stimulation or without it. It's my problem and I'll have to deal with it.

Sincerely,
(Dot Weller)

Lynn Calmes Kohl

71ST EVAC. HOSPITAL,
PLEIKU—JUNE '69 TO JUNE '70

Lynn presently lives with her family in Greenville, Wisconsin. She is active in the Fox Valley Vietnam Veterans Association, a member of the PTSD Advisory Board at Tomah VA Medical Center in Wisconsin, and belongs to the Vietnam Veterans of America. She is very active as a Girl Scout leader and in numerous school activities.

These past few years have been extremely difficult—not only for me, but also for my husband, Ken, and the girls (we all still attend some form of counseling). We are hoping the worst is now behind us. We realize this is something that will be with me for the rest of my life, but hope that with continual hard work and mutual support, I will some day be able to lay that ghost to rest. . . . My heart goes out to those families that are going through this or will have to go through it. . . .

My mother tells me that since about age two I must have wanted to be a nurse, because when someone was sick I'd bring the aspirin, I'd hold their hand, or anything like that. It's interesting, because in high school, when you're taking career aptitude tests, the first thing that I was supposed to be was an English teacher, and the last thing that I was suited for, according to the test, was nursing. I think I should have listened to them, I don't know. They might have been right.

I graduated from high school in 1965. I applied to a few nursing schools but was most interested in Mount Sinai in Milwaukee and was accepted. In our last year there—in fact it was a couple of months before we graduated—a few of us were sitting around talking when a fellow student came in and said, "Gee, I just heard of an opportunity you girls might be interested in too." She met this fellow—I think it was one of the recruiters—and he was talking about Army nurses and how if you were graduated you could go in as an officer and you'd get your choice of duty stations. They were going on some kind of a training mission down in Florida, so he invited us to come for the weekend to see

235

what it was like. Four of us went down, got wined and dined, and it was kind of nice, so we thought about it. We decided that if we stayed in Milwaukee we'd get in a rut, because we already were. And we thought, "Gee, you know, you get your choice," and Fort Ord, California, sure sounded nice. I had been against the war—I didn't think we ought to be over there—so I asked the recruiter what were my chances of being sent to Vietnam. He said, "No way can they send a female unless you volunteer." Well, I certainly wasn't going to volunteer, so I signed on the dotted line.

We went to Fort Sam for basic training, then to Fort Ord and were there a couple of weeks, I think, when I got orders for Vietnam. I went to my commanding officer and started explaining to her that there had been a mistake, that I didn't volunteer. She just looked at me and then got this little grin on her face and said, "Did you get that in writing, Lieutenant?" . . . and within a few weeks all four of us had orders for Vietnam. Fort Ord was very nice while it lasted. The interesting thing was, as it got time for us to go, the gal who had talked the rest of us into joining went AWOL, got pregnant, and left the service, in that order, and the three of us were on our way to sunny Vietnam. We've never heard from her since, which is probably a good thing, because we might strangle her or something.

I got there June twelfth, 1969. Our flight left Travis AFB, and we were all on the plane together going there, but once we got in-country they split us up, three different hospitals. We had hoped we'd be together. I went to the 71st Evac Hospital at Pleiku in the Central Highlands. It was a surgical hospital built mainly to treat soldiers from the 4th Division and the Air Force base nearby. They came to us either directly from the field or from an aide station. My MOS was post-op nursing, but to my complete horror, I was placed in the OR, as they needed a replacement and I happened to be the next body through the gate! That in itself was extremely traumatic because in nursing school I had had a very bad experience in that area.

Before we left Fort Ord, one of the nurses who was just coming back told us, "Whatever you do, before you go, buy all kinds of sexy underwear, black lace bras, anything just to remind yourself that you're female, because after a year in your combat boots and your fatigues, you're going to forget." This was her advice and we did; all of us went out and bought things like that except, of course, everything got moldy and mildewy with the heat and the red dust—Pleiku is noted for its red dust.

The morning I started in surgery I thought I'd be getting an orientation of some sort. I went over to the surgical unit to find out what it was like and what I'd be doing. They had a lot of casualties. The head nurse told me just to go in and observe for that case to see what would be expected. I was supposed to be a circulating nurse. I remember it was a really bad case—a GI with multiple wounds from head to foot; his right arm was just hanging by a couple of tendons, and I knew it would eventually be coming off. There were a couple surgeons working on him. One of the surgeons looked up and saw me standing there, and he didn't realize that I was brand new, but it made him angry to see someone just standing there doing nothing, and he threw a scissors at me and said, "Don't just stand there. He's going to lose that arm anyway. Cut it off." . . . So I did. And I remember the sound; there was a pail underneath, and I remember it hitting the pail. That was the end of my orientation. . . .

For prepping, they used those big straight-edged razors. A case that came in—they had to do some work around his head, and of course, just coming in from the field, he had a big bushy beard and stuff. They told me to shave his face. Well, I had never used one of those doggone things. So I'm sitting here trying to shave and my very first swipe I put a nice gash into his cheek, and I remember the anesthesiologist saying, "Be sure to record this: 'First incision made by Lieutenant Calmes.' " Then they gave me a straight-edged razor, sent me back to my hooch, and said, "Now I want you to shave your legs." And I tell you, you shave your legs with that once or twice and you learn how to handle it awful quick.

The days and nights just went into each other. At minimum, shifts were twelve hours. Sometimes we had a day off on Sunday, or one day during the week if you weren't real busy, but I don't ever remember not being real busy. I remember that we didn't have enough doctors, and when we had a push on, the nurses, the corpsmen, or whoever was there, had to do a lot of the minor surgery. They'd show you once how to do something, like a debridement, in a time when it wasn't a real critical situation, and from then on you were on your own. I think of that now sometimes and wonder if I did any damage to the fellow or if I saved his life or what I did; you just don't know. And you never knew, out of all the fellows that you took care of, if they lived or died or what, because at any stage along the way, they might have lost their life.

We were rocketed and mortared—Pleiku was known as Rocket City. There was a time, very close after I got there, that I did send a will to a friend of mine in Milwaukee. I didn't want my family to know. I kept telling them, "There's nothing to worry about. We're safe here." But I really didn't think so; I never thought I would leave there alive.

The MARS unit was right behind us, and the Air Force base was over on this side, and 4th Division's over here, and our big red cross is in the center, so it's hard to tell just who they wanted, but they managed to get us quite often. The day before I left, we got hit three times. I remember after the second time that day I was thinking—you know, you heard so often of a fellow getting killed on his last day, and I thought, "Wouldn't you know, today's the day!" That's how I got promoted from second lieutenant to first lieutenant. Two of us were sent to headquarters for the ceremony, and just as we got over there we came under rocket attack. So they put us in the bunker, and we sat there for I don't know how long; it must have been an hour or so. The colonel finally said, "Come on over here—crawl over on your hands and knees—we'll just carry on with this. You may as well be a dead first lieutenant as a dead second lieutenant." So that's how we got promoted, on our knees during a rocket attack. Those things I remember very clearly.

But you remember crazy things like the movies that you

could go to if you had some off-time. And of course they
never had them in order—the third reel they'd have on first,
and then they'd have the first reel and then the second
reel—well, nothing ever was together, but you sat there
and watched it. And during times when we were being hit
a lot, we'd have to wear our flak jackets. I remember once,
this Special Forces fellow asked me to go up to the movies
with him. I had on my dress and my sandals and my flak
jacket and my helmet. And I had just gotten a care package
that day and it had Cracker Jacks in it, so here we are,
going to the movies . . .

Then one night he asked me and another girl if we
wanted to go on a jeep ride. So we said, "Well, that sounds
like fun." I had on an orange outfit, and it's night, and
we're out there in the middle of God knows where. When
I think of it now, we could have been killed! I mean, we
had to be crazy. But at the time it sounded like fun, so we
did it, and it was fun. We hit a mud puddle, and it came
up over the jeep, and we were mud from top to bottom,
just laughing away and not even thinking about where we
were and what was out there. We could very possibly not
have gotten back alive.

I stayed in surgery the whole year—that's where they
put you, that's where you stay; I had no choice. In fact,
that's where I met my first husband. He was a corpsman,
an OR tech. He was stationed at Fort Belvoir afterward,
and I was stationed at Walter Reed. I got out of the service
in October, and in November we were married. He was
still in the service until that following June. He had four
years of pre-med in and thought he was going to go on to
become a physician. However, he changed his mind while
he was at Fort Belvoir when he heard about the physician's
assistant program at Marshfield Clinic in Wisconsin. It was
an on the job training type of situation. So after he got out
of the service we made our first move to Marshfield. And
guess what I got to do in the hospital there? The only
position open was surgery! It just kind of follows me. I
worked there until my first daughter, Michelle, was born.
Then we moved from Marshfield to Appleton. I needed to
get a job; my husband had quit his. He came home one

day and said, "I quit. We're moving to Appleton," just like that. The personnel person asked what I wanted to do and, looking at my career background, said they had an opening in surgery. I didn't want to go back in surgery again. I asked what else was available, and she went through the list, but nothing sounded like anything I really wanted to do. And she said, "Oh well, we have an opening in the nursery, but I suppose you're not interested in that." I said, "Well, I don't have any previous training in this." She said, "That's all right. We'll train you." So that's how I got in OB, and that's how I spent most of the rest of my nursing career. And then one day my husband said we were going to move to California. His family is out there. He had other motives, but I didn't realize what they were at the time.

We bought a house in Costa Mesa. I went to work at Hoag Memorial Presbyterian Hospital at Newport Beach in the nursery and the postpartum floor. I decided that I wanted to go back and get my degree, because Mount Sinai was a three-year diploma school. It was beginning to look like if you didn't have a BS degree, you weren't going to have a job. I happened to be reading the newspaper, and there was a little ad in there saying that there was a program at Pacific Christian College, and it was a BS degree in management that was designed for nurses, so that you could go into management in a hospital. I worked nights at the hospital, then came home and got my daughter to school. I quickly lay down and got two and three-quarters hours of sleep, and then I had to go and get her. Then I studied in the afternoon, went to school from six to ten, and then I was back at work. I ended up getting straight As, and now I'm going, "How did I ever do that?" I ended up getting my BS degree in nursing in management, which came in handy a little bit later.

Then my husband informed me that he wanted a divorce, so I now needed a full-time job. I went to work at Santa Ana—Tustin Community Hospital in the Alternative Birth Center as a homevisit nurse. I loved that; it was the only job I ever had where I felt guilty getting my paycheck. But that just lasted the summer, because I had a lot of problems with my ex-husband and, for Michelle's sake, decided to move back to Wisconsin.

I came back and for the first time in my life when I walked into a hospital I was unable to get a job. They weren't hiring at the time, and after a couple of months, when I was down to my last pennies, I did get a job as supervisor of the obstetrical unit at a local hospital, which I enjoyed, and I was in that position until June 28 of 1980, when I had my second daughter, Kristy. (I married Ken Kohl in September 1979 and gained a stepdaughter, Tracy.) The hospital wanted me to become an assistant vice-president and take on pediatrics as well as the OB department, but I felt that with a new baby it was just too much responsibility—I was already spending long hours at the job I had. So I told them I had to turn it down, and after my leave I wanted to come back just as a staff nurse part-time. When I came back, they informed me that nothing was open, so I extended my leave, and after that leave they informed me nothing was open yet. I knew a gal who knew the supervisor in surgery, and she said that they needed some people in recovery room. It would be a relief/on-call position, and I wouldn't be able to get benefits or anything, but it would get my foot in the door. So for a year I worked in the recovery room as a relief/on-call nurse.

That fall I learned that I had post-traumatic stress disorder, and I started counseling for it. And my supervisors knew about it. My head nurse and some of the staff knew also. This was in the fall of 1981. . . . Well, there were things ever since I got back from Vietnam. It started in the first year—just little things that I couldn't put my finger on, depressions and things. My personality changed drastically. I thought maybe it was because of my marriage; it was not the best. At the time my husband was in active PTSD—within the first year that we were married. The first six months were fine, and then it was downhill after that. He was active; maybe that's why mine was more subdued, because his was really out in the open, with the rage and the depressions—it was to the point where he was talking suicide. So one of us had to keep control, I guess. At first I thought I had postpartum blues after I had my baby,

Michelle. But I knew it couldn't be postpartum blues when it went into weeks, months, years. After a while, I really thought I was going crazy and started having thoughts of suicide myself. But I was sitting at work one night, and I don't remember what magazine I picked up, but there was an article on PTSD. At the end of the article was a list of signs and symptoms. The lightbulb goes on: "Oh, my God, that's it! I'm not going crazy; I have this dumb PTSD business." At the same time I saw a program on television about PTSD. There was a phone number to call—it was a hotline in our area—so I called and was directed to the Fox Valley Vietnam Veterans Association. They had a rap group, and I started going to it.

I continued working in the recovery room. I had problems when we had critical patients. It wasn't while taking care of the patient—although I preferred not to, because it just put me right back in Vietnam—but later on, when I was home. If I had a real critical patient with the tubes, maybe on the respirator and things, then it really bothered me later, and I'd have nightmares that night.

In September of 1982, we were told we were no longer going to be under surgery. We were going to have a new supervisor and would have to work in ICU as well. There were seven of us on staff. Two quit right away, and out of the five that were left, the head nurse was the only one who said she'd stay; the other four of us actively started looking for another job. My former supervisor had said that she would talk to this new supervisor about my PTSD. It became apparent to me that she never did.

The day after Thanksgiving I was called in early; she said she wanted to talk to me. In the beginning of November I was due for an evaluation, and when I asked my head nurse about it she said, "Well, I'm working on it. You know, with all these changes I'm behind." So I never got my evaluation. I went to this meeting, and she hands me an evaluation that was terrible. At the bottom it says, "We consider you incompetent, a safety hazard to your patients, and you are terminated as of this minute." So I've been unemployed since November of 1982. I've not been able to get a job in or out of nursing because of that evaluation.

It's interesting, because in order to terminate a person, you're supposed to have three pink slips—they're like warnings—and I've never had a warning; I've never had a reprimand for anything. I've had no complaints from staff, doctors, patients; I had nothing but good evaluations in my record, but once I talked to her about the PTSD I'm suddenly incompetent. Although I've even done surgery myself, I'm suddenly a safety hazard to my patients . . . end of nursing career!

Well, I was not in a real good position emotionally, and that kind of put the frosting on the cake. I was having a very difficult time and—at the height of the PTSD I would say—so I did decide to apply at the Tomah, Wisconsin, VA Medical Center to go through the Post-Traumatic Stress Unit. It's an in-patient, open-ended program. There are less than a dozen of them in the country. I caused quite an uproar because they had never had any females, and when I applied and met the criteria, they had to take me. I understand that I caused a lot of havoc with things like, Where do you take a shower? Where do you sleep? They had just one big room that the fellows slept in. Well, they decided that they had to find something else, so there was a storeroom that they cleared out. It was right there next to the fellows. First of all, they were going to put me on the women's ward—it's mainly dependents, and it's a locked ward—but the fellows complained. They said, "Hey, she doesn't belong there; she belongs here," because a lot of the therapy is rapping with each other. That is a great part of the therapy, especially at night if you can't sleep—you sit there and talk to either the staff or the fellows. So that's when they found the storeroom and set up a bed in there. The fellows had it all worked out; they were going to stand guard over the shower. But the nurses had a locker room downstairs, and there was a shower in there, so they would give me the key and everything worked out fine.

They had had the gamut of fellows. No matter where they worked and what their job was over there, they knew how to treat them, but they never had worked with anyone who had been in a hospital setting or a female, so they weren't real sure what to do with me. It seems with the

fellows there was always one or two specific things that
they could pull out that was really bothering them, but with
me it was different. They wanted me to pull out one or two
main things, and it was so difficult. In fact, I don't really
think I did. . . . There were a couple things that I mentioned that I had nightmares about, but for me, Vietnam
was just a continuous flow of bodies, one after the other
from the day you got there until the day you left. I was
there for about six weeks. I got the most that I could out
of the program, but unfortunately I didn't have anybody
there who had a similar experience, so even though it was
good, it's still not quite finished as far as I'm concerned.

My first husband and I were both in Pleiku. On June 7,
1972, my first daughter, Michelle, was born. When she
was born, she had an eye defect. Most people don't notice
it, but I know it's there. She had severe stomachaches ever
since she was born, even though I was nursing her. As she
got older, she'd have headaches and always the stomach
problems. I had testing done; they never found anything
that they could put their finger on. When she was five, I
believe, I finally got so angry I said to the doctor, "Look,
I want some exams done. I want some answers; this is just
not normal." He accused me of being an overanxious
mother. I said, "Either you run some tests or I'm going to
get another doctor." So just to appease me, he thought
he'd run some blood work. Well, he called at home and
said, "Wow, her blood work is really off. It's almost like
rheumatic fever, but there's some things that are not quite
right. I'm going to call it a subclinical rheumatic fever."
He treated her for rheumatic fever. When we moved back
to Wisconsin and I went to a pediatrician there, he looked
at the lab work and said, "My gosh, something is definitely off here." He said she didn't have rheumatic fever—
there's no such thing as subclinical; you've either got it or
you don't. And she's got all these skin rashes, problems
with her knees, pains, a lot of pains. I've got a lot of things
too, Agent Orange signs and symptoms, but she has more,
many more than I do. Of course, I just feel like she got
double dose, because both her father and I were over there.
As far as the pains and things, "Well, it's growing pains."

They always had an answer. I'd say to them, "Do you know anything about Agent Orange?" "Uhh! Agent Orange, of course not. I don't know anything about that nor do I want to. It's not that; don't worry about it. That's a government problem." Of course if you go to the VA they say, "Well, we do our Agent Orange studies, and that's all we do. We don't handle children or anything like that."

Over the years it's gotten progressively worse. She had 20/20 vision until two years ago. She went from 20/20 to 20/40 in one eye, so I took her in and he said, "Well, watch it for a year, bring her back, and eventually she'll probably have to have glasses." That summer we were on vacation, and we'd be saying "Oh, look at that and look at this" while we'd be driving along, and she couldn't see it and she was really getting upset. We thought she just didn't look fast enough. So when we got back I said to Ken, "I'm not going to wait till school starts. Let's take her in now." I took her in, and he put up the biggest sheet that they have with those big letters and asked her what they were, and she says, "I can't see it." Well, he got really mad at her, and he said, "Look, I'm too busy for this. Don't play games. I know you can see that; you were 20/40 and 20/20 less than a year ago." Well, I know my daughter, and I knew from the way she was acting, she wasn't playing games. And she was really getting upset because he was telling her she was lying. She said, "Honest, I cannot see that. I don't know what it is." Well, he did the exam and he apologized; she was 20/200 in both eyes. He said he had never seen such rapid deterioration. She was nine. Now she is up to 20/350 and 20/375.

It's always so many things. At age ten, last summer, she came to me one day and she said, "Mom, I can't feel my hands or my feet." So she's got the numbing of the extremities already—now, these are advanced signs. She's had two knee surgeries. The doctor is baffled because he thought, when he went to do the first surgery, that with the signs and symptoms she was exhibiting, she had what they called plica buildup. Well, when he went in there she had some, but not enough for the signs and symptoms. After that surgery she went to school and she was injured, a direct hit with a soccer ball, and she started having trouble all over again. And then the dog ran across with the chain and pulled her legs out from under her, and she went smack-dab on the cement. So we went back in, and she had this band of something like scar tissue, but it wasn't scar tissue. He removed that, then he said, "It's two times in. Everything should be fine." Well, I had her back again this summer because she was telling me that it felt the same again, and now it's both knees, and he said, "I've never had to take anyone back three times. I'm not going to operate right now." And I'm glad, because I was going to tell him no more surgery because that would be three surgeries in less than a year, and with that amount of anesthesia on a young child—I was not going to let him do it. He said, "She's just going to have to suffer with the pain for now until we can go further." She has all these things at age eleven and I've got to think what she's going to be like at age fifteen or twenty and what the future holds for her. So I get very upset when people tell me there is no such thing as Agent Orange, it doesn't exist, it's all in your head . . .

You don't think about yourself—you're used to the aches and pains and things—but when your child is suffering, then you get very angry, especially when nothing's being done. She's had x-rays, she's had tests, and they can't ever find anything that they can put their finger on, and yet things are not normal. It just makes you angry when you see her suffering, an eleven-year-old suffering so much, and there's nothing you can do. . . . She's said to me, "Can't you do something, Mom?" What do you do? What do you say? "No, I can't. I don't know what to do."

Maureen Walsh

U.S. NAVAL SUPPORT
ACTIVITY HOSPITAL,
DA NANG—AUG. '68 TO SEPT. '69

Maureen lives in Annapolis, Maryland. She is a nurse practitioner of traditional acupuncture in private practice there. Since leaving the Navy in 1974, she has completed a BS degree in nursing; attended the Oriental Medical College of England, College for Traditional Chinese Acupuncture, where she earned two degrees; and received a master's degree in pastoral psychological counseling, in 1981. She is currently enrolled in the master of social work program at the University of Maryland, "in the hopes of some day influencing public policy in health care as regards transcultural medicine availability in the U.S."

I N AUGUST OF 1966 I TOOK MY OATH IN THE NEW
Federal Building in downtown Boston. After women's officer school, I went to Quonset Point, Rhode Island, to the
naval air station there and spent two years, which was a
varied experience, being around the planes and the ships
as well as the naval station hospital. I had a lot of experience flying in the planes and went through the low pressure
chambers so I could fly in jets. I got to spend a lot of time
on the ships, especially the carriers. I was head nurse in
the dependents' units and also the emergency room there,
and then, because we were near Groton, Connecticut, got
involved with submarine medicine as well.

At that point I was rather addicted to military nursing,
and of course, the social life wasn't any small part of it as
well. Vietnam was starting to become prominent in the
military picture, and I decided that I would volunteer to go
over, much to my mother's dismay. My chief nurse dis-
couraged me. She said, "You know, you're very young.
They're only taking people who are very experienced, and
you shouldn't go near Vietnam unless you've had a lot of
experience." I decided after I got to Vietnam that there

was nothing in the United States that could ever prepare me for that, absolutely nothing. But I was adventuresome, and I decided, what the heck, might as well go. So, I entreated the chief nurse to endorse my request. She did, and said, ''I do it with a lot of reservation. I know that you can do the work, but I really worry about your lack of experience.'' Sure enough, three months later, I received orders. She was more surprised than anybody, but I wasn't; I said I knew I'd be going anyway, because that was my intent. Ever since I was a little kid I wanted to be a Navy nurse and be stationed at the naval academy—of course, I had all of this glamour idea. The other thing, I wanted to be in a war zone or someplace where I could really experience my skills, et cetera. . . .

Well, that bubble burst after I got over there. It was September of '68. The memory is very vivid. I remember coming in to the airport at Da Nang, and it was raining of course—we were coming into the monsoon season. We got off the plane and really went through a culture shock. Everybody had guns; people were lining up; there were people in the airport sleeping all over the place. There was nothing but artillery from one end of the airport to the next. There were a lot of Vietnamese people walking around very, very depressed-looking. Off in the distance we could hear the guns exploding, and I thought to myself, ''My God, this is like a John Wayne movie.'' You could actually see the explosions going off in the hills. But the eerie thing about it was, people were walking around like automatons. The explosions were going on, but nobody was paying any attention. Every time something would explode, I could just feel my heart skip a beat; it was both exciting and very frightening.

We unloaded at what seemed to be an old courthouse. It was dusty but it was the only place where the inside was dry. We sat down to write out the endless papers that you have to fill out when you go from one place to another in the military. As the explosions were going on, the desks or the tables that we were writing on would raise up off the floor. And the guy who was talking to us was talking nonstop like this was just ordinary traffic going by outside.

Anyway, we got to our quarters, which was in the east end of Da Nang, right along the South China Sea. It was a beautiful place, paradoxically, very beautiful and very hostile at the same time. We were right off the beach, where Seabees were on one end of the compound and the Marine engineers on the other. Across the street there were helicopters and the Marine airfield, and then beyond that was the beach. Marble Mountain was to the left as we were looking out to sea and to the right was Monkey Mountain. Behind us there was a Vietnamese village, and probably about ten miles out there was another mountain range, Hivan Pass. The hospital was made up of Quonset huts. It was the largest combat casualty unit in the world at the time. I don't remember how many personnel were there. There were hundreds; it was like a little city in itself. We lived in a Quonset hut and, according to the standards of Vietnam, lived rather luxuriously. I mean, we had our own toilets—we even had a washing machine! We each had an individual room with the metal military beds and a desk, but at least we had privacy. The Marines and Seabees had made a patio out in the back with a fence surrounding it. We would often pull up a chair, grab a beer, and watch the war as we could see it going on in the mountains north and south of us. Our chief nurse let us rest for about twenty-four hours to go through the jet lag, and then we were hustled onto the wards.

Each unit, which was one Quonset hut, had five corpsmen, with about thirty to sixty patients. And each of the huts would be divided into orthopedics, surgery, medicine, intensive care, or whatever. There were several of these huts lined up, and each had a walkway entrance to it so we could get from one to the next. The walkways had bunkers along them. The Navy nurses, because we had so many corpsmen in each ward, would be responsible for like three hundred to three hundred fifty patients, and what we'd have to do is go from one building to the next, get the report from the corpsmen, and take care of the sickest patients.

The first two nights I was there we didn't have any incoming or anything, though we could hear it in the peripheral areas. But my introduction to Vietnam nursing was on the third night as I was walking outside, going from one building to the next, checking the patients—and I was feeling overwhelmed as it was. From the mountains behind us, the Viet Cong were sending in mortars and rockets, and I heard this tremendous roar go over my head. I never heard a rocket in my life. I didn't know whether it was a plane, or a helicopter—I couldn't imagine what it was. Phew! This red, flaming thing came flying over, and I thought, "Oh, my God, that thing's from outer space." Well, when I heard that whoosh I went into one of the bunkers, and I know that I did not reach the bottom, because I felt all this stuff crawling around down there. I think I hit bottom and bounced right back out. I knew they were rats; they had to be rats! I said to myself, "Dear God, am I going to get bit by a rat and have to go home, or am I going to get hit by the shrapnel up here?" I decided it would be more honorable to be hit by the shrapnel, such a choice! So I just kind of buried into the sidewalk, and as I was kissing the concrete I looked up to watch all of this action. As I turned my head to the right—we were sort of on a hill on a sand dune—I could see the Marine base receiving rockets. As they went in I could see the planes explode. Oh, my God, this was like a movie! I couldn't conceive that I was really there. I was a participant, but I still didn't feel like I was going to get hit, because I really wasn't there; it was total denial.

Finally, everything stopped and I didn't know whether to get up. Navy nurses wore white uniforms over there, and we were walking targets. The Vietnamese village—we called it "the vill"—the Viet Cong vill was right behind us. Often times our people would take sniper fire at night. I didn't know about the sniper fire—that came a few days later—but I took my white hat off. If I had had something to put around me I would've, because I knew instinctively I was a sitting duck out there. So I just got up and said, "Well, I guess I'm in Vietnam, and I've got to do the best

I can,'' looked down to make sure I hadn't wet my pants, went on to the next building, and walked into the ward. Some of my corpsmen had been there six or seven months, and this was a routine night to them. I must've looked as white as my uniform, and they started laughing as I came into the unit. They started teasing me about getting into a little action already. I could've clobbered them. So I guess I got my initiation; that was it. I was frightened as hell, and I was excited, yet on the other hand, if I let the emotions run away with me, I would've been totally incapacitated.

As it was, I was fighting inexperience; my former chief nurse was right. I was really flying by the seat of my pants as far as going into these units and checking the patients. To make up for my inexperience, I'd read the chart, check all the IVs, dressings, and casts several times for each patient. Each person had enough "plumbing" to make the average plumber marvel. I mean, there were machines on every person—suction, respirators, monitors of all sorts—everybody had multiple intravenous fluids infusing, catheters, and all sorts of sundry tubes and drains. By the time you weed through that to find the poor individual under it all, you couldn't really make him out. It was incredible!

I really had to stifle the emotions in order to be able to focus in on what was happening to each and every one of those patients and to keep all of that data in mind, write everything down, as well as talk to all of the corpsmen. I didn't even know all of the corpsmen at that point; I didn't know all of the patients. I would hope and pray every time I would leave a unit to go to the next one that I wouldn't find so much devastation, because already I was overwhelmed from the other wards. But I found similar situations on every ward. I think I had five wards that were my responsibility. And that's what we did when we worked the night shift. I had so much responsibility and so much to do on each of the units that I couldn't worry about the extraneous goings on outside.

Nights were especially difficult because this was the time when people who were wounded would be very frightened—moaning and groaning and calling out. Marines were incredibly stoic. It was surprising that they didn't cry out more than they did. There were a lot of times when they died on us at night. I mean, I would go from one unit to the next and have three, four, five Marines die maybe in the period of one night. Some of them in my arms. I'd be holding them, and they'd be hanging on—"Oh, I don't want to die!" You have to say, "Well, God, I can't get involved, I can't get involved," but it's pretty damn hard not getting involved when you see a nineteen- or twenty-year-old blond kid from the Midwest or California or the East Coast screaming and dying. A piece of my heart would go with each! You knew that their families would be getting a visit from the Marine Corps two days later. It was all I could do to hold back the tears, and we did hold back a lot, which I think was very unhealthy. It started very early; we had no way to really let loose with each other. One of the things we found is that we were all so extremely busy that we didn't have *time* to let loose with each other. The other aspect was that there was some sort of a feeling with nurses at the time that we were all volunteers that went over there. Since we were volunteers, we had to take what we got and not complain about it. The "shut up and do your work" mentality.

We also had to put up with the hostile environment as well. Besides the incoming, there were the rats, there were the snakes, there were the monsoons. We would often go down to a ward that was flooded from the monsoons. We were taking care of patients . . . There'd be rats in the water; sometimes there'd be snakes there. That bothered me more than anything. . . . We also took care of the Viet Cong and the NVA. This brought us down to the realities of war—there were young men there from the opposite side. They were the same age as our own fellas; most of them were even younger. They didn't want to be there any more than we did.

It took me about two days to realize that it was such a mistake being over there. We were so pumped up when we went to Vietnam, so patriotic, so full of American idealism, and when we got over there, it was nothing but a sham. The war was going on—there was no sense to it, there was no sense of "Okay, we're going into a battle. We're going to take over some of the geography; we're going to hold it, then we'll go on to the next part; we'll take over that. Then there will be peace." Our guys would go in to a hill or a village, get the hell beat out of them, and then we would receive the casualties. The next day they would be pulled out of there. Then they'd go back another week; we'd take more casualties. It was like that for the entire time we were over there. Marines were getting shot, they were getting mutilated, and there was no purpose; there was no rhyme nor reason to it.

So besides dealing with our own emotions and then dealing with that, we were in conflict between anger and grief constantly. There was just no resolution to any of that. Even when we went into town there was evidence of the Vietnamese taking advantage of us. The black markets were set up all over the place; they were milking us from every single angle that you could imagine. But we took care of *them*, we took care of them well. I remember the Viet Cong were like jungle rats, surviving in the jungles. Their skin was scarred like leather. They were very unsocialized. The average twenty-year-old looked like he was forty, fifty, sixty years old. Some of them I became quite attached to. The NVA were more educated, and a lot of their officers were very fluent in English; some of them had studied in the States. God, they didn't want to be there any more than we did. What we found was that the women, the NVA and VC women, were very, very vicious in behavior. I remember one night I brought a dinner tray to one of them, and she was on a bed with two casts on her legs, having had abdominal and eye surgery and all of the usual plumbing. I gave the woman a tray and turned around to get a sheet, and she had picked up a fork and was going right into my back. I just turned around in time and knocked it out of her hand. That was typical of the female behavior—they never gave up; they tenaciously fought to escape.

I want to talk about the intensive care unit. The other units were nothing compared with what the intensive care units were like. Many times when we were on duty and there were a lot of casualties coming in, the doctors would necessarily be taken to the triage area. That left the nurses and the corpsmen to do the best we could on the units. We couldn't call the doctors to do some of the things that were physician-related. For instance, patients would pop bleeders on the ward; they would start bleeding under their dressings. What we would have to do is make decisions about . . . We'd have to go in and clamp off bleeders. And it was rather a touchy situation because, you know, it looks pretty clear when you're in the laboratory or the operating room, but if you're not a surgeon, it's pretty hard to tell one artery from a ureter. It was anxiety-producing, to say the least.

Several times when we would have incoming, the mortars would blow out our regular and emergency generators. Of about twenty patients in the ICU, there were usually ten to fifteen on respirators, with chest tubes, and when the electricity went off, you can just imagine what chaos ensued. We often had to do mouth-to-mouth or trach-to-trach breathing for these people until the emergency power came on. We would have a few ambubags. We'd be throwing them around like footballs from one end of the unit to the other. So we lost people that way too. It was so frustrating, and a lot of times we'd have to give up breathing because we were so exhausted we would have passed out. That happened four or five times when I was on duty.

One night I was walking through one of the units that was right off the helicopter pad, when a mortar came in and exploded. Shrapnel came in the door—went right by me, under my legs. Another piece came in as I was counting narcotics for one of the corpsmen at the medicine cabinet near the door. The shrapnel went through his eye and through his head, went through the medicine cabinet, exited through the unit on the other side, and lodged in the wall. God, that was awful, that was awful to see that.

Another night that we had some incoming, we were walking along the walkway and I saw one of the mortars hit smack-dead on one of our units; it exploded. There was not a lot of screaming and yelling, but mostly what really hit me was the stench, the burning flesh. The Marines never screamed, which is incredible, their training is incredible. I remember going into the ward. The lights were all out, so I couldn't see a thing, but we knew there was a lot of activity. I'm not so sure I would've been prepared to see immediately what was happening. I had a flashlight with me . . . opened the flashlight and there was just chunks of flesh and blood all over the wall. Wounded men had been wounded again in the unit. Four of our corpsmen were killed that night. One of our nurses that was out going from one unit to another got down just in time. The way the shrapnel came it would've decapitated her had she not been down. I don't know how any of our nurses missed getting hit—by some miracle.

There were times when, as I say, the doctors weren't immediately available, and we had to make major life-saving decisions. One night, as a typical example, I was on a neurosurgery unit. We had a lot of casualties, and the doctors were all tied up in triage. I had a young man that was put on the unit, and the doctor said, "You've got to do the best you can with him." As soon as the doctor left, he went into respiratory distress, and I had to do a tracheostomy on him, and God, there was no equipment on the unit to do something like that—most of our patients went to the operating room to have something like that done. I just had to put a slit in his throat, and all I had was a ball-point pen; I had to unscrew that and put the tube of the pen into the trachea, which is a common thing actually—it's the only thing you had on you. There were a lot of those kinds of things going on that we had to do, things that we were never taught.

I'll never forget this one night. I was sitting next to this bed, and a young corpsman came in . . . and I looked at his name, of course. I had known him in the States. He was one of the fellows that was at the naval air station with me, but when I had seen him, I didn't recognize him because his wounds were so severe and numerous. There's no way you can save somebody like that, but the most incredible thing is that he was clear—he was talking with me; he knew who I was. I was holding the one hand that he had left, and as I was talking with him, he said, "I know I'm not going to live." . . . I remember him telling me to contact his mother, and he was telling me how much he enjoyed our friendship, and he said, "Please don't leave me." This young man was losing blood at a tremendously quick rate, and what amazed me is that he was still so clear. He grabbed my hand and I talked to him for as long as possible, and I just felt that grip loosening and loosening and loosening. The only thing I could do was sit there and pray with him. I knew he was going to leave this holocaust; he was lucky. I just told him good-bye.

Many times I'd have fellows that would come in the ward—especially the Navy corpsmen, some of whom I had trained—and some of them had been stationed with me at the units back at Quonset Point. That was horrible, seeing those men come in wounded. They were just like brothers to us, because the Navy nurses and the Navy corpsmen and the Corps WAVES had a very close bond. We worked very very closely and went through a great deal together. You knew their families, where they came from—you knew everything about them. And to see them come in—they were just like having your own family, own brothers, get killed. Those are some of the memories in the intensive care unit.

It sounds like there was a lot of gore over there, but there were good times as well, in between. We used to have lulls in the war. When we had time, we played. When we were not too tired we used to go over to the officers' club. Once in a while, in the one day we had off a week— if we did have the day off—we would go over on the beach.

We did a lot of things, also, in the community. I volunteered to go on the civil action patrols. We went out a number of times with some of the corpsmen, Marines and physicians that used to volunteer to go into the villages to see patients. And my eyes were opened out there too— people living in these slovenly, dirty huts—dirt floors— with the chickens and the ducks. We'd go in there and deliver babies in the filth and the crap. We went to the orphanages, played with the kids, and took them to the beaches every now and then.

Some of us got in to town; it was more or less off limits—you know, we had to deal with the sniper fire and everything else. Most of the time we didn't tell the chief nurse we were going in. I had a friend who was a Korean; he would pick me up on his motorcycle, and we would go to the different restaurants downtown. It was a dead giveaway that I had been there, because of all the garlic and kim chee and everything else that they used—it was awful-smelling.

The saddest thing that happened for me over there too, among all those other things, was I lost my fiancé. He was a Marine pilot, and I was with him the night that he died; he was going on a mission. I was sitting in the officers' club, and I knew he wasn't coming back. I practically begged him not to go, but there's no way he couldn't go. It was his job; he had to go. And he was shot down. The worst thing was that I was not allowed to grieve for the whole time that I was there. . . . I don't know if any of the other nurses really knew about it. I told them, but it was just one of those things that you didn't—you couldn't share because everybody else had their own little world of grief. Quite frankly, each of my friends, each of the nurses out there, was just totally saturated with their problems, with their own fatigue. . . . And again, the stiff upper lip-type martyr syndrome of nursing didn't allow for that to happen. I think I was more able to talk to the other Navy and Marine friends that I had out there. We had quite a relationship with the Marines that were around us; they were always in our club or took us out. They were more or less our confidants. I think my Marine friends knew more about me than the people that I actually worked with. They used to pick us up with their jeeps. I remember going out on a date with somebody riding shotgun . . . rather a lot of fun. I'll never forget, one night I was going out to the officers' club with one of my friends, and it was kind of a strange sensation having somebody go on a date with a .45 around his waist and a rifle on the dash of the jeep. We went through this village and somebody took a potshot at us, and I remember the bullet coming in and over my head and behind his and out through the other end of the jeep. The attitude that we had: we looked at each other and laughed. What else could you do?

Well, what I can say is, I did come back from the holocaust, from that horrific experience over there, with a very peaceful philosophy, a very changed value system about life and death. We came into California—when I saw that Golden Gate Bridge I wanted to reach down and hug it. And by God, when we got to Travis Air Force Base I got down on the ground and kissed it. I remember having to stop there overnight and going to this swimming pool where all the officers' wives and everybody were chitchatting about the day's events. I thought to myself, "My God, I have been in hell. These women are sitting around talking, and they have no concept of what is going on over there." I was extremely depressed. But I knew I was coming home the next day. I was met in Boston by my folks. It was great to see them. I had requested to come to Annapolis to fulfill my dream, but it was for a different reason this time—it was to come back here for peace and quiet. I didn't want to go back to one of these huge hospitals. I didn't want to see any more carnage. There's nothing more pastoral and more quiet and soothing than this water around here.

I had injured my back when I was about three weeks away from coming home. I didn't tell anybody. What had happened is that the rockets came in and I belly flopped on the floor and really tore up the back. It gave me a lot of trouble when I came here to the States, shortly after I started working on the units. The horrible part about it was that I had a lot of pain and problems that I was going through, and I couldn't get anybody to believe me. You know, they were essentially saying, "Well, you're just a baby" or "It's all in your head." For about three years I went through all this pain. I had gotten orders from Annapolis to Bethesda Naval Hospital, and I finally went through surgery. They found a lot of damage in the back, so at least that vindicated me, but still I decided right then and there I was going to get out of the service.

I really didn't know what I wanted to do. I had reached the epitome of what it was to be a nurse. There was nothing I could possibly do in the United States that would equal that experience. My fellow nurses that had been over there, incredibly, never asked me what I went through. We went through an ignominious kind of a situation where, a couple times in Annapolis and in Bethesda, I did some things on the units that were not considered nursing responsibilities—but out of reaction, you know, gut-level reactions—and got chastised for it. There was no level of understanding that maybe I knew what I was doing, maybe it was okay for me to do what I was doing even though it wasn't accepted protocol. It was clear to me that I could never go back to being the kind of nurse I was before I left for Vietnam.

When I had my back surgery, I was temporarily retired from the service, and I went back to school at the University of Maryland to get my degree in nursing. It just so happened that one of my professors had had acupuncture, and she had suggested that I go through it, because even after surgery, I still had a lot of pain. The Navy kind of wrote me off and said, "You know, its a degenerative process. It's just going to get worse. You have a choice— you can retire; we'll separate you from the service—you have a choice." I accepted the fact that I wanted to be separated from the service, because I couldn't see a future in the Navy anymore. Somehow all the, as I call it, "poop and circumstance" didn't mean anything anymore. It was a lot of . . . bullshit as far as I was concerned.

I started having the acupuncture treatments, and pretty soon things started coming together for me—and things started unraveling at the same time. A lot of the old stuff had started coming back—from the war zone, you know, as it often does. Things clear out when you start taking a natural therapy such as that. I was getting better and better, and finally I realized that, "Hey, I went through my hell, went through my training and education; all of the experiences were for me to do something like this." I went back to school to study acupuncture. I went to England to study at the College for Traditional Acupuncture in Oxford. Then I came back and did some clinical work in acupuncture and decided that I needed to deal with the spiritual role in healing as well. I went to Loyola College and got my master's degree in pastoral psych counseling to add to my bachelor's degree in nursing and the degrees I was getting in England for acupuncture.

I am now in my own private practice—doing nursing as well, but the kind of nursing that I know and feel ought to be done. I'm doing acupuncture and I'm doing counseling. I have one patient now who is a World War II veteran. He's gone through a lot of hell; he was a Navy man on a ship and had seen a lot of killing and wounding around him. This man is in his sixties, and he was still having these horrible, horrible dreams about the war. I sat down with him and listened to him and said, "Look, I know where you are; I know what you're feeling. I've been there." He looks at me as if saying, "I can't believe this is a woman who understands." Since he started treatments, he hasn't had any more of those dreams—after thirty, forty years. But it's because of my own feelings of where I need to deal with him—the holocaust he has been through—I can put myself in that position.

It really hurts every Veterans Day, when I see the Vietnam veterans rising up and getting so upset about not getting benefits and so forth. It starts opening wounds. You never forget what you've gone through. When the prisoners from Iran came back, I was shattered. It seems every time I get to a point where things have healed, or I think they have healed, something comes up in the news, and all the wounds start opening like Pandora's box. My question is, when is it all going to end? How much do you keep? I don't think you ever get rid of it. From all experiences, one can either become shattered or take the experience and incorporate it, learn from it, and make a positive thing from it. As a nurse, I really feel for the Vietnam veteran that came back to nothing. Most of us nurses were able to come back to professions; we weren't ostracized by bosses. We were just ignored, but we weren't ostracized in the fact that we were Vietnam veterans and therefore second-class citizens. I don't know, I have not really talked to any of my compatriots out there—surprisingly. I don't know what they're feeling or what they've done with their lives.

I was just thinking that my formative years in nursing have all been spent in the Navy. Whatever I've learned and gained and experienced, whether good, bad, or indifferent, I've learned in the Navy. That's what I took out into civilian life. A lot of my philosophy and the way I deal with problems is based on what I learned in the Navy. I may get upset at little things, but major crises—I'm just right there, cool, calm, collected. The ironic part is that when I came back I was supposed to forget the skills and the responsibility that had become second nature, so ingrained in me. I don't feel any regrets; I feel like I've pulled myself up. I've gone through school, I'm doing what I want to do, and I'm using the experiences probably with a deeper understanding than I ever would have, had I not gone over there.

With each person who goes out of my office from the acupuncture treatments in harmony, if they feel more peaceful, then somehow I've vindicated the war. I guess what I'm doing vicariously through them is coming to peace, coming to terms in a creative way. I certainly haven't prolonged the agony, I haven't prolonged the war, I haven't prolonged the chaos, but in fact have chosen something that is creating harmony, and I guess that's the testimony to my life now.

Postscript:

On August 9, 1985, Maureen Walsh was severely injured in a car accident. She awoke four days later in the Shock-Trauma Unit of the University of Maryland Hospital.

The rescue helicopter concept and shock-trauma treatment saved my life. I awakened to the sounds of the ICU staff and harmony of that Unit's familiar support machinery. I was not fearful, but at peace knowing I was cared for just as we nurses cared about the patients in Da Nang. In an eerie and ironic way, my accident allowed me to come full circle and experience the fruits of the seeds planted in Da Nang, for I was part of the Navy ICU staff there who set up the prototype of the Shock-Trauma Unit. Now I see that what we learned in Vietnam is being fully applied here. It is a legacy of the living— for more lives will be saved in peacetime than were lost in that war.

Jane Hodge

95TH EVAC. HOSPITAL,
DA NANG—JULY '69 TO JULY '70

Jane is currently director of operation and medical services for a health maintenance organization in Seattle, Washington.

I firmly believe that if we (Nam vets) don't move beyond dealing with the actual war itself and recognize that each person brought their own unique problems into the war and thus their reaction to it, and deal with those as well, there will never be recovery. Rap groups are necessary for a beginning, but they are not the whole answer. We have to move beyond them . . . I would urge anyone not to stop with rap groups but to follow up with professional counseling.

A LITTLE BIT ABOUT WHY I DECIDED TO BE A NURSE.
When I was five years old my dad was in a tuberculin
sanatorium and was admitted only after a lot of hassle because they didn't want him on their death statistics. He was
one of the first civilian patients ever to receive streptomy-
cin, so he got well in spite of them. When I would go visit
him, there was a nurse who wouldn't allow us to sit on
Daddy's bed, and every time I did she'd spank my butt
and put me down on the floor. So I decided I'd be a nurse
so I could go around and spank little kids. And although
the reasons changed during the years, the decision to be a
nurse never changed. When I was growing up I was a real
strong Baptist and really felt I had a calling to be a nurse.
So I went to school in Charlotte, North Carolina, at Memorial. I had the opportunity to enlist while I was in nursing school and the Army would pay my tuition. I'm just a
little hardheaded and decided that I didn't want to be ob-
ligated to go in the service. If I decided to do that, it would
be a free choice, not something I had to do.

I graduated from nursing school in '63 and worked in
obstetrics until '68, when I decided to go in the Army. My

dad fully expected the first letter he got to be from the brig, because if some fool came along and told me to do something and I didn't want to do it, I'd say, "I will not." And he was almost correct. I was dancing in the officers' club one night with a colonel who was married and had five kids. His hand kept wandering down toward my tush, and I told him to move it and he wouldn't. I said, "Sir, they spent the last six weeks teaching me that I'm an officer first, a nurse second, and a lady third. The officer has asked you to move your hand, the nurse has told you to move it, and the lady is about to slap the hell out of you." Which I promptly did. He threatened me with a court-martial for assaulting a senior officer, and I said, "Fine, but we won't go for a simple court-martial; it will be a general court-martial, and I'll invite your wife and kids in to see why you had your hand on my butt in the first place." He decided that he didn't want a court-martial.

I had an interesting experience when I was in basic, because I went in as a first lieutenant, so that automatically made me a platoon leader. In my platoon was a lady who had joined the Army from the Haight-Ashbury district. Why she ever joined the military, nobody ever knew. Unbelievable! She was the most nonconformist human being that ever breathed the breath of life. Everybody picked up on that, so every time we had an inspection, if her hem was off a quarter of an inch, everybody was in deep trouble. So I spent six weeks in basic, trying to keep her from getting us all thrown in the brig. On the night before we finished, we were in the officers' club, and she walked in with her pea jacket on, and it looked like she had nothing on down to her shoes. She took the pea jacket off, and she had an open-worked white lace dress on with a beige body stocking under it. I thought all the senior officers in there were going to choke and die, because it looked like she was totally naked. Everybody looked at me because I was her platoon leader. And I say, "Don't look at me! I didn't dress her, for God's sake!" The next morning I was in the office of our senior nurse who was in charge of us in basic. Royal flaming bitch is the only real word to describe her. I was in her office more than I was out on training maneuvers in basic, so we never had a strong relationship except real adversarial.

I went to Fort Ord, where I was stationed and really loved it and met a man who became real important in my life. I stayed there for eight months, I think it was. Anyway, I hurt my right leg; I had a huge hematoma in my calf, and when the hematoma was gone I had thrombophlebitis. While I was in the hospital for that, I got orders to go to the Philippines, which I did not want to do. I went through the process of trying to get out of the orders and couldn't. They said I had to go. I had a profile that I couldn't sit longer than two hours. I mean, a profile as long as my leg and still had to go. Couldn't fly, so they decided they would book my passage on an aircraft carrier, where I could walk all I wanted to. . . . They were hellbent and determined I was going to the Philippines. So, I said, "Okay, if I'm going to the Philippines, I'm going home to North Carolina to see the family before I go."

I was home for two days, when I got up and went into the bathroom, and I was coughing up blood. I looked down—my fingers were kind of blue, and I was having a little bit of difficulty breathing. There was nobody home but me and my mom, and she tends to be a little hysterical; I couldn't figure out how I was going to get to the hospital without having to put her in the ambulance before they did me. I had told them that I had to have blood drawn because of the medication I was taking, so I walked in the kitchen and said, "Mom, I need to go to the hospital to have some blood drawn." And she said, "Okay." Never really looked at me, and when she drove a car she never looked right or left. We got in the car, and by the time we got to the hospital, I was blue up to above my wrist. We pulled into the back by the emergency room, and I said, "Mother, you're going to have to go inside and tell them to come and get me." It was the first time she looked at me, and I was blue around my face and really couldn't breathe. I had thrown a pulmonary embolism from the thrombophlebitis, and I was really quite sick.

When the doctor called the Army in California to tell them that I would not be able to go to the Philippines, they accused him of lying. They would require proof that I was dying, essentially. So he, having just gotten out of the Air Force, was a little irate and gave them a few choice words. Anyway, they canceled my orders to the Philippines and restationed me at Fort Ord. I stayed in the hospital at home for—I think it was—two and a half weeks, then went to Fort Jackson for several weeks. I was the only female officer in the hospital as a patient, and they didn't have any beds for female officers, so they had to put me in the generals' suite. Then they med-evac'd me back to California.

I was on convalescent leave for four weeks and went back to work full-time on an OB ward. They came over one morning and said, "You're the only captain that we have who is not a head nurse, and the head nurse on the orthopedic ward has just been transferred. You are now going to be head nurse for orthopedics." One of our wards was solely for Nam returnees . . . so an awful lot of guys came through there were not only physically scarred but very emotionally scarred.

We had one kid who had a broken femur and was in a spika body cast. He had been a Lurp and was scared to death to lose his temper because he was afraid he'd kill somebody. He wasn't sure he could control himself enough not to kill. On that ward we rarely admitted anybody who was not a Nam returnee, so that everybody could support each other, and what have you. But because the other two wards were full and we had a bed empty, we admitted a buck private who was in basic training. He had a mouth on him that wouldn't quit, and he kept smartin' off at these guys, which didn't set too well. One morning he smarted off to the kid who was a Lurp, and I heard this horrible commotion on the ward. I went back there, and the first person I saw was the kid in the spika cast. He was over against the wall, and I didn't even see who was on the floor. For some reason I went to the guy in the cast first, and he said, "I killed him. I know I killed him." I said, "He can't be dead. He's making too much noise. Don't you hear his mouth?" I finally got him to realize that he hadn't killed the kid. I turned around and looked at the kid, and it was very apparent he had a broken jaw. I said,

"There is a sidelight to this: you won't have to hear his mouth anymore because it'll be wired shut." So we didn't bring him up on charges or anything, mainly because I think we agreed to agree that he fell down. He agreed that he would agree that he fell down, because he didn't want anything else broken. Nobody threatened him; he just knew that it was okay that he fell down.

But it was really very sad to see the guys come in, especially the ones who were physically disfigured, because you'd call their families, or they'd call their families, to tell them they were there. They tried to put them in a hospital as close to their homes as possible. I hated visiting days, especially when there were people coming for the first time. You would talk to them and try to tell them what condition their son was in, and they'd say that they understood. You'd tell them, "Okay, you have to realize that he's gonna be looking straight at your face, and no matter what you say, what is going to register in his mind is what he sees on your face, and *that* is what is important." And I've seen more guys turned into just real psychiatric cases because their family would walk in—"Oh, I'm so glad to see you"—and their faces would just be a mask of horror at what they were seeing. The poor guys would lie there and they knew. Even though their families, after a while, could accept what they looked like and what was happening to them, it never made a big difference because the first thing they had seen was total rejection. It was real hard to work with them after that because no matter what you said to them, it didn't matter. I found that to be true after I got to Nam. They would think if we, as nurses or as females, could look at them, take care of them, and handle what had happened to them, that their wives or their girlfriends or their mothers would be able to, too. And sometimes it probably turned out that way, but I saw so many times that it didn't. . . . It just broke my heart to know what I was sending them home to. . . .

I was never a real conventional Army nurse. I mean, I wanted things done, but I always believed you could get people to do things more by asking them than you could by ordering them to. That always bothered the Army, mainly because it worked. I mean, the guys on my ward and the people who worked for me would have stood on their heads and spun for three days if I'd asked them to, when they'd have told somebody else to kiss off. They knew I wouldn't ask them to do anything that I wouldn't do myself, and they knew I very rarely gave an order, but when I asked them to do something, that's what I meant. The Army was always bothered by that, and they were bothered by the fact that my ward was run every day just like it was when the IG was coming. I always figured that if you did it right every day, you didn't have to worry about inspections. So when they'd announce inspection and I didn't get all bent out of shape, that upset them. Then it would upset them even more when the IG would come and my ward would pass with flying colors, because of the staff's attitude. They never understood that if you just did it every day, you didn't have to worry about it. Needless to say I was not high on their list of people for career school.

It was real strange, the person that I was dating was career military, and I drove him crazy too. One day I went by the PX, and I had on my white uniform, and I had not put on the stupid cap that you have to wear. The main reason I never wore it was because of what everybody called it. So I was coming out of the PX with no hat on, and he and his first sergeant were coming in. Well, he was a major, so I saluted him. But then he stopped me, pulled me to a point of attention, chewed my ass out from one end to the other because I was not in uniform. I stood there trying real hard not to say "You just go to hell." His sergeant was with him, and I knew that was part of the reason he was doing it, but it still didn't make me any happier. When he came home for supper that night, he said, "You know what the sergeant said to me after you left? He said, 'You really mean you're going home and eat her cooking today? If that was my wife, she'd poison me.' " I said, "No. I'm not cooking. After all, I'm not in uniform. . . . You can cook."

He got orders to go to Nam, and I decided I was not gonna sit back here and wait to be notified that he was hurt or dead. So I requested orders for Nam and thought full well that they'd be denied because of the medical profile that was in my records. So, with a little creativity they gave me orders.

We were required to fly over in our class A uniforms; nobody issued females fatigues before we went. And, of course, you fly twenty-something hours in this plane. And those silly little high-heeled shoes they made you wear— when we arrived you couldn't find the shoes, our feet were swelling so bad. Nobody dared take their shoes off, because we'd never have gotten them back on. We got into the replacement place, and I got orders to go up to the 95th Evac at Da Nang, and that was in July of '69. Then we went down to get issued our fatigues, and I wear a size 8½ women's shoe, which I think is equivalent to a 7 men's boot. The only boots they had were size 9½ men's. So that's what we got. I could put five pairs of socks on and you still wouldn't have been able to keep the damn boots on, but at least when the feet swelled, you had room for them.

Then we had to get it all together and get out to the airport, and flying up to the 95th was my first experience flying in a cargo plane with goats and geese and chickens and Vietnamese and everything else. And ducks get airsick. Chickens get airsick. But they don't vomit. So, needless to say, the aroma was not good. We arrived at the 95th, and I was assigned to a five-by-eight room that had nothing in it but a metal cot and half a closet. And it was hotter than livin' hell. I mean, I've never been that hot ever in my life, and I'm from the South, where it gets hot with humidity.

They told me I'd be working nights on a med-surg unit to start with. I started orienting on the surgical unit, which consisted of eighty-five beds. After I'd been orienting about four days, they informed me, because I was a senior captain, that I was to be night supervisor of the whole hospital. I said, "Glory to the world! I mean, I'm not a military person, folks. I don't think you really want me to be this." And they said, "Too bad. That's what you are gonna be. You'll just have to learn to be military"

I had been having a nightmare for about three weeks before I went to Nam and had had it a couple of times after I got there—that I was working triage and my friend came in on one of the litters. On my first night orienting as night supervisor I walked into the receiving unit and we had casualties coming in. They knew I'd never been in the receiving unit, and I said, "What can I do to help?" and they said to set up IVs and this, that, and the other. I started pulling IVs off the shelf just like I knew where I was, and it was just exactly like it was in my dream. . . . So when we finished that night, I told somebody about my dream, and as a result, when we had casualties coming in from where he was stationed, they'd never let me triage, which I really appreciated. But I knew, I knew as well as I knew my name, that sometime during that year he was coming into that ER. He did not, however, which was fine with me. After I came home, he was missing in action for six weeks before he was found, but he was never wounded.

I oriented as the night supervisor for three days; that was it—"You can have it now." We had eight wards with something like eighty-five patients each ward. A psych unit, an ICU unit, a POW unit, and of course, the receiving area, OR, and the recovery room. The first night I was working by myself, the people called from receiving and said they needed help. I'd heard choppers coming in, and I was trying to get down there. I hadn't worked in an emergency room since I'd been a student. I walked into the receiving area, and as I went through the door I said, "Which side do you want me to start on?" They said, "Start on the right." I went around the end of the partition, and I was face-to-face with two at-the-knee amputations that had tourniquets on them. I thought, "Holy shit. What do I do with two AK amps?" It was almost like—I mean, I knew what to do—it was somewhere in the recesses of my brain, and with help from the corpsmen it really came back quickly. I did what I needed to do.

The worst part was, you didn't have time, and after a while, you didn't have the ability to give these guys . . . any amount of real emotional support. I know that one night this kid came in, and he was so . . . he was just going to die, and there was nothing we could do. He'd been hit in the chest as well as everywhere else and was really having trouble breathing, and his trachea was messed up. He knew he was gonna die, but he was conscious. And he was just petrified. I asked one of our new surgeons if he would put an endotracheal tube in it so that at least he could die without drowning in his own blood. He said no. I said, "Fine, I'll do it." He said, "No, you won't. You'll take care of the patients that are gonna live." I pulled the set over, started to intubate him, and the doctor said something else to me. I threw the tube and scope at him and barely missed his head and picked up the other one and intubated the kid. Then he could breathe. I stayed with him until he died—it didn't take him long. . . . But the look that came over that kid's face when he could breathe and he knew he was going to at least die peacefully was worth anything that happened.

So it was minutes like that in a year of being there that . . . You knew what you were doing was right. The fact that we were in Vietnam might not have been right, but the guys who were being shot up weren't the ones that had that choice to make. That's why I think I was able to work and live under the conditions that we did for a year. It's because the kids—not all of them were kids, but a lot of them were—didn't have a choice about being there, and the least I could do was take care of them. They would come through there and then would be gone in just a short period of time, and you began to feel like you were in almost like a processing house, just passing things through. It was just . . . a completely different psychological trip for you. On the one hand, you wanted to fight the injustice of being there, but there wasn't any way to fight it. There wasn't anything you could do except be nonconformist when you were off duty, which we were. I mean, totally nonconformist off duty.

One night I went into the NCO club with some enlisted Marines. I had on jeans and my officers blouse with my captains bars on it. I had on a Marine sergeants hat—and flip-flops. I walked in and neglected to remember that if you dropped your hat on the bar, you bought a round for the whole place. And I had had just enough to drink that I wouldn't have cared if I'd remembered. I sat up on the barstool, dropped my hat on the bar, and wound up buying a round for the whole place, which, over there, wasn't too bad. I mean, drinks were not that expensive. The sergeant who worked in the nursing office was there. Oh, I neglected to tell you that about four months after I arrived in Nam, our chief nurse left. She was no jewel, but the one who replaced her was the woman who had been my CO in basic training. So her sergeant went over and told her that her night supervisor, Captain Hodge, was over in the NCO club, drunk, with a sergeants hat on. She sent word for me to come over to her office. And she never did really do much to me. Mainly because, I think, she realized that I didn't really care what she did to me. She gave me a tongue-lashing. That didn't bother me. She should have waited until I was sober, then at least it would have bothered my hangover. But being just generally nonconformist—it was your only real rebellion against the system.

About eight weeks before my date to rotate, my combat boots hit on the back of my leg exactly where I had hurt my leg when I had phlebitis. I developed phlebitis again, and they couldn't regulate my clotting time. Nothing real big. They were giving me subcutaneous heparin to try to dissolve the thrombophlebitis, and subcutaneous heparin doesn't absorb real quickly. So they finally med-evac'd me out, and when they pressurized the plane, all the subcutaneous heparin went into my system. When I got to Japan they ran a clotting time on me and almost croaked. I think my clotting time was something like three minutes. They said, "You can't go to the States like this." I said, "Why not? If the plane crashes, it's immaterial. I'll just die quicker. I mean, what the hell!" Then they med-evac'd me on to Scott Field, and I was protesting going to North Carolina. I wanted to go to California.

On your first day at Scott Field you can have anything that you want to eat. And because the food at the mess hall in Da Nang had been so terrible, the Marines would keep us supplied with food. The main things they could reappropriate were lobster tails and steaks. I had eaten lobster tails and steak three times a day for three hundred days. I was so sick of it I thought I was gonna throw up if somebody put another lobster tail in front of me. And until this day I will not eat lobster. But the Marines would get it for us from the Navy. The Marines never had it, the Army never had it, but they'd reappropriate it from the Navy admiral's mess. (Also, when I got to know the Marines— we were up on Monkey Mountain one day, and one of them stepped on my foot, and he said, "Excuse me," and I said, "What did you do?" He said, "I just stepped on your toe." I said, "You can step on half the shoe, and you'll never find my toe." He said, "What are you talking about?" And I said, "The Army only had 9½ boots, so that's what I'm wearing." He says, "What size do you need?" And I said, "7," so off they went and came back with a pair of size-7 boots. They had them for the Vietnamese troops that were with them. They found out the rest of the nurses down at the 95th were in the same shape, so they brought us all boots from extra supply.) After they finally got me to Scott—this sounds a little schizophrenic; I can't stay in one place—the things we hadn't had to eat were fresh vegetables, bacon and eggs, and tomatoes. The dietician asked me what I wanted to eat, and I said, "I want two tomato sandwiches, and I want a half pound of bacon on each sandwich." She said, "Are you sure?" I said "That's what I want." When dinner came that night there were these two huge bacon, lettuce, and tomato sandwiches. I ate until I was sick. And when I was in the bathroom throwing up, the guy came. I said, "If you take that tray I'll break your arm." So I came back out and was a little less gluttonous the second time around. I ate it in stages, and it was the best thing I think to this day that I've ever eaten in my life. Then they med-evac'd me on to Fort Bragg, and I was there for two or three weeks.

The first day there, they neglected to tell me that the parade ground was just across from the hospital, mainly because nobody was real accustomed to female Vietnam vets. And if they were, they thought that the female vets were off somewhere. I don't know where they thought we were in Nam—somewhere where you never heard shooting. The first night I was on the ward when they started retreat. I was about half asleep, and they fired the cannon. I came out of bed, ripped the IV out of my arm, and was trying desperately to find my helmet and my flak jacket. And couldn't. This female second lieutenant came down the hall—heard all the commotion—couldn't figure out what was wrong with me because she'd never been told about Nam vets, and there was blood streaming out of where my IV was. A sergeant who had been to Nam and had worked with Nam returnees walked in the door and told her to leave me alone; he talked to me until he could get me to realize where I was. They put me back to bed and then told me the parade ground was across the way, and they would make sure that I was awake at retreat from then on.

From Fort Bragg I went home on convalescent leave and began to be real aware that people were not pleased with veterans who were coming home from Nam. I had known that when I was in California. But somehow I think I felt that during the year I was over there, it would miraculously change. That people would not spit on you for being in uniform. Nobody in town wanted to know about Nam, and if I said I'd been over there they looked at me like, "What are you talking about? No decent human being female from the South would go to Vietnam." That's the distinct impression I got, and it was enough, combined with some other things, to make me begin to repress the whole year. And I did. The Calley trial was going on shortly thereafter, and even though I felt strongly about it, I didn't say anything. And that's real unusual for me, because I tend not to keep my mouth shut. But I tended to work hard enough or drink hard enough, one of the two, that I couldn't think about it and didn't have time to think about it, and I always thought that the experience was there if I wanted to recall it, until eleven years later.

I had a very traumatic experience in the job that I was in and as a result was not working. That was the first time since I'd come home that I had the time to try to figure out what had been making me so terribly angry for ten years. I would get superangry over just little things. People who didn't practice quality medicine drove me insane. And I wasn't sure why. I started looking for a female support group, and there weren't any. Then I saw the article in the paper by Jan Ott from the Seattle vet center. I got in touch with her, and she told me that they were not going to be starting a group until the fall. I tried working it through by myself, but I couldn't remember. I could remember people's names, but I couldn't remember anything about the hospital. Then, even when the group started, listening to people talk, it was like I was divorced from it, like I was an observer. So I decided if I didn't get in touch with Nam, with what happened to me there, then I didn't need to go to group and I was never going to work it out.

I'd known that there were people who worked through hypnotherapy to regress you through things, but I'd never really thought a lot about it. I started calling around to see if there was anybody who did that type of work and was told that there was. I went to this man and spent—I think it was—four sessions with him. I began to remember some of the things from Nam, but because I don't like to lose control—even though I was assured that he couldn't make me do or say anything that I didn't want to—I didn't trust him enough to really get to all of it. I was continuing to go to the women's group all this time, and when I'd go, things would begin to come back to me. Some of the things I have remembered, I really rather I hadn't.

I was in a helicopter for the first time since Nam; it was at the air show out at Boeing. And if it hadn't been for the guy who was showing the helicopters, I probably would have decompensated right here in the middle of God and everybody. I made up my mind that I was going to get in a helicopter again. I started to step up into it and broke out in a cold sweat—I wasn't sure what I was going to do. All I wanted to do was run. He started talking to me, and the first thing out of his mouth that I remember hearing was "Where were you in Nam?" I evidently told him. He kept talking, just a straight blue streak, and I can't tell you what he said, but when I began to calm down, he said, "Are you okay?" I said yes. And I said, "How did you know I had been in Nam?" He said, "You'd be surprised how many people come to these air shows just so they can confront something they can't confront in civilian life." Then he said, "Your eyes and the cold sweat. I wasn't sure which way you were going." I said, "I wasn't either."

Since then it's just been a gradual progression of dealing with what I can and accepting that there are some things that will never be dealt with. I have adopted the attitude of the Alcoholics Anonymous creed. Just give me the strength to deal with what I can. Give me the strength to know what I can change and what I can't. And to know the difference. Some of it I've been real comfortable to put back into the subconscious and say, I know what you are, and I've dealt with you. There's nothing else I can do about you, and you're gonna affect the rest of my life."

I have looked at my darker side and accepted it, and now it doesn't matter to me if anyone else does or not. No one can absolve me of whatever guilt or discomfort I had about Nam by "welcoming me home." I and God must do that. No one can cause me to feel guilty if I don't allow them to. If I have met the "Monster" and it is me, and forgiven myself for my shortcomings or excesses, and feel comfortable that God has forgiven them also, then I don't need anyone else's forgiveness or approval. I can live with myself and, in turn, with the world.

Above: *Jane Hodge by the 95th Evac Hospital sign, Da Nang, 1970.* **Below:** *"What about me?" No room for Maureen Walsh in a bunker at the Naval Support Hospital, Da Nang.*

Above: Sandra Collingwood of the International Voluntary Services visits the grandmother of the Vietnamese family with whom she lived while in language training. They had been celebrating Ancestors' Day. *Below:* Sandra with children of Binh Ba Island, 1968.

Right: Maureen Walsh with a fellow nurse and young Vietnamese patient at the Naval Support Hospital, Da Nang. *Below:* Dot Weller in the American Friends Service Committee Rehabilitation Center, Quang Ngai, with Vietnamese grandmother, daughter, and her four-year-old son. The daughter had lost both legs below the knee; the son was having reconstructive surgery on his foot.

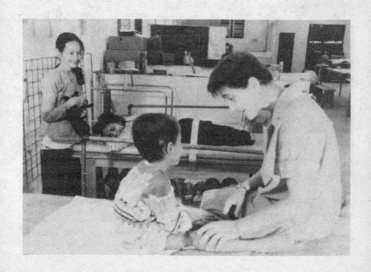

The prosthetic shop in the Quaker Rehabilitation Center. Vietnamese workers ignored the vises, preferring to sit on work benches and hold the wood blocks with their feet. Photo by Dot Weller

This child, a triple amputee, was walking and semi-independent after one and one-half years of daily rehab at the Quaker Center. Returned to her family, she was poisoned—considered a "mercy killing" in this war-torn society. Photo by Mark Jury

Micki Voisard

CIVILIAN AIRLINE FLIGHT
ATTENDANT—FEB. '69 TO JAN. '71

Micki lives on a ranch in northern California with "one husband, three dogs, two horses, and one cat." She has her own video taping business, and as a videographer her life is "definitely unstructured." "I still see a lot of similarities between what I'm doing now and what I did as a flight attendant. I have to be very flexible with my time and energy, and I have to try and remain neutral without taking sides. Some days it reaches the point of absurdity, then I go out and run through the mountains with my husband and the dogs—and things become clear."

The first time I saw Andy was when I took my position on the tarmac at the bottom of the aft ramp. In a few minutes we would be loading passengers from the return trip home. This was Bien Hoa, it was close to the jungles and for many men, when their time was up, they came in straight from the hills, so to speak. Andy was one of them. He caught my eye because he was the first guy in line at the gate, dressed in camouflage, heavy boots, jumping up and down and waving his process papers like he couldn't wait to get to the john.

From where I was standing by the aircraft 100 feet away, I could see the biggest smile on any face in all of Asia. He was making a spectacle of himself and all of the crew members had noticed him. Our senior attendant told us to keep an eye on him, he probably had been drinking. But, I didn't think so. If you could define joy, we were witnessing it before our eyes.

When the gate was opened, Andy came barreling out of it like a rodeo steer. He spoke in an Alabama drawl, but the fastest drawl I'd ever heard. So fast, he spit as he talked. After kissing my hand ten times, then kissing the bottom step of the ramp he lumbered into the cabin. Once inside, Andy picked his seat like it had his name on it. He chose the seat next to the window by a wing exit and what was my jump-seat for landing and take-offs. After securing all passengers we went to our jump-

seats to prepare for take-off. I took my seat near Andy. Waiting for the plane to take off I definitely could smell Andy. But it wasn't liquor I smelled, it was the jungle. I smelled that smell often and he reeked of it. We were still waiting to take off, so I turned my head slightly to look at him. He looked at me, smiled and as soft as this big guy could possibly speak, he said, "I'm goin' home." I believed him. No one could ever have uttered those words more sincerely than he.

Throughout the flight, we were all drawn to this awkwardly large person and so were several of the men on board. When we got to Japan my crew got off, but I continued on with the new crew. My vacation had started and I was coming out of the hills too. I could relax on the trip home, but that wasn't going to be possible since Andy wanted to talk all of the way back.

What was so different about him was the innocence he managed to still maintain even after seeing combat for 13 months. He talked of what he had learned in Vietnam and also of the letters he got from home. Home was a small town in Alabama. 250 people in the town, to be exact, and everyone of them wrote to Andy while he was gone. They told him not to try and be a hero but to stay alive and come back with all of his teeth in place. He said that that had been difficult at times but he managed, mainly because 250 people believed he could do it.

Andy did not budge from his seat during the entire flight. We were all getting a bit concerned. A human body can only carry so much fluid, even one as large as Andy's. But he held out and never even stood up to stretch his muscles.

When the wheels of the aircraft touched the runway of Travis AFB in the States, the usual cheering took place. Except for Andy. I looked toward his seat and he had his big face pressed against the window as far as he could press it without breaking through. Tears were streaming down his face and he wasn't trying to cover them up. He was saying in that still soft voice, "I'm home, I'm home."

(From Micki's journal)

I TOOK ON THE JOB AS A NIGHT ATTENDANT WITH A
civilian airline flying into Vietnam because I heard the
money was good. It was, and somewhere along the way I
convinced myself that this would be a perfect opportunity
to save some money to continue my education. This was
in 1969. I knew there was a war going on and that I would
be flying in and out of the war zone on a regular basis.

I went through six interviews in two weeks, going from
one to another, and there was a process of elimination. I
didn't know what that process was until we had completed
the six weeks of training and some of the girls didn't make
it. It was like going through your final vows in the convent
or something; you had to complete all this training, get the
shots and pass the tests, then you still might not make it.
I found out only after graduation that we were actually
selected through handwriting analysis! I remember writing
several stupid little paragraphs on why I wanted to be a
stewardess, and they were using these to find out your personality traits, to see if you could handle this kind of thing.

I was real good at what I did because I have been cheer-
leading all of my life. I really was a cheerleader in high

school, and it just seemed to carry on through; I still am at times. When we went through the training they didn't give us any beauty training, like they did in the other airlines. I would come across other crews and would talk about their training, and they would say, "Oh, we spent three weeks doing things on our hair." And I went, God, we never spent three hours doing that. But, one thing about the company I worked for, they really were up on emergency procedures; I mean, that was essential. They were trying their hardest to prepare us for something that they themselves did not know was going to come about.

What they didn't prepare us for, and did very little work on, was how to work with 215 GIs on board the airplane, and I don't think anybody can prepare you for that. We would ask questions—you know, "What are they going to be like?" Their typical response would be "Boys will be boys; men will be men." That is the way it was left, and thinking back, what people are calling sexual abuse today was what went on all the time on those airplanes. I think it was up to you as an individual. When something happened to you, you reacted to it. The second time it happened, you had a choice of acting or reacting . . . and there is a big difference there. I learned that as a survival method. Whether anybody had any personal contact with you or not, you understood where you fit in. And it wasn't always in the best light; I never saw women as being in the best light with a lot of the men in the military.

Our headquarters was in Los Angeles, but the main stewardess headquarters was in San Francisco, and we had a contract with Travis AFB. We were connected with the Military Air Command (MAC), which is their airlift. During the war, the military needed their transports to fly equipment rather than troops, so this was contracted out to private companies like Continental, Flying Tigers, Pan Am, TIA, World, et cetera. My second home base was in Japan. The company had a hotel there and we had privileges at the Air Force bases.

Our trips lasted seven to fourteen days, during which time your whole life had to change. Your social life went with you like your suitcase did; you had to make it happen right there. And you couldn't wait until you got home because the company ended up screwing you, making sure that if you planned something, it wasn't going to happen: those two weeks skiing in Tahoe would suddenly become a turnaround flight back to Vietnam. It happened all the time.

We flew from Japan into Cam Ranh Bay, Bien Hoa, Da Nang, Tan Son Nhut, and generally they were seventeen-hour round trips. You flew in, waited for them to clean the plane and reload passengers, and then flew out. It was a long haul. That was if nothing happened. Sometimes you flew in and didn't come out until a couple of days later because of mechanical problems with the airplane or rocket attacks.

The very first flight into Vietnam I was in awe of what we were doing. I was walking around with my mouth open, going, "Wow!" A limousine came to take some dignitaries who were on the flight and then a school bus for the officers. The draftees were herded into this big, open cattle truck and were driven away, just like cattle going away to slaughter. There was no glory, no John Wayne stuff; this was war. . . . This is what people are so willing to do today, and it angers me, but if every mother could see her son going off like that they wouldn't accept it. It was a disgusting sight.

On the average trip you would see twelve hundred to fifteen hundred guys, and to this day, being the visual person that I am, my mind is filled with faces that I can bring back any time. I call them the faces of Vietnam. It was interesting to me when *Life* magazine came out with an issue called "The Faces of Vietnam." It became a turning point in my life as a flight attendant going into the war zone. We were flying from Yokota, Japan, to Travis AFB, taking a group of guys back from Vietnam. I had galley duty; it was real late at night, and I had nothing to do so I picked up a magazine, and on the cover was the face of a GI. *Life* was dedicating that issue to ending the war. So I started looking through page after page of faces until one of them was very familiar. A guy I had gone through school with. I looked at it and thought, "He can't be dead." I

started reading all the captions under the photographs. Then
it hit me that he was dead. . . . He was the hometown all-
American boy. Every girl in my high school was in love
with him; he was the special one. He was president of the
student body and was the quarterback on the football team;
he had a scholarship. The whole town gave him a sendoff
party . . . to Vietnam. . . . They sent him off to war. And
when he was killed, it was amazing what happened. His
father committed suicide; his mother had to be institution-
alized. People just couldn't accept this. They mourned for
weeks. When I saw his picture, it just hit me—so many of
the guys on these flights who weren't going home, so many
of those faces.

On one flight, we got caught in a B-52 bombing mission.
It's interesting, I think if I had given it any more thought,
I wouldn't be here today; I'd be in an institution, I'm sure.
We were just outside of Da Nang, heading to Japan, filled
up with troops going home. I was looking out of the port-
hole of the aft galley door, just admiring the view, and
thought I saw something go by real fast. And when you
are up in the air you feel a little uncomfortable about that;
there is just not enough room up there for something that
close going that fast. . . . Then I saw it again. I looked
down the center aisle of the airplane, and all the people
who were window-watching were pointing to something.
Then the captain came on and said, "That was a B-52
bomber that just flew by us." It turned out that they were
flying above us. They were in a bombing raid and were
maintaining radio silence. One of them dropped down to
see what this blip was on their radar, and it was us. So, it
had to go through the chain of command for them to stop
and let us through. (This is my interpretation of it—what
we were picking up from the captain.) I remember going
up front and seeing the looks on the passengers' faces.
They had just gone through thirteen months of horror; they
were going home in a civilian aircraft and are put under
this stress . . . How could this happen?

Well, at first you couldn't see or hear them; then we got
to this point where you could look out the window and see
the bombs down there, hitting below us about thirty thou-

sand feet. It was so silent—so clean—it was incredible. And for a good half an hour we sat there, strapped to our seats, waiting on pins and needles for our plane to clear the bombing area. We just wanted to do a right-hand turn and get the hell out of there! You felt like a mosquito in a shower: how are you not going to get wet?

In those years, I was three different people, three personalities. I had to be a cheerleader for the guys going over. Then on the way home, I had to tell them about things that I didn't want to tell them. The country was not welcoming heroes anymore. They were so happy to be going home; you didn't want to break their hearts and say, "But, it's not going to be good. It's not going to be what Mom and your sisters have been writing. They are going to expect you to be the same guy that left."

I would go home, and my parents would say, "It's okay now, Micki. Why don't you forget it while you are on vacation?" Even if what I wanted to talk about was terrible, I still needed to do it, but nobody wanted to listen. One time—the first time I had ever been shelled, in Cam Ranh Bay—I came home twenty-four hours later, and my boyfriend had tickets to the play *Hair*. He called me up and said, "Can you be ready in half an hour?" I said, "You won't believe this—I just had a terrible experience. I don't think I want to go." And he said, "Every time you go on your trips all you do is talk about that stuff. . . . I spent twenty-five dollars on these tickets, and I hope you are going to be ready." I was stupid; you know, I put on my clothes and went. So, I'm sitting there looking around the room, thinking, "Just twenty-four hours ago, I was in a bunker, and here I am watching this antiwar play. . . . What am I doing? Am I crazy?" I walked out.

And I began wondering what the hell I was doing. I was flying over there, getting paid to be in the war. I'd come home and find myself going to Berkeley and marching in the antiwar demonstrations. And, after reading the *Stars and Stripes* newspaper, which I had to hand out to each seat on the return flights, I couldn't believe what they were passing off. I had to do that because it was my job, but I justified it by taking a whole bunch of those newspapers home and burning them at a demonstration. Everybody was burning their draft cards, I burned *Stars and Stripes* newspapers. That felt good to me. For three years I was playing so many different roles; it was so confusing. Why? How could anybody stay in there that long? And it was no longer the money. I mean, I wasn't even saving money. The guilt that I've had the last fifteen years is, Why in the hell *did* I stay for that long? Well, I was twenty-one. Who knows what you do when you are twenty-one years old. And if I look at my cultural background—I'm Catholic. I remember going into confession and making up my sins. I felt guilty that I didn't have all the sins down so I could give my penance, so I made them up as I went along. Then one day, I was talking to a couple of friends, and they said, "Well, who doesn't make up their sins?" Nobody believed in it, but they still went in there and did it. We didn't question those things. And I believed in the president . . . believed that there was somebody in charge. That was a big slap in the face—as I went through the war, I discovered there was never anybody in charge of that war. . . .

Cam Ranh Bay was a target because it was a main artillery base, and Charlie figured that out in a short period of time. Every time we would bring ships in, they probably were sitting there with their binoculars, watching them hauling in all this ammunition and putting it in the warehouses and Quonset huts around Cam Ranh Bay. Then they would go, "Okay," and they would blow them up. On one particular flight Cam Ranh was under fire when we came in; we didn't have a choice because we were low on fuel and couldn't go to an alternative airport. It was take your chance while you have it. The captain told us that there was all kinds of junk on the runway; they didn't know what to expect.

He did a great job landing, and then we sat there. All the lights were off in the airplane, the air conditioning is off, everybody is sweating, and you couldn't see faces because it was so dark. . . . You can feel 215 people in there. . . . I had to wait for six rings from the captain and then pull the emergency door, and the emergency slide is supposed to inflate. I'm flying number two position, sitting in the front jump seat and straining to hear six rings through all this "pow, pow!" And the plane is shaking. . . . I'm going, "One, two . . . I think I hear . . ." Finally the six rings come, and as I jumped out of the seat, I got my leg caught in the seat springs somehow. I had this feeling like I had my dress stuck, and being in such a frantic situation, I just ripped myself out and grabbed for the door. The slide didn't open—it just fizzled out! I am panicking because I could see everybody else letting their guys out. I have about fifty guys just sitting there in this dark coffin, waiting. There were three officers in front of me, and one said, "Let's go hand over hand." So, they went down and made, like, a chain ladder, and about halfway through he says, "It's your turn." I said, "I'm supposed to be the last one off the airplane." He says, "Get down there, lady!" and they practically threw me down. Then on the tarmac, I'm going, "Where am I? Is this Cam Ranh Bay?" In training they had shown slides of where there were bunkers at the various air bases. We had that information, but the troops on the airplane didn't know there were bunkers. They are saying, "Where do we go now?" And you go, "Oh, I saw slides of them once . . ." I mean, I remember the slides, and they showed the blue coral reefs in the background, and you thought, "Oh, that should be easy to find." You didn't realize that none of this is going to happen during the day—it is going to be dark. . . . Who is going to be looking for blue coral reefs?

Then some guy pointed in one direction, and I remember looking back at the airplane and seeing reflections in it like the whole earth was blowing up . . . lights, explosions . . . I thought, "Oh, Micki, you blew it. You were supposed to be the last one off that airplane. . . . The rules said . . ." I was even going to go back; you know, I had seen too many Goddamn John Wayne movies—"Oh, leave me here, you go ahead"-type stuff. I didn't know that I was hurt. I had cut my foot down to the muscle, and I ran on that foot through all the glass and debris on the tarmac. But the only thing I remember when we were running was the smell of sulfur everywhere. We got into the bunkers and stayed there for two hours—stood there, it was so tight.

Then finally they moved us into a warehouse, and that's when I discovered my foot was hurt. Some guy said, "Eeew, you've got blood all over your pantyhose." Here we are, there are rockets going off outside, and the guy is still looking at my legs. I'm going, "Goddamn it! Some guys are . . ." But he was just trying to tell me that I was hurt. There was a medic right there, and he said, "Let me look at that. You do have blood on your pantyhose." I looked down at my foot and almost fainted!

After it was over, they refueled the airplane and got our crew on board. The medic had reported my injury to the senior stew, and she wrote it up. When we got to Yokote, I went into the hospital on Tachikawa air base and spent the night. Then the company flew us home, since our plane was damaged and was going to be worked on in Japan. We flew home thinking, "Oh, we'll probably get two weeks off, maybe a bonus . . ." They gave us a turnaround! I was back in Vietnam in forty-eight hours! I mean, any excuse you would give them was not good enough, or bad enough. I called them up and said, "God, last night we were shelled in Vietnam. I'm really not feeling very good." They would go, "When can you be back on the line?" It was amazing. It was nothing to them. . . . You meant nothing to them. So, that was gnawing at me: "Well, why the hell did you stay there then, Micki?" I lived with that for years. The reasons I came up with, in addition to my Catholic background, was I knew I was on to something. . . . Having a journalistic background, I was intrigued. It kept me going. I knew that the discrepancies were just too great, and that I had privileged information in my position. I could walk around as freely as can be, photographing and talking with people. I could ask any person what their side of the story was. . . . It was amazing . . . the stories, the confusion; nothing made sense, nothing.

The value was more than I could ever pay for, and the time that I spent in Vietnam was a significant and valuable period in my life. It haunts me to this day. I would not have traded it for anything. I was not injured over there to an extent where I was incapacitated, I didn't see my best friend die—or a lot of things that people saw over there—but I had my life on the line every time I flew in there.

And I had to deal with sexual abuse. I saw men masturbating all the time on the airplanes. I remember when I was new, having one stewardess tell me, "Never take a blanket off a sleeping GI." Then, once in a while, someone in Los Angeles who had forgotten we were hauling troops would put sanitary napkins on board, so we had to check out the lavs to see if there were any sanitary napkins. But there were times when we forgot or the guys would bring them on themselves. They would put ketchup down the center of the napkin, lay it in the middle of the aisle, and wait for your reaction. The first time it happened to me I was real embarrassed. Then there was the guy who got stuck in his seat belt; you were to save the day, helping him with it while he sits there with a big smile on his face and everybody around him is laughing. So, you learn the art of seat belt deployment by verbal command. Or, the guy who asks for a pillow and, as you reach up to get one, he has his hand up your dress. . . . You learned to never do things impulsively. You won't believe this one: the guy who follows you to the john to see if you locked the door. They would wait until you got comfortable, then jerk the door open, and everybody down the aisle could see you! So, to me right now, thinking of those things, it seems incredible, but it got to be routine. There were a lot of bad apples, but there were also guys that would let you know that they didn't approve of what they saw going on. A lot of them would come up and say, "I'm real sorry that happened to you." They weren't all older guys either; some were just young kids. You saw where respect came from.

Even now I have a way with men that . . . Fortunately I came out of it not hating them. I knew a lot of girls that ended up that way. They were having difficulty dealing with the men on the flights. I was able to function and talk with the GIs the whole time; it's just that I found myself giving commands all the time. In order to survive, I had to challenge them. They would challenge you, and if you could speak louder and be more authoritarian, then they would buckle under to you. Just my sense of survival, I guess.

Then there is the story about the bomb on our airplane. It was a pressurized bomb which, they figured, was supposed to go off above twelve thousand feet. It had been planted by one of the Vietnamese who cleaned out the airplane. We used to just stroll off the airplane and go down to the beach while they worked. . . . Well, that stopped real fast! The military started coming on board and standing there with M-16s pointed at these guys while they cleaned the plane.

I was in the aft galley with another girl, whose jump seat was right in front of the coffee maker, and on takeoff, it came out and hit her in the back of the head. She was actually holding it in place with her head—this big, heavy thing. We started pushing and shoving on it, trying to get it back in place and asked a couple of guys who were sitting near there to help us. Finally, we called the flight engineer, and he came back to check it out. We were all milling around, getting things ready for meal service, and meanwhile the plane is climbing. The night engineer looks in behind the coffee maker with his trusty flashlight and says, "Oh, my God, everybody get out of here, right now!" Here is this happy-go-lucky-type guy who suddenly goes into instant fear. He says, "There's a bomb here." I remember standing there with all this coming back to me. I had been pushing on it, hitting it! Now, all of a sudden, I can't move; I can't even walk past that thing.

The captain came back, they discussed it, then went forward and talked with somebody on the radio in Cam Ranh. They were pretty sure it was a pressurized bomb and told us to level off and stay at our altitude until they could get some kind of a bomb squad together down there. Then we had to return, and it was up to the captain to bring that baby in as light as can be . . . and not make any drastic changes in altitude . . . slowly bring it down. The captain left the door of the cockpit open, and everybody on board was included. He let us hear the communication of he and the ground crew. They were joking and discussing this openly. Everybody felt 100 percent better because they were able to participate in this. He let that thing just glide into Cam Ranh Bay and landed. Everybody cheered! There were a lot of different kinds of heroes in that war.

I was telling someone this story, and they said, "Oh, you mean the *North* Vietnamese planted the bomb." I said, "No, a South Vietnamese." They said, "But we were fighting *for* the South Vietnamese." It was just amazing how people thought the war was that black and white: "Here is the north; all the bad guys live over here. Here is the south, and all the good guys live there, and we are saving the good guys, keeping communism away."

Then you come home, and they give the body count each night at dinnertime. They say, "North Vietnam lost fifteen hundred and we lost thirty. Isn't that great!" You know, to me that's where we really lost it, on that body count. Because people would be sitting there watching the six o'clock news, saying, "That's not too bad, only thirty guys. . . . They lost fifteen hundred. We are doing a good job over there." Nobody thought of thirty individuals. . . . Those guys got lost in there, somehow. Fifty-eight thousand people got lost in that body count. See, and I'm still playing both sides. I still have to say that I recognize everyone who went over there believing that they were giving the ultimate for their country, their lives, but I recognize the war also as being a big mistake. The Vietnam War was the pits, to put it mildly, but anybody that went over there—my God, the credit wasn't given to them. And still is not. I can't use Vietnam as an excuse for the times that I'm not productive or under stress or whatever. I've done that a few times. I've accepted it, and I'm able to act upon it in a positive way. How can that be positive? It can give you the strength to go on to face things that are more important in your life. I think the significance of Vietnam *will* come out one of these days—I think it is beginning to happen right now.

What I got from Vietnam were a lot of valuable things that helped me in my life. Discussing it with my counselor, I said that I didn't feel a lot of anger. She said, "Micki, you do have anger." I never thought of it this way, but I realized that my anger was directed in deciding I was going to be antiestablishment, that I was not going to work in a structured situation like that again. I didn't believe in the Easter bunny and 'Cinderella or that life is better if you drink Coca-Cola. And because of my Vietnam experience, I found that there wasn't anybody else in charge. I was always in charge. . . .

It will stay with me forever, but I'm getting to the point where I can separate my life from Vietnam. Maybe each year I can let go of a little bit more. Sometimes, when I'm down, one word looms up as big as life: *Vietnam* . . . Then I go, "No, Micki, don't do that. It's not fair to use that as an excuse!" I have to reach for the things in my life that are positive and bring myself back to this present moment.

Doris I. "Lucki" Allen

U.S. ARMY
INTELLIGENCE OPERATIONS,
LONG BINH—OCT. '67 TO
MARCH '70
SAIGON—MARCH '70 TO SEPT. '70

After serving three years in Vietnam, Lucki Allen returned to the U.S. as an instructor, Prisoner of War Interrogation, at the Army Intelligence Center and School, Fort Holabird, Maryland. She worked as a special agent with both Military Intelligence and Defense Investigative Service until her retirement, as a CW3, after thirty years of military service in June 1980.

Doris is currently a psychology Ph.D. candidate, studying at Wright Institute, Berkeley, California, and doing her dissertation and study in organizational psychology, on life management systems of persons with hidden, periodically manifested and nonobservable physical disabilities. She works as a private investigator and lives with her family in Oakland, California.

THE STORY OF MY LIFE BEGAN FIFTY-SIX YEARS AGO; I'm almost fifty-seven. On Friday the thirteenth, 1950, I went in the military. I'd been teaching school, and I went to Jackson, Mississippi, and told them I wanted to join the military. I was going to be an officer at first, and I said, "No, I'm not going to be an officer. I'll go through the ranks." At any rate, they let me in—that's the way they put it: they let me in.

After basic training they asked what MOS I would like to be, and I wanted to join the band; I was qualified. So they sent three of us black women over for an audition with the WAC band, that's Women's Army Corps Band. I was playing trumpet, one woman was playing clarinet, the other was playing percussion. They gave me the fourth trumpet part, they gave the other lady the fourth clarinet part, and the percussionist was doing whatever she was doing. But if you know anything about music—those are really the hardest parts. You really have to concentrate, and you have to know what you're doing to be doing this du-pity-dupity-du or whatever. As we were playing, the commander of the band, Chief Warrant Officer Allen—no

kin, believe me—had made some prearranged signal with
the rest o the band. She was standing up there directing
us—we were playing "Under the Double Eagle," I think—
and on the signal the rest of the band stopped. Then you
heard nothing but this fourth trumpet part du-pity-du and
this fourth clarinet part do-do-do-do-do and the drum going
oom-ba, oom-ba. We kept playing because the director was
still directing. She was getting so exasperated that we kept
going, following her directions. To us it was, you know,
follow directions, do what you're directed to do. I wish I
could show you how Miss Allen looked. Afterwards, the
regular members in the band congratulated us and said,
"Yeah, you guys did real well." And we know we were
in the band, right? Miss Allen called us in and told us that
we did fine, but sorry, they couldn't have any Negroes in
the band. So, well, that was my first real touch with how
they want you but they don't want you.

Right after that rejection, they sent us to become entertainment specialists, which entailed nothing but putting on
soldier shows. One of the fortunate things was that I did
get a chance to play a gig with André Previn—just messing
around at the Presidio in San Francisco.

I went to Japan within a year after joining the military,
and when I came back I was stationed at Camp Stoneman,
California. My sister, Jewel L. Allen, was my commander.
I caught lots of flak from that because they thought we
were colluding or doing something or going with each other
or something. But when they closed Camp Stoneman, they
wanted her to go to one end of the earth and me to another
end of the earth. And I think that's because as sisters, we
were real loving sisters, but when it came to being soldiers,
we were soldiers.

Oh, there was another incident at Stoneman which was
downright prejudice. I had been editor of a newspaper when
I was in Japan. They didn't have an editor for the newspaper, so I was a college graduate and I spoke English well
and they said, "Okay, you're it." Here I am a PFC, and
I had all these other high ranks working—in a sense, working for me because they were doing the reporting and I was
doing all the editing. When I got back to Stoneman I was

supposed to be on newspapers, and I went in and told the sergeant, "Hey, I'm supposed to be doing some kind of newspaper work." The captain called me into his office and directed me to "go empty those inkwells." They were on his desk, those old-time inkwells. One had red ink in it, and the other, green. Why call me? I was a corporal. There were five men, PFCs, in the office. I was a woman, and he called me in to empty the inkwells. I picked them up, took them outside, in my very starched dress, washed them out, careful not to get dirty, brought them back in, set them on his desk, saluted him, and walked out. I went directly to the sergeant and told him that he had other people in here of lower rank who were not trained like I was and that I did not appreciate that. I think that was one of my first really assertive acts, knowing it's all right to assert yourself in the military and say, "Hey, I don't want to do that."

Another important time in my life, in the intervening seventeen years before I got to Vietnam, was at Fort Monmouth, New Jersey. I was running the education center and doing public information, and my boss wanted me to go out with him. And I said, "No, I don't mix business with pleasure." So he saw to it that I didn't get promoted. Even though there were not that many promotions to be had, there were what they called blood stripes. In other words, if somebody did something wrong and they lost their stripe, somebody else could get it if you were highly recommended. He never recommended me because I wouldn't go out with him. We had a good working relationship, but I . . . Well, I didn't get promoted for twelve years. I was sergeant then. I was stagnating and in that same no-win situation while I was at Fort Monmouth, and I said, "Well, I'm going to have to do something." I applied for lots of things, lots of places, and they would always tell me, "Well, no, your MOS is too important. It's critical, so we can't send you."

They finally, though seemingly reluctantly, let me go to language school. I went to the language school in Monterey, California, to learn French. I was no longer in public information. I had become a French linguist when I finished school. I just knew I was going to go to France. But that was during the time that President de Gaulle said that he did not want Americans in his country any longer, so I didn't get a chance to go to France.

I went to Fort Bragg in North Carolina, where I had a problem, again, getting promoted. What eventually happened there was, one day I saw all these guys walking in, thirty-two of them to be exact, walking past my desk and standing there in their class A uniforms, looking sharp, and I said, "Geez, I had no wind of a formation today. Why are you guys dressed up?" They said, "We're going before the board." I said, "Come on, what board?" They said, "We're going before the promotion board." And me, in my naiveté—if you can use that term—said to myself, "Well, hey, Lucki, your stuff is so together; you're a good soldier. They know how good you are, how efficient and professional you are. You don't have to go before the board." Then I sat there and started thinking, and I jumped out of my complacency and got very upset. I told the sergeant major I wanted to speak to the colonel. I always walked in informally, but this time I *marched* into the colonel's office, saluted him, and forty-five minutes later I walked out of there. While I was in there, I was telling him how good I really was, how well trained I was, and my mother and dad raised no idiots . . . the whole bit; I expounded respectfully, but I was really venting. When the board is convened for promotion, that's the only board for that month; you just couldn't change that. This was on a Wednesday. Well, I guess about five minutes after I went back and sat at my desk, the colonel came through my office and went out the door—where he went, I don't know. When he came back he looked as if he was sort of in a huff. He called the sergeant major in, very formally, and the sergeant major came to my desk and said, "There will be a promotion board held for you on Friday."

What had happened in all of that—and this is not just reflection; I knew then what was happening—had I not said anything, had I just let it go, I'd probably still be the same rank I was then. When I did go before the board I came out fifth out of the thirty-three people. I would've been first but they threw out all of the education points for promotion because they looked at mine and I just messed up the curve completely. You know, I was already a college graduate, I'd taught school, I'd taken everything that the Army had to offer as far as extension courses, I took extra college courses in speech and a few other things I hadn't had. Too many. So they threw all of them out. I still came out number five. But the point being that you have to have the sense of how they were going to promote everybody else and not include me and just not say anything about it. Maybe it would've gone along and I'd have had to wait another month; this might have happened again. I believe that my assertiveness paid off. So I finally got promoted there.

Another important incident happened. When the Dominican Republic uprising happened, I was stationed in Fort Bragg, North Carolina. I was in military intelligence by then: a prisoner of war interrogator, a French linguist, and I also spoke Spanish. I had all the skills that they really needed. But for whatever reason hey had, I was not sent to the Dominican Republic. It wasn't that I was asking to be sent, but according to my records, I was one of the highest qualified persons. Why not send me there, okay? They didn't do that.

At any rate, in 1967, I volunteered to go to Vietnam. I was working in strategic intelligence at that time. I wanted to go because I kept hearing what I thought must have been lies—all of this couldn't be true, the information that was coming back to me. And I got information not only through regular intelligence channels, but also from overseas newspapers and the regular media. There was a lot of conflict for me in knowing who was telling the truth, so I said, "Well, I know whatever it is I know, and I may as well be there too. I'm gonna be a part of this." Instead of just sitting back here and knowing that I had an expertise that was needed, it was better for me to be there. Not to fight and not to shoot guns and not to kill people, but I looked at it rather that my intelligence would save lives, as opposed to taking lives. Two months prior to the time that I left Fort Bragg, I did not read anything having to do with Vietnam. I didn't read reports; I didn't read newspapers; I almost didn't listen to the news. I'd kind of close it off when it came to what was happening in Vietnam. The reason I did this is because when I got to Vietnam, I wanted to be open-minded and unbiased and be able to work from there.

When I got to Vietnam, my paranoia started really showing. I don't remember the day I got to Vietnam, but it was either the thirteenth, fourteenth, or fifteenth of October, 1967. Going over, I was the only woman on the plane with all the other GIs. What I spent my time doing while I was on the plane is reading newspapers and doing the entire order of battle. This was possible because in newspapers they had given locations of all of the American troops from division headquarters down to platoonsize units, exactly where they were in all of Vietnam. So I kept saying to myself, "Here I am sitting on the plane being able to figure out where all of our troops are." I said, "My God, the enemy must be . . . They know!" I think I got paranoid reading that paper, you know. But I already had my cover story—"When I get to Vietnam I won't know anything about anything, and if I get captured, I'll be okay." The cover story I had made up was that I was an expert on the M-16. I knew why it jammed, when it jammed, what was wrong with it; I knew everything about it. I don't know a thing about the M-16 right now, but I had that weapon so heavy in my mind . . . And if they got me I was going to tell them that the only thing I did was take complaints about the M-16. I was going to say, "You know yourself it's a horrible weapon and that your AK-47 is much better than our M-16." Wow, listen to that fantasy!

When I got to Saigon, to Tan Son Nhut airport, dressed in my nice, clean cord uniform, I was looking sharp. They were calling off all these units and all these names, and I did not hear my name once. I don't care where you are, you hear your own name. I was just standing here, and all of a sudden the airport was clearing out, right? But I don't see it clearing out because I'm standing with head against the wall, because when I got there I see all these people that I knew were Vietnamese, okay? For whatever reason, I knew they were Vietnamese, and I saw these cameras, and people are clicking their cameras, and why are these people in here taking pictures? Oh, my God. Not realizing this is their airport—it wasn't military; we just happened to land there. I was standing with my face against the wall— "I hope they don't take a picture of me, oh, God." And that kind of wore out, but that was my introduction. Then I finally found somebody, and I said, "Listen, I'm here, you know, you must have a place for me." And I didn't want to tell them I was military intelligence. . . . Well, anyway, that was all my own anxiety.

They finally decided where I belonged, and I went down to wherever that place was where all the other Army women were sent, and they'd given me this white towel and white washcloth, so I could take a shower. And I think I have a beautiful brown color, right? I got in the shower and started washing, and I said, "Oh, my God, what's happening?!" My washcloth, absolutely, so help me God, was brown, and I thought I was turning white. You don't know how panicky that is—this is the honest truth. I just got panicky, and I almost started crying. . . . Do you realize how dusty and dirty Vietnam was? And this was a matter of being there just a few hours. Imagine, the first day there, and all my black's coming off. Well, I got over that.

The next day I started working. I was in intelligence. For my first year in Vietnam, I worked in the Army Operations Center (AOC), Headquarters, United States Army, Vietnam (USARV). I was the only specialist-7 at the time; there were only twenty-two spec-7s in the military. I was in the "Two Shop" in the AOC and was the only woman in there. I remember one of my humors came up one day. When the general walked in, nobody, none of the men in there, wanted to tell him that his fly was open. I told him his fly was open, and everybody glared at me. I don't think they liked that. The general says, "Oops, thank you," and zips his pants up.

Another general, Air Force General Ryan from Pacific Command in Hawaii, came for an orientation. I was directed to give the orientation, which included a complete rundown of the current military operation throughout Vietnam. I remember it kind of disturbed me, because they put five very plush chairs for the general and his staff to sit in, and I was wondering, "This is Vietnam. Why are you putting plush chairs there for somebody to sit in? I'm talking about war!" When I finished briefing General Ryan, he walked over to me and said, very loudly so that everybody in the AOC could hear it, "I've been CINCPAC for"—whatever time it was—"and I've had lots of reports from over-here in Vietnam and been all over Vietnam, and this is the best and most honest report I've had yet, because you stood up here and dared to tell the truth." And everybody else was very excited about this. I think there was a lot of anxiety behind the fact that I was the only spec-7 in there. Well, being spec-7 had the connotation of, you're either really great or you're something special. Being a woman had lots to do with that. My credibility was with me—I had it—but a lot of people couldn't believe, or didn't want to believe, that a woman could actually be making decisions or analyses—and their being correct.

I think the first time I was really tested was when I called the Tet offensive. I had been looking at my notes and reading everything. I had all these reports that I'd read through; I was pouring over them and really into it. Then I wrote a paper, and I titled it "50,000 Chinese." What it said was, we had better get our stuff together because this is what is facing us, this is what is going to happen, and it's going to happen on such and such a day, around such and such a time. I had never heard the word *Tet*, it just wasn't part of my vocabulary. I didn't know that there was a Tet celebration, like maybe a lot of people in foreign countries don't know that we celebrate Easter or Christmas. But I put the date down and said it's going to happen around this particular date. When I took it in to the G-2, the intelligence officer said, "Well, I don't know about this." And I said, "We need to disseminate this. It's got to be told." Well, he sort of believed it and said, "I'll tell you what to do. I want you to take it up to Saigon and run it through and see what they think there, what the G-2 at MACV thinks about it." I said okay, and I got in my jeep and went on up to Saigon.

When I walked in I knew that it had to go through and

be scrutinized by about fifteen people. It seemed like that, but it really went through only four or five. When I walked in there, the sergeant came up to me and said, "Can I help you?" And I said, "Yes, I'd like to see the G-2. I have something et cetera, et cetera.'" The captain came out: "What do you have?" I said, "I'd like to see the G-2 et cetera, et cetera." And he said, "Just a minute." A major came out, and I showed it to the major, and he said, "Well, just a minute." He handed it back to me, this paper I'd written. I guess it was a page and a half. He walked back in there and said, "Maybe you better go talk to the colonel." The colonel came out, got the paper, took it back in the back, they discussed it, I imagine, and they came back out and said, "Well, we really don't know if this is . . . No, I don't think we better, no . . ." I know that they knew there was substance in it. . . . I don't know why I said that—I don't know, but they must have, because too many people took too much time to discuss it, whatever it was. Maybe they just saw it as logic, I don't know. I did this at least thirty days ahead of when this was supposed to be, and I think one of the things that might have scared them off was that I titled the report "50,000 Chinese," and there were not supposed to be any Chinese in the country; these were supposed to be Vietnamese, Viet Cong, North Vietnamese Army, okay? Maybe calling them Chinese made it unacceptable to our headquarters. At any rate, the date came, and I was right . . . but Tet, believe me, is history. Tet is history. Well, I'm not an "I told you so" person, but I most certainly felt very good for having at least tried to warn our brass, and even though we lost so much, I felt inside myself that I had done what I was supposed to do.

Another incident. The order came to send a convoy up to Song Be, and I warned the colonel that they shouldn't because of a possible ambush. I outlined enemy locations and the site of a possible ambush. "Well, ahh, I'm sorry, we're going to send it anyway." They sent the convoy up. . . . We're talking about five flatbed trucks blown up, nineteen wounded, and three killed. We lost a lot. You know, when you're talking about a flatbed, you're talking about lots and lots of ammunition that gets wasted because it got caught in an ambush. I even told them the probable location of the ambush. About two days later, when it was time to send out another convoy, the colonel came in and asked me, "Hey, by the way, do you think we ought to send this convoy up there today?" What happens with that is, somewhere your credibility is being questioned. Not that I had to establish any more credibility. As far as I was concerned, I was doing a sincere, caring, very professional job. So the onus was not on me to prove my credibility; the onus was on them to listen.

I guess the things that really stick about Vietnam is knowing you give them something and what you give is reliable and valid, but biases can creep through. There are a lot of things that they might have been biased about me with. I was a specialist as opposed to being a sergeant. I was black instead of being something else. I was enlisted instead of being an officer—especially in the milieu where there were only two enlisted people, and I was one of them. There was a master sergeant and myself; the other twenty-eight were officers. Being a WAC, whew! You know, "Women have no business over here, WACs especially." You know, there were a lot of things at my age—let me see how old I was, about ten years ago, I was in my forties. Ten years ago?? That's almost fourteen, fifteen years ago, wow, geez! How vivid it is! But somehow you have to say, "I'm going to either keep doing it, or I'm going to get bitter and I'm not going to even bother with this anymore."

Two more incidents—I'll make them short. One had to do with a chemical round (82-millimeter mortar) I heard about. A friend up in Tay Ninh called me up and said, "Hey, we've got something out here that's different." I found out that there was a chemical round, and it was the first time we knew about a chemical round in Vietnam. I made a couple of phone calls and a couple of little "calisthenics" and came up with the fellow who defused it. I brought him down to my headquarters, and we sat and he told me all he knew about it. I got it all drafted up in this big picture, telling exactly what one should expect if a "dud" 82-millimeter mortar round hit an area. I published it in a document called "Weekly Intelligence Estimate Update," which went out everywhere in Vietnam. Sometimes people don't read things—they throw them in trash cans; sometimes people do read things.

It happens that a Marine commander at Qua Viet, the 3d MAF area, up by the DMZ, happened to read it like he was supposed to. He read this article on Wednesday, and on Friday they were attacked. And the enemy was using the chemical round. He said, "Do not touch it," and they didn't touch the round. They found out later that it was actually a chemical round. The 3d MAF commander called back down to the USARV and asked, "Who put out the information on the chemical round? I think whoever it was should be credited with saving a hundred and one lives and be given at least the Legion of Merit." Well, my colonel was quite amenable to that, but by the time it got watered down I don't remember if I even got a thank-you. I did get a big thank-you from myself again for having done something that was really productive. Later they said I couldn't have a Legion of Merit because number one, I was a woman; number two, I was enlisted; and number three, it was not in actual combat—it wasn't in a shooting situation.

Another incident that was . . . Geez, I think about these years later . . . it was Tet of 1969. Almost the same thing was happening, but I had wind from my sources that rockets were being planted outside of our perimeter around Long Binh. They were using 122-millimeter rockets. What they were doing is just laying them on the ground and covering them with earth. They intended to use these ground mounds as launchers. They would put them down there, cover them up, and you just couldn't really see them from the air. This information was coming in to us; we had agents out there— we had woodcutters just like they had woodcutters, so to speak. I had been getting all these things across my desk and talking to all my friends that would call me on the hotline—that I was not authorized to have at my workplace—saying, "Hey, by the way, did you hear about such and such?" And the reason they'd talk to me is because when they'd talk to somebody else, nobody would want to do anything about anything. I wrote up a report saying that I figured there were at least five hundred rockets spread out around our perimeter. Something hit me all at once, and I said, "Jesus, this has got to be told right now." So I went down to II Field Force to the operations center—I was the only woman that normally ever went down there—and I was telling the sergeant major standing beside me what was happening, and he said, "Just a minute." Then a lieutenant came over. I don't know why they always did that with me; I went through more echelons and chains. So I said, "What are you guys doing about all this stuff?" "Ahh, there's nothing out there" was the reply. And it went on up the line. The colonel comes out, asks me, "Do you have an SI clearance?" I said, "No, but I'm not talking about SI clearances. I'm talking about what's happening right now," you know. He says, "I'm sorry, we can't talk to you. We don't have anything to do with that."

By that time, I'm really worried—these rockets were pointed at our compound. I have always thought that if I take care of me and you're riding with me, then you're taken care of. If I'm safe, you're safe. That was the first time in Vietnam I ever cried absolute tears. I was so angry when I walked out of there. I was angry that I knew what I was talking about and they didn't listen. This happened on the eighth of whatever month it was. On the tenth they put out a couple rounds of duster fire, 40-millimeter duster fire, and they had a couple of secondary explosions. The next night, they did a flyover and got four more secondary explosions, okay? On the twelfth, they put out whatever they put out, but they got 117 secondary explosions up to a hundred feet high in the area that I was talking about. And I sat back and, again, felt very smug and snug and comfortable and thanking God, because had they not done it, we might have been hit again, another Tet. And I think a lot of people would have been killed. The things that I did were not big, in one sense, but had I not been assertive behind whatever it was I was saying—and I'm not saying that a lot of other people did not come to some conclusions—I don't know what more could have happened. What I am saying is that a person must be assertive enough to say, *"Do* something about it, please!" or even be willing to say, "I don't care what you do with the information, just here it is." If fifty million people take credit for it, I don't care.

Well, I stayed in Vietnam for three years. I came home a couple times during that. I came home on leave, had a marvelous time. I don't want to give the impression that all my time in Vietnam was spent . . . well, all my time was spent working. A lot of my time was spent really enjoying the camaraderie. There was a togetherness in Vietnam you wouldn't believe; most of the prejudices, for a while, went away. Even though blacks were into their black-power salute and a few whites had their confederate flags and stuff, there was a togetherness that I think you can only get in times of peril, if I can use that term.

I kept getting orders to go to Fort Bragg, North Carolina. I got five sets of orders to go to Fort Bragg while I was in Vietnam. I kept telling them, "I'm not going to Fort Bragg. I'll stay here." I was living in a hotel in Saigon my last six or seven months, and I had to walk to work. That was a trip, a combat tour in itself, walking up and down the streets of Saigon. But it got so bad I used to . . . They didn't want us to carry weapons in Vietnam; women couldn't carry weapons. Doris I. Allen carried her weapon. Make no mistake I carried a .45. A couple others of us, friends of mine, carried weapons. That .45 was mine and I loved it, and I'm going to say it now: I still have it. I used to be able to cock that thing behind my back—maybe I was getting skittish or whatever. I had seen my name on captured enemy documents as one of the persons to be eliminated, and that's scary. The first time they told me that they had found a document with my name on it, it was on a list of intelligence personnel to be done away with, to be eliminated. I felt kind of, well, important—"Hey, tell all your friends how important you are," you know. Then the second time, I actually saw it. It was on a captured enemy document. The third time I saw it I happened to be assigned to the translation branch, in charge of the interpreters section at the Combined Documents Exploitation Center (CDEC) in Saigon. And one of my supervisors said,

"Come here, Ms. Allen," and he put the captured document in my hand. I told him two and a half months later I was going home. It really got kind of scary. Then when cowboys on motorbikes would come by me and try to rip off my briefcase, it was just time to come home. I was getting skittish, getting nervous, and I might have blown somebody's head off. . . .

But at any rate, they finally got me back to Fort Bragg anyway. You know, when people want you, they get you. When I got back to Fort Bragg, I put on my uniform and I walked in, and I know I was looking good—a new warrant officer, WO-1. I had three rows of good stuff here on my chest—you know, all those pretty little five-cent ribbons you put on your chest on this side—and I had three ribbons over here. I walked into the office, and the colonel was sitting behind his desk, and in his office were sitting five other colonels. He says, "We have just the place for you. We're going to put you in CONTIC." The same outfit I was in before! I said, "Just a moment, sir," and he says, "Yes?" I said, "I must say this: I'm not given to vulgarity, and I'm not given to profanity, but I think I've spent my time in hell." And he says, "What? What do you mean?" I said, "I just got back here from Vietnam, where I spent three years. Before I went to Vietnam, I spent four years at Fort Bragg, North Carolina, and I think that's enough time in hell." He said, "Oops. Okay, where do you want to go?" Okay, that was another example of "if you don't tell him, you don't get it." I'm not saying that other women haven't told what they wanted, you know, and been assertive, but I'm saying that if we don't do that, then we are doomed as far as I'm concerned. And I think that's one of the reasons that I was able to do thirty years in the military—because had I not been able to talk for myself and not feel afraid to do that, then I think I could not have survived as well.

When I got back from Vietnam, I guess I did not have the problems that some people had. Maybe that was because, as I told you, my sister had been my commanding officer back at Camp Stoneman and she was very in tune to me. I became an instructor at the intelligence school in

Fort Holabird, Maryland. About a year later we moved the intelligence school to Fort Huachuca, Arizona, and within a matter of a year, I became a full-time special agent. So my life was all working when I got back, as opposed to being put out on the street—put out to pasture, so to speak— and being left to the mercies and the tendernesses of those people who did not like Vietnam vets, especially here in the state of California. Some people went home to some places, and they were heroes, and that's not that they were looking to be heroes, they were just looking to come home and—"Please welcome me home. I've been away." I think it was easier for me because of my sister on the one hand and the fact that I was really working on the other.

Actually one of the biggest shocks to me was that I had less money to spend. Within a month of leaving Vietnam I had been promoted to warrant officer. As a spec-7 having as much time in service as I did, I made more money than a warrant officer-one, newly promoted. So I lost that money. I was also collecting combat pay and interrogator specialty pay, so my shock was more like coming back and "Geez, I'm broke!" I wasn't eating as well—over there it was good steaks. Make no mistake, I ate very well in Vietnam. All that heat—I had an air conditioner in my room. I worked hard but I played hard. I had a nice, nice fellow who thought the world of me, and I thought the world of him. Every day he'd bring me a quart of Crown Royal. I didn't usually drink the whole bottle every day—unless I had to go to the bunker.

But that was a different time. . . . You had to sort of get crazy over there. Then when you got home, there was a lot of camaraderie lost. Nobody even really rapped about these things, and then things start going through your head. A good friend of mine, a nurse, told me that when she got back and saw that she was not being welcomed back, she internalized it and put it upon herself and said, "The only reason I'm feeling that way is 'cause I left that guy on the gurney, and I got to go back and take care of him." I think a lot of Vietnam vets have not been able to air and say what was happening. Again I'm very fortunate to have my sister that, even right now when I try to get crazy or whatever, says, "Come on, knock it off" or "Hey, this is what's happened to you." I think we all needed that somewhere.

After I retired in 1980, I never had to go out there on the street and look for a job. A friend of mine called me a month before I got out. I hadn't talked to him for five years, and he says, "Congratulations on your retirement." We had a nice conversation, and he said, "By the way, what I really called about is, I'd like you to come work for me." So the bottom line of that is that I did become a private investigator with his company, and we still work together. The other thing that really helped me is that I'm working on my Ph.D. So what I've been doing—I've been working; I haven't given myself a chance to fall. . . . It's still there in my mind, but it has not come out to really haunt me, okay? Like I say, I keep busy, and now that I'll finish my Ph.D. next year, I'll have to find something to do, something to keep me going. Another thing I haven't been willing to do in one sense is to walk the picket line, but I might have to go start doing that.

Now you have the story of my life, my entire life.

Charlotte Capozoli Miller

95TH EVAC. HOSPITAL,
DA NANG—FEB. '70 TO FEB. '71

Charlotte lives in Baltimore, Maryland, and works as a psychiatric nurse in an acute care setting. She is raising two children and pursuing her education on a part-time basis. "I am professionally committed to the concept that before anyone can administer to the health needs of an individual, one must recognize the *dignity* of human life."

She met me at Baltimore's Penn Station. It was early in the morning, and she had come almost directly from having worked the night shift. We sped off on a Cook's tour of Baltimore. Then, after serving me a huge meal, Charlotte began talking about Vietnam.

We went to an empty downtown bar, looking for a place to unwind, then found a happier, boisterous place down on the waterfront. I missed all the commuter trains back to D.C. and finally grabbed the 8:05 while Charlotte's son, Byron, had to settle for a hot dog instead of dinner.

It was dark on the train—my mind realizing the mistake that I had made in trying to crowd too much into a hectic schedule, discovering how difficult it is to say good-bye to someone who has become so close to you in such a short period of time—exactly the way friendships were made during the war. And in a way, the war is still doing that to us.

A MALE NURSE THAT I HAD GONE TO NURSING SCHOOL
with and I decided to join the Army with the purpose of
going to Vietnam on the buddy system. So I walked in to
a recruiter and said, "Can you send me to Vietnam?" He
said, "Have a seat!" I think within four weeks we were at
officers basic in San Antonio, Texas, then went directly
from officers basic to Vietnam. As a matter of fact, thinking about this, he and I were the only two in the whole
class that were going directly to Vietnam. After six weeks
of basic, we traveled to San Francisco, and within twenty-
four hours, we were in Long Binh. That was February 12,
1970.

I was the only female, other than the flight attendants,
on the plane with about two hundred men who were coming into country. I was so nervous when I got off the
plane—there was one man on each side of me who took
me by my elbows, and my feet never touched the ground;
they just literally carried me into the airport and set me
down. Jim and I were assigned to the 95th Evac Hospital
in Da Nang. We flew in a C-130 north to Da Nang, got in
to the hospital around two or three in the afternoon, were

met by the chief nurse, and showed to our quarters. I guess we were only there about two hours, and we heard this large explosion. Well, needless to say, I hit the dirt! I was scared to death. There was a rock quarry on the other side of the peninsula that dynamited everyday at four o'clock; nobody warned us. They used to call you the FNGs, which were the "fairly new guys"—there's a more explicit meaning, but I'll eliminate that. And you could always tell who the new people were, because we were reeling and shaking in our boots.

Then we were assigned to our areas, and I spent about two months on a neurosurgical unit that was just an extreme amount of responsibility with a heavy patient load. We had twenty neurosurgical patients, and then on the other side we had twenty surgical patients, a heavy load of IVs, dressings, et cetera. Also, the way the government paperwork is set up for nursing in hospitals for transcribing doctors' orders is just very redundant and time-consuming. I was always getting in trouble because I didn't get the paperwork done on time, but my patient care was always good—I always took care of the patients first. We had GIs and Vietnamese civilians and children; we also took care of prisoners of war in our hospital. It was a whole gamut of experiences, not only in terms of the injuries that you saw but your emotions and reactions to that.

I guess the few things that strike me the most were the long hours, the heavy patient load, the lack of any kind of positive reinforcement—just the expectation that you were to produce, and everything on a very negative basis: "Captain, your blouse is too short. Captain, you don't have your hat on." I was allergic to Army wool socks, and my mother sent me mens', like, argyle socks from the States, and because my pants were too short, you'd always see these plaid socks sticking out of my boots. The chief nurse was always on my case about that, and the colonel said, "Well, one of the highlights of my day is to see Capozoli walking down the hall with her bowlegs and her wild-colored socks, so leave her alone."

I guess about a month after I was there, they had a dining in at the general's mess. That's when they send an Army

Chinook helicopter to pick up the nurses, all dressed up in their civilian clothes, to fly across the peninsula to be the escorts for the generals and colonels and the high-ranking officials of the multiforces there. It was incredible to think that that occurred in a war zone. The best linen, china, lobster, steak, servants with their linen towels over their arms, pouring the wine—I mean, there was war going on within minutes of you. You were there to entertain the general's officers. If you didn't comply, then certainly you didn't get invited back. Well, that was fine with me. I guess the real issue was that they kept us late and we couldn't get the flight back, and they had to drive us through the city at night in open jeeps, which was very unsafe and frightening. We couldn't get back on our compound because it was after midnight, and the guard at the sentry post didn't care if you were the president. Then the next day I got in trouble for being late. Well, my mouth has always gotten me in trouble, and I said, "Colonel, I volunteered for Vietnam. I don't owe the Army anything for my education. I'm here as a volunteer. Yes, I'm in the military, but this is a crock of shit. I'm not a high-class lady of the night for these men that are old enough to be my grandfather." So, needless to say, I was never invited back. Then I was labeled a troublemaker, and it never stopped for the two years I was in the military. Captains just don't tell colonels what they think, where to go, and what to do when they get there.

And also, for us as women, who could we socialize with? You socialize with the doctors—they were geographical bachelors, or they were, perhaps, individuals that you didn't age-wise or identity-wise have a lot in common with. They were really macho, and they worked very little. I mean, when they worked, they worked very hard—I'm not discrediting them in any way—but they did their surgery and left. So if there were days when they didn't have any surgery, all they had to do was come and make rounds and leave. But we worked there twelve to fifteen or more long hours a day, everyday, sometimes twelve to fifteen days in a row if staff was short. I mean, it was just incredible.

When I think back now about that, I don't know how we did it.

I think every woman that served there—I'll tell ya, they can't tell us anything. I mean that. And even now, in civilian life, you do a job and you're really good at what you do and you can handle a lot of things at one time. It almost becomes a drawback; you almost get punished because it alienates you from other staff. Everyone wonders, ''Who do you think you are? What are you trying to prove?'' I'm not, it's just . . . we are good at what we do, and that was the mecca. The difficulty lies now in trying to be able to apply it and not being criticized for it. It's almost as though you're viewed as having something wrong with you. Does that make any sense?

Getting back to Vietnam—you know, coming into the country, you're not only adjusting to the military life, but also to a strange country, to a new way of doing things. Then, added to that, you are dealing with the idea that you're in a war. Everything by itself as an entity was a tremendous stress, but when you lump all those things together—I mean, we who deal in psychiatry talk about helping patients improve their coping mechanisms and dealing with little bits of things at a time—that was a situation where you really didn't have any control; you had to deal with all of those factors at one time.

Initially, I don't ever remember being afraid, but now that I look back, I think at first I was afraid for maybe a week, and then you kind of romanticize it and deny it; you assimilate with the group, where you don't wear flak jackets and helmets and ''So what, there's a red alert.'' I can remember, I was only there about a month or so and there was a red alert in our hospital. The Marines who were standing guard on the POWs were running around with their weapons locked and loaded. We were supposed to put mattresses over our patients and wear our flak jacket and helmet and stand guard at the door, and all I could think of was, ''What if nothing happens and I still have to get all these IVs out and these dressings?'' So I kept on working, and I couldn't work in a steel pot, so I didn't wear one, and the flak jacket only slowed me down, so I didn't wear it. I just kept on going and reassuring my patients. When I think about it now, I was terrified, but you could never admit it or deal with your own emotions and feelings because if you did, you could never continue on doing anything meaningful for anyone.

I worked in the neuro ward for about two months when I asked to be transferred. They had an opening in the receiving and pre-op area, and that's where I spent the rest of my year. We took the patients right off the choppers and brought them into the receiving area and did the triage. Anyone who had so many multiple injuries—head wounds, frags in the eyes, facial or oral surgical wounds, chest and abdominal wounds, orthopedic wounds—we deemed them train wrecks. That's what we called them—train wrecks.

All the specialists would come in. We would initially establish lines and pump in the blood and stabilize the patients, minimally clean them up, and then send them off to the OR. I mean, guys came right out of the field with their fatigues on and their grenades in place. You had to secure them by taking away their weapons, and some of the guys would be so disoriented, they didn't want to part with their weapons. You'd have to have the men in the registrar's office try to talk them down to give up their weapons and reorient them so that we could get to them. I became so proficient at starting IVs that they used to call me in to the operating room to put in jugular IVs. It just became automatic that everyone got at least two lines when they came in. And then we had to deal with shortness of supplies. I can remember leaving duty and going to donate blood and going right back to work because we'd be so low on blood, and many of us did that.

I guess one particular incident that I think about now on a quite frequent basis—I don't think I ever stopped thinking about it. An orphanage was rocketed, and I think we put about two hundred kids through the receiving and pre-op areas. These were children from infancy to adolescence. I mean, literally had their eyes blown away, their shoulders—you could see all their bone structure just blown away—limbs. One kid came in with an arm between its legs—intestines out on their abdomen, brains out on their forehead, blood everywhere. I can remember saying to my mother in the tape I sent her, ''Mom, I had kids coming out of my ears: they were on chairs, they were on desks, they were on the floor, they were in the hall, they were stacked up, they were everywhere.'' That was just incredible, that was just incredible. And I guess the intensity of that situation lasted about fifteen straight hours. Some of the women and teenagers who seemed so innocent were really VC by night. When a chopper landed and GIs came in half-blown away—maybe the next chopper were women and teenagers, and you didn't know if they were the VC, if they had done that to the guys. . . . You dealt with that in a sense of suppressing your feelings or your questions so that you could go on and function. I mean, the intensity of what we dealt with—when I really think about it now, I don't know how I or any other person could've done it. It's phenomenal. I think we're fantastic. I do, I think we sit on the right hand of the Father. And whatever there is in the hereafter that's positive, we have a direct nonstop flight.

One particular young man was an officer—and I've been to the Wall a couple times, but I've never been able to look up his name because I only remember that his name ends in *ski*—he was a train wreck. He lost his spleen, lacerated his liver, had half of his intestines blown away, had two broken legs, a broken arm, multiple frags in his body, had his head operated on, had oral surgery done, lost part of his lung—and we stabilized him. He developed every complication in the world, from hepatitis to pulmonary emboli to a cardiac arrest. We brought him back to the point where we would sign up for overtime essentially—nurses would special him on our off-duty time because he required so much care; he needed one or two nurses just to take care of him. So we'd do our twelve-hour shift, then we'd break up the other time by specialing him. We had to get special permission to keep him longer, because he was not stable enough physically to air-evac out. Through all the complications, he came back, and he just had a wonderful, wonderful attitude. He was truly a fine human being. He was due to leave about two weeks before I did. His one request was that he had some film that needed to be developed, and I told him I'd take it to the PX and have it developed and send it to him in the States at home. He just loved us all. . . . Anyway, he promised that wherever I was in the country, he would come and take me out to dinner. . . . He was sent to Japan, and when I left Vietnam, our plane landed in Japan for refueling, so I ran into the airport to call the hospital to tell him hello and see how he was doing, and I found out from them that he died . . . and I've never been able to forget that because we worked so hard. . . . It just was so unfair.

When I see the news now about Beirut and Grenada—those guys are over there—they couldn't even lock and load their weapons. And when I see their families on television now . . . The same thing is happening, and we're not doing anything about it. Our officials are doing the same thing. They're telling us what they want us to know. They're setting up another situation where our troops are going to be fragmented, and they're going to experience delayed stress—or they'll give it another name and write up additional symptoms. . . . And I don't know if it's really worth it, because just like Vietnam, Lebanon has been torn by war for hundreds of years and it's religious in nature, and those are issues that people will never resolve. So no one learned from the loss of Ski's life. And the brave men walking around this country today who are physically disabled or psychologically not home yet, or even the women that have taken care of them . . .

The doctors—when they did their surgery, it was very intense and sometimes long hours, then they had periods that they didn't have to operate. They made rounds, and they were gone. If you had a problem, you dealt with it. I mean, you had standing orders, and you used your judgment and your common sense; you did fine, and things went real well. I put chest tubes in, and I sutured, and I debrided wounds and suctioned open, gaping cavities, and I practically did cut-downs. I mean, now I can't give a Tylenol without some other person telling me it's okay. When I came back to civilian life, I worked in an emergency room in Pittsburgh, and they wouldn't let me start an IV without being supervised by the IV therapy nurse. I probably put in more IVs in that year than she ever saw in her whole life! Jesus, it's incredible. And I have a real hard time now, in civilian life, when people go to give me an evaluation of any kind. I guess I'm arrogant, or maybe I'm grandiose, I don't know, but I have a real hard time with it, because I think, "Who in the hell are you to evaluate my skills?"

After Vietnam I can't equate it, I can't find it again: I can't find that "A team" that went in there and did the work; I can't find that closeness, that sense of caring. Then on the other side of the coin, because it was a replacement war, it seems like every time you made friends with someone that you could identify with—someone with whom you could sit down and talk about your innermost feelings and thoughts and share your secrets—they were always leaving. You were always saying good-bye. And I find myself now not getting that close to anybody, not investing any more, because it's like being in Vietnam—as soon as you get close, for whatever reason, it's time to DEROS. I work, I take care of my children, I volunteer at the vet centers, but I find socially I've withdrawn a great deal. It's really too painful. . . .

One thing I want to talk about is the monsoons. I hate rain. If it's a shower and it makes it nice and green, that's okay, but when it's dark and dreary and overcast, it reminds me of the monsoons. Your clothes never dried and your room never dried. I ended up sick. I had a temperature of a hundred and five, and they admitted me to the hospital with an FUO—fever of undetermined origin. They were going to med-evac me to Japan, but I refused to go because we also had a typhoon while I was there. I was really terrified that the plane was going to fall out of the sky, and where would I be? In the South China Sea somewhere. I'd rather stay there and take the risk of at least dying among people I knew.

During another typhoon, the water was coming up as high as the buildings down on the shore. Our commander was going to take us up to Monkey Mountain. The Marines had evacuated Monkey Mountain because the winds were so high they had taken the rooftops off the buildings. He was taking us up there, and I said, "If the Marines left, I ain't going." And I wasn't. I made a pizza in my electric skillet and had two bottles of wine, and I ran around from place to place passing out my pizza and wine. And I sat with my feet propped up and watched all the lifers evacuating their stereo equipment, their refrigerators, putting them in jeeps and ambulances and taking them to dry land. It was hysterical. They fled, and I stayed and waited out the storm. We listened to some great music, and some of my favorite people were there. And one particular gentleman that I had an amorous affair with, we made some good love in the rain while everyone ran around.

Getting ready to leave, it was customary to throw a DE-ROS party. Because most of the people that I socialized with were the enlisted guys, I asked to have the party in the NCO club. Then, with the permission from the commander, the officers could also come. I had to take the club officer to the commander to get permission to have my party, and he gave permission. I paid the money and arranged for everything. And they had everything. I mean, we had steaks, hot dogs, hamburgers, free-flowing booze, beer, wine, and we had a band.

The next day, which was the day before I was to leave country, the commander sent a runner to my hooch to get me to come to his office and demanded to know why I had my party in the NCO club and who gave me permission. I said, "You did," and he said, "I never did any such thing!" Well, he should've known not to bother me with a hangover, and I said, "I beg your pardon, *sir,* but that's a lie." I got the NCO club officer and brought him to the colonel and said, "Now, you tell him in front of me that you didn't give the permission." He said, "Capozoli, I'd court-martial you, except you'd have to stay here longer, and God knows what you'd get us into." He took out five dollars in MPC, and he gave it to the NCO club officer and said, "You put her on a plane tomorrow, and I don't give a good Goddamn where it's going." And that was my farewell to Vietnam.

We left and went down to Cam Ranh Bay and were there

about three days, waiting to get on a manifest. The last night we were there, the place was rocketed. We lost electricity and water, and I was in the shower washing my hair, no less. I had this soapfilled hair and came running out, found a water tank, and used it to get the soap out of my hair. The sentry was saying, "Captain, Captain, we're on red alert! We're being rocketed!" And I said, "Well, dammit, if I'm going to die, I'm going to die with clean hair!" I didn't think we were ever going to get out of that place.

When we arrived in Fort Lewis, Washington, we saw the McDonald's golden arches, and everyone on the plane went crazy. And when we got down, people got out of the plane and knelt down and kissed the ground—that was the tradition. Going through the airport, there were a lot of antiwar protesters in there throwing fruit at us and screaming obscenities and calling us all kinds of names. And interestingly enough, the two guys that carried me off the plane in Vietnam were back on the plane to come home. One guy was a Green Beret, airborne—he had seen a lot of action out in the jungle; it was just miraculous. We had our own little homecoming and didn't leave the West Coast for another day. We just stayed out there and stayed together. I mean, we were, like, holding on to each other and sharing stories and drinking, just staying together, and we cried . . . and we parted . . . and we came home.

I guess if I had to summarize it, Vietnam is one of the more positive experiences in my life. The only other experience that equates that was having my two children. And I feel Vietnam impacts on my life in every way because that experience becomes a part of you. It helps formulate your present attitude, your philosophy, your problem-solving method and coping skills. I see myself as a strong person, but that experience is something that only in the last few years of talking about it and dealing with it and working through it have I become more healthy. It's sort of the dichotomy; it was so good and yet it was so awful. It was so good because of the intensity, because of the relationships, the survival, the challenge, the learning experience. I mean, I truly appreciate life far more. I think I value a human being far more than the average person. I tend to look a little harder for the positive and the good and try to walk that extra mile more readily, because I saw so much death and destruction: I saw the outcome of when people stop communicating.

Penni Evans

AMERICAN RED CROSS, SRAO
CAM RANH BAY—MAR. '70 TO
AUG. '70
LONG BINH—AUG. '70 TO OCT. '70
CU CHI—OCT. '70 TO DEC. '70
QUANG TRI—DEC. '70 TO MAR. '71

Penni resides in Santa Rosa, California, where she works as an employee relations/affirmative action specialist. "I enjoy the outdoors, hiking, and photography and share home with two people of the feline persuasion." She does volunteer work for a local Vietnam veterans organization, through which she shares her concern for other women who served in Vietnam, "the invisible minority."

Over the years, there have been very few people I could talk with about Vietnam because when I did, the comments were "Women in the war zone, what are you talking about?" or "You were over there supporting babykillers?" or "You were a hooker"—all this kind of stuff . . . and just for openers.

I have one friend, Mary, who is one of the people that I could share some of my experiences with. One day she introduced me to a man who was a Vietnam veteran. In the conversation she said, "Penni was in Vietnam." And he said, "You were in Vietnam?" I said, "Yeah," real quietly, like I didn't really want to talk about it. He asked, "What did you do?" Mary said, "She was with the Red Cross." He looked at me and said, "You were a Doughnut Dolly?" . . . He got up, walked over, pulled me out of my chair, and gave me this big bear hug. "My God, thank you!" he said. "I didn't know how to thank you over there; my buddies didn't know how to thank you. . . . You are fantastic!"

I HEARD ABOUT THE PROGRAM IN THE LATE SIXTIES, when I was in college as a political science major. A friend of mine worked at the career center, and we were trying to find an interesting job for me. I wanted to travel, and I like working with people. We heard about the Red Cross program, got a recruiter to come out, and it sounded really interesting. I thought, "That's what I want to do," rushed my schedule up to twenty-two units so I could graduate a semester earlier, and then found out that they didn't have any openings for the program until June. I graduated in December 1969 and went back to Indianapolis to stay with my parents. I'm a northern Californian by birth, and it doesn't snow and sleet like it does in Indianapolis, and I was miserable.

Then, sometime in January, I got a call from them—"We have a group going over in March. Are you interested?" I said, "Sure." So they flew me down to Saint Louis for an interview. They accepted me and said, "We have openings for the Korean group and the Vietnam group. Where would you like to go?" I said, "It snows in Korea doesn't it? I think I'll go to Vietnam." Believe it or not,

337

that was one of my major reasons for going—that and being a political science major, thinking, "Maybe I can find out what the hell is going on in Vietnam." Also, I really wanted to travel, to get all the benefits: a stereo, china, go to Hong Kong, have jewelry and silks made . . . all the good stuff. When I had been at Colorado Women's College in Denver, I had dated airmen from Lowry AFB and really kind of understood some of the loneliness and concerns they had being away from home. I thought maybe I could help.

I went to Washington, D.C., for two weeks of "training." They gave us uniforms, and we all hemmed ours too short. In fact, when I look at the pictures, I go, "Oh, God!" That was when the mini was in.

We learned about military etiquette, how to read military insignia, and what we were supposed to do in representing the Red Cross on duty and off. Be feminine, don't swear, don't date enlisted men (unstated, but there). We were to be nonsexual symbols of purity and goodness . . . be sister, mother, girl next door, but don't have affairs; that's a no-no. What they didn't tell us was what to do about the rumors, the comments, the come-ons . . .

Then we spent a week in San Francisco waiting for a flight out of Travis. Four of us went to Menlo Park to a chapter there, where we folded bandages, we literally folded bandages! On our last day they said, "Your mission today is to look at San Francisco and let us know what you find." So we had the whole day to explore and went out that night to Fisherman's Wharf. People found out that we were going to Vietnam, and they bought us drinks, dessert, it was incredible. I mean, that's what we had going over, this fantastic support.

After processing in Saigon, I was sent with one other girl to Cam Ranh Bay air base. We went up in a C-130, and I was pretty nervous. When we landed, my impression was, it was a sandpile, a huge sandpile. We were shown our hooch, which was in the nurses' compound. It was like a Spanish-style adobe, built in a U-shape with a patio in the center with a gate at one end. There were four rooms in the hooch, and the girls had made one of them into a party room with a stereo, refrigerator, chairs, and a rug. There were a few nurses there who were really neat ladies, but unfortunately, we basically segregated ourselves from them. The hooch was on the street right next to the night line, and you would hear the rockets and small arms fire during the sapper attacks at night. . . . Incredible.

We had two clubs at Cam Ranh, and I was there for five months. There were eight women in the beginning, and then it dropped down to six. At Westside club we had volleyball, pool, table shuffleboard, and a library. We rotated working in the clubs and going out to the units on a regular basis. Thank God for that. I hated the clubs, for the most part—there were some guys that I couldn't stand. The guys that I did like really made the tour easier. I mean, these were nice men, from an eighteen-year-old kid all the way up to a grandfather, all races and religious persuasions—just a cross section of America.

There were Caribou squadrons there; most of the jets had moved up to Phan Rang. I made friends with a lot of the pilots and crew chiefs. That was one of the neat things there—everybody that worked on those planes and flew them were like a family; there wasn't a lot of rank distinction. I remember one day—I wasn't in the country very long at all—sitting with a ground chief for a squadron while he was waiting for word on three of his birds . . . and . . . we waited and waited. I was with him when he found out that they had all gone down, two of them in flames . . . no survivors on any of the planes. That was my first communication that this was a real war, that people got killed. I remember crying, and one girl at the center asked what was wrong. When I told her she said, ''Well, you've got to get used to it.'' That was it. I started withdrawing and saying, ''I'm not going to let it get me.''

The club was essentially a social place for people to gather. The ''program'' runs that we made were a lot different. There were two kinds of runs: what we called our base run, which was to units on the base (within or just outside the perimeter), and then we had our forward runs. These were way out in the boonies: Ban Me Thuot, Ban Don with the Special Forces camps . . . wherever artillery groups were, and APC units that might be in the middle of a clearing for a day . . . If they wanted us, we went there.

The programs were about forty-five minutes in length. We carried everything in what we called "prop bags," which were big green canvas bags with a couple of handles so a girl on each side could carry it. We were working with from five to as many as seventy guys, but usually five to twenty, and we went out in two-girl teams. The programs used cliché formats, like Concentration, covering any subject under the sun, from advertising to zoology. We would make up new programs about every six weeks: do the research, come up with the format, make all the props, and then deliver it.

Out in the field, we would do our programs up against a tank or a tree, in a hangar or a mess hall, on a bunker, in a jungle clearing or a muddy field filled with APCs, wherever. The whole purpose of it was to bring American women out to the field to let the guys know that we cared. A touch of home, a chance to take a respite from the war and the realities of their situation. Whether it did any good is still debatable; it depends on who you talk to.

Our program was so unique, because we saw more of Vietnam than probably almost anyone else. We saw more of the guys, how they lived, what they did in their own environment, and were dealing 95 percent of the time with essentially able-bodied, healthy people. It was the other 5 percent that was the killer, because we were not prepared—not that any of the nurses or others in the medical profession were prepared for what happens in a war, but we had *no* training whatsoever. So, out in the field, some GI would say, "Hey, Joe got hit yesterday. Would you take his stuff back to him?" You would go into the hospital and walk through the wards of torn up, mutilated bodies with . . . wounds that are so big they can't be covered properly, naked bodies, legs blown off . . . and where do you look? What do you say?

I was in four units. After Cam Ranh I went to II Field Force at Long Binh. They had strictly forward runs. I was only there about six or seven weeks, then went to Cu Chi and five weeks later to Quang Tri, where I finished my tour. Cu Chi was mostly all runs. We tried to open a mini-center, and it just didn't work. A Red Cross woman was killed, murdered, in Cu Chi the night before I was originally supposed to go there. We got a call about six-thirty in the morning—"Don't let Penni get on that plane!" We knew something had happened but didn't know what, and we all had friends down there. And until last year, I carried around a guilt that if I had gone down there the evening before, things would have changed, that she wouldn't have been killed. I went through totally unreasonable guilt for all these years.

At Quang Tri the reality of the war really hit. Our office was in the hospital, and some of the medics and corpsmen thought it was really neat for us to go in and write a letter for somebody. . . . I mean, these poor people were so blown out of their skulls with pain and medication and were so torn up that they didn't want us there, but they didn't know how to say no. That was during the Laotian invasion, and I lost friends. . . . You would party with people, and the next day they weren't there. Or we would be programming to guys in the field in the morning and then go to an aid station in the afternoon, and there they would be. . . . or go up to Alpha 4 and see a bunker by the chopper pad that had just been blown up. . . . These were guys that we had joked around with, and now they were gone . . . gone.

We flew on a lot of helicopters, and I am very prone to airsickness, but I only got sick twice. Some turkey was trying to impress us and did a couple of hammerhead stalls—which are totally illegal, but they learn how to do it so in case of a stall there is a way out of it. You go up real high, cut your engines, and the force of gravity, as you fall, spins the rotors and starts your engines again. The other time, we were up by Khe Sanh. The chopper right ahead of us took enemy ground fire, and we took evasive action. We were going along, following the contour of the land, up and down real fast, and I was very, very sick.

And, it seemed, by Murphy's Law, when a Red Cross girl gets stuck on an unscheduled overnight, her period starts. It happened to me up in Khe Sanh. I was somewhat prepared, but I ran out real quick. We were stuck there because of fog and couldn't get out. We spent the night in an ambulance backed up to a bunker. And we are hearing all these weird noises that are muffled by the fog: incoming, outgoing, small arms fire, flares going off setting up really eerie colors in the fog. I mean, absolutely surreal. It was like the scene on the river in the film *Apocalypse Now*. But this ambulance was our camp for the night. They found a couple of sleeping bags for us, and that was it!

Then, what happened the next day is a story in itself. Pat Rowan and myself went out with this assistant field director who came out to "protect the Red Cross girls." How he was going to protect us, I don't know, but he thought that it was his duty, the chauvinistic SOB! He wanted to go out to Lang Vei, which was the site of a severe massacre during the Tet offensive and the bombardment of Khe Sanh. Well, we go out in a jeep, with no radio—I think we had field jackets and helmets—with this guy and a driver with a .45 on his hip . . . and that was it. We see a bunch of guys, stop and pass out calendars, just talking to them—we didn't really program. They are going, "Women! Women!" Then we kept driving and driving and finally came to a truck. The guy says, "What the—are you doing here?" The assistant field director says, "We are looking for Lang Vei." "Well, you missed it by about three klicks"—or whatever it was—"You are in Laos!" So we turn around and finally find Lang Vei. There is an armored car unit there, and these guys are just blown away—they've been in the field four and a half weeks, and here are some round-eyes out in the middle of the jungle. Meanwhile, we had missed about three chopper rides already, and nobody knows where the hell we are.

We finally get back, and by this time I am getting awfully raw from the hand towels I was using for my protection, and I'm walking in a rather funny way. I am going to look up a doctor who is there, when someone says, "Okay, you are getting out of here." The general had found out we were still there—this is Khe Sanh; it is incredible the action that is going on there! The general says, "I want these girls out of here, now!" We went out on a chopper. It was foggy; you couldn't see. You would look out and see the side of the mountain right next to you! I remember the pilot saying, ''We'll give it a try, and if we can't make it, we'll go back. . . . If we can find our way back.'' I don't know how we made it.

There was another time in a chopper, when it suddenly took a steep dive and landed next to a road where there had been an accident. We brought in a young ARVN woman who had been injured. I held her in my arms as we took her to the hospital. I couldn't do anything for her; here I had this red cross on my shoulder . . . I couldn't do anything but hold her and tell her everything was okay. . . . And I remember more than once flying with body bags in the chopper.

Then there were some super times. I remember once down south, we flew into this chopped-out clearing, walked down a grade, through a little stream, and up a steep slope to a group of guys there from the 199th LIB, the ''Redcatchers.'' They were in little pup tents; they had been there for a while. We programmed to them, and the next day, through some error, were sent back to the same group. There was no other scheduled run, so we sat and talked to them, just chatted and shared tea. It was great, and we thoroughly enjoyed ourselves. Then we went out to another group and programmed. They were an APC group that had just taken two hits—no deaths, but some bad injuries from a road mine. As we were on our way back home to the base, the chopper pilot said, we just got a radio request to go to a certain coordinate.'' Then he says to us, ''Look out the window.'' We looked out, and it was the guys from the 199th who we had been together with the past two days! They were waving and tossing smoke up at us and basically saying, ''Thanks, we really appreciate you.''

We were out on this run, way out in the middle of nowhere, and our chopper transmission failed when we were about ten feet off the ground—we were lucky—so they were trying to find another bird for us. They were waiting for replacement parts, then the replacement bird came in and it broke down. Another one came in, and it was a supply chopper going over to a small radar outpost. So I flew with them to the radar post. (The girl I was working with was coming down with "Uncle Ho's revenge" and not feeling very well, so she stayed there.) I took a bunch of short-timer's calendars; it was going to be a real quick ten- or fifteen-minute stop. We landed and were getting out of the chopper, and I heard thump, thump, thump! I thought, "That doesn't quite sound like outgoing." They took me to this bunker real fast. I stayed there, talking to the guys as they were unloading supplies, and I keep hearing these explosions. The ground is shaking, and dirt is coming down off the bunker, but nobody seems concerned! I was a little nervous, but I just thought, "Hey, it's outgoing." Well, I found out later they had taken fourteen mortar rounds while I was there, and they were all really worried about me and very relieved when I came back.

We finally got another chopper in, and they were flying us back to base. We took ground fire . . . and when you are flying in Vietnam, you've got the doors open with the gunner . . . and if you go up high it gets really cold, especially at night. So we are circling around up there, and I'm freezing to death! They were watching the firefight and waiting for the gunships to arrive, being the observer, telling the artillery where to fire and the guys on the ground where they should go. This is going on for an hour. Meanwhile, *nobody* knows where we are. No one had bothered to radio that we had been stuck at this base all day. Our other runs hadn't heard from us, nobody knew where we were, and they were about ready to send out the Marines to find us. We assumed that the base had made contact, and when we landed we got our asses chewed! That night we went over to the club, and that's the night that I got an Air Medal and a Bronze Star. . . . Two of the guys that were with us that day—one had a Bronze Star and the other the Air Medal—held this great ceremony and gave me their medals "because of my coolness under fire, et cetera."

Then, there was the whole concept of wearing those stupid little blue uniforms. When we were in the centers they were fine, but not out in the field in mud up to our knees or in helicopters where the crew chief is saying, "Okay, everybody roll your sleeves down." (In case you crash, you get that two seconds to get out without getting badly burned.) We had no sleeves to roll down! And the chopper pilots loved to torque up their engines and have the dresses fly up over our heads. And you think that is feminine? BS! That is not feminine. We had no flak vests, no helmets, no bunkers to go to. Talk about feeling vulnerable! And scared, and having no power . . .

And I was so damn naive. When I went over there I had had, like, three sexual experiences. I was almost a virgin, but not quite. None of them had been anything to write home to mother about, much less to anybody else. I was going to protect the image of the Red Cross, because that's what they told me I was supposed to do. So I did not have one sexual affair when I was in Vietnam, though I really fell in love about three times . . . and supposedly I was having mad, passionate affairs with at least two of them. I mean, it didn't do anything to protect my image or the image of the Red Cross, and I just totally blew the opportunity of a lifetime! Then the whole fact that we were supposed to be hookers. What was that saying? "Nurses do it for free, but the Red Cross girls charge." We were supposed to be making all this money on the side. It was like, no matter what we did, if someone wanted to think of us that way, they were going to do it, because that was their need for some reason.

There was one incident—it was on New Year's Eve in Quang Tri—that totally destroyed a lot of my illusions. He was drunk but very sincere when he said, "You are not doing us a bit of good. All you are doing is teasing us: 'look but don't touch.' You are a bunch of cock-teasers, and you shouldn't be here." That's when I began to wonder, "My God, are we really helping? Or are we hurting these people?" I still vacillate; I really don't know on that score. I do know that I resent the hell out of not having taken advantage of some of the opportunities that were there, and I resent the fact that I wasn't mature enough to be there. Not many of us were, to be honest. . . .

Yet I am now, fourteen years later, proud of being a Doughnut Dolly in Vietnam. During those years there have been some difficult times. I didn't realize the impact that

Vietnam had had on me, on my perceptions, but I recognized a common thread that I couldn't touch nor understand. I denied a major event in my life. I turned off emotions, resented the hell out of authority and normalcy, and felt I couldn't fit into society. I've had more than six jobs since I returned, with the longest lasting barely two years, and long periods of unemployment. None of the jobs were satisfying for long, although I enjoyed some of them, but when I set goals, I'd get blown out of the water. I finally stopped making goals.

I had severe depression, recurring nightmares, start-reactions, and was fearful of things that represented Vietnam. There were two periods in my life I seriously thought about suicide as a viable option. I think I'm too much of a survivor to go to that extreme, but even the thoughts scared me. I went through three separate therapy sessions lasting three to five months each and never really understood the issues or pain. Vietnam wasn't discussed much—it was unimportant, so I thought—and I thought I was crazy having Vietnam still with me years after. Relationships with men were with the same type of person: those with the inability to make commitments, users in a way—"safe" in that there didn't have to be a closeness or vulnerability. A few times I thought I was in love, but it was more with the idea of love, not the person. So many times I wondered, "What is wrong with me? Why can't I love?" or "Why do I choose impossible candidates?" et cetera, et cetera. Again, that common thread that was intangible but very strong.

There has been a lot of lost time in those years, loneliness, frustration, medical problems relating to stress without understanding why or even how, wanting to succeed, wanting love and recognition, yet running, putting up barriers—my own emotional claymore mine perimeters.

It wasn't until the SRAO reunion in September of 1983 that I realized I wasn't alone, nor crazy, that the nightmares weren't mine alone. That weekend was a turning point for me. It touched on the common thread I'd wondered about for years but was never able to define. Seeing women I hadn't seen since Vietnam put me in touch with a sisterhood of caring friends, both old and new. It was so encompassing and emotional. It was love, caring, and most importantly, an acceptance—words spoken of feelings I had thought but never spoken, a bond formed from a common sense of uniqueness and pride in who we were and what we did. It is so hard to describe the feeling of that reunion—the joy, love, support . . . It was a touching of souls and a discovery—for myself, of myself.

Cheryl M. "Nicki" Nicol

91ST EVAC. HOSPITAL,
TUY HOA—FEB. '67 TO SEPT. '67
523D ATTACHED TO
8TH FIELD HOSPITAL,
NHA TRANG—SEPT. '67 TO FEB. '68

Nicki lives in a beautiful new home in Gig Harbor, Washington. We arranged for her to pick me up in town. Then she had trouble finding her way back, and I didn't find that a bit odd as all the roads look about the same around there.

In the next few hours she introduced me to four other women Vietnam veterans who live in the area, fed me a huge lunch, and went through her entire Vietnam scrapbook, all the while talking nonstop about her life in Vietnam and after Vietnam, back and forth, almost as though the two were inseparable in her mind.

After settling down and putting her "official" version on the tape, she offered to drive me back to my friends' home in Tacoma. As we drove, this woman of enormous energy, who does volunteer work for the Tacoma Mountain Rescue Unit, the Special Olympics, and in numerous Vietnam veterans organizations, began telling me, almost as an afterthought, how she had been forced to retire from nursing because of a debilitating illness. About the pain that she suffered, and how much she missed nursing.

I WENT INTO THE ARMY IN MARCH OF '66. I WAS LIV-
ing in Delaware, working in an absolutely nowhere job,
and I watched one too many Huntley-Brinkley news reports. They showed some field hospitals and things like
that, and I decided that I wanted and should go to Vietnam.
They had said on one of their news broadcasts that they
needed operating room and nurse anesthesia people. So I
joined the Army, and in April of '66 went down to Brook
to officer basic. We had a guaranteed first assignment, and
I put in for Letterman because I wanted to see my family.
But while I was down there, I decided no, I want to go
right to Vietnam. So I started sending in all these papers.
After we'd been there about four weeks, everyone in the
class had to go get shots of one type or another. Those that
had red flags were the ones who had to get cholera and
typhoid shots, and I had a red flag on mine. I went up to
them and said, "Well, I'm not going to Vietnam. I'm going
to Letterman right now." The sergeant just looked at me
and said, "Sorry, honey, you're going to Vietnam." So I
got all the shots, and about eight months later I left.

I was with the 91st Evac Hospital, and they had pretty

much handpicked everybody for it. The 91st was at Tuy Hoa, and there were a lot of us at Letterman who were going, so we knew everyone. A lot of us were an older group, not just right out of nurses training. All the nurses flew over together, and the enlisted personnel and some of the doctors were already there. They had some of the buildings up, but a lot of people were still in tents.

We spent, I guess, the first six weeks building our hospital. There was just this great big sand dune and cement slabs. I can remember using two-by-fours to smooth out the cement for the tropical buildings. What we ended up with were Quonset huts all in a row. The first Quonset held pre-op, lab, and x-ray. They were right off the triage. The next two Quonset huts were operating rooms; we had three tables in each room. The next after that was our workroom, where we cleaned our instruments, put our sets up, and the other side was offices. The fourth one was post-op, recovery room. When it was done, the inside looked a little tacky, and we tried to figure out something we could do for it. Tuy Hoa air base was ten or fifteen klicks from us, and so we made a proposal to our chief nurse that we get some wood from them to put in the Quonset huts. We got our enlisted people from the OR and some of the doctors in on it. They took us over, and we started having a big party with the Air Force people at their officers' club; the guys were more than happy to see round-eyes. And when we got everybody pretty well smashed, our guys came up in a deuce-and-a-half and loaded up all this plywood that was there and snuck off with it. Most of us weren't drinking. We were pouring the booze anyplace we could because we didn't want to get drunk, and then as soon as we got the high sign that they had the wood, we left. We spent the next two or three days putting that plywood up, and we got a beautiful stain for it. The place really looked sharp. Then a week or two after that we invited the CO of the Air Force base to come over, and he brought a bunch of his men with him. As we took them past the OR we thanked him very much for his wood, and he just laughed. I mean, that was kind of what everybody did, you know, moonlighting, scrounging. We had two or three guys in our unit that were darn good at it.

The group was very cohesive because everybody worked together. Then our chief nurse put out an order that the nurse officers could not speak to the enlisted men except in the line of duty. But the enlisted men were the ones who were punished if we were found conversing with them. One of the guys got sent to Cam Ranh Bay to unload ships, and he was one of the best damn people that we had in the recovery room. She broke us up quite a bit. After a year's time they would have what they call a rotational hump, where everybody would have to leave at once. After six months they sent ten of us down to Nha Trang and sent ten of their people up. She said that it was just one of those things, how it happened, but they sent the ten of us that fought her most of the time on policy and things. Nha Trang was in kind of bad shape at that time, and they sent three of us to the operating room. So that broke up the original group; the rest of them stayed at Tuy Hoa the whole time. There was a lot of flying back and forth between the two places after that, you know, because most of us were going with someone. I was going with a dentist from Tuy Hoa, and we saw each other almost every week, at least once, for a few hours if nothing else. It wasn't too far. My roommate in Nha Trang was going with a guy who flew a plane called a Beaver, and he'd fly us back and forth. Another one was going with a guy that was in an artillery unit that had a couple of choppers, and he was always glad to fly us back and forth. So you found ways to work things out, and you very seldom ever went by the book.

I remember our first mass casualty; we had about twenty-seven patients, and they were all Vietnamese. They were supposed to be having some kind of free election, and the story as we were told was, a Viet Cong girl about sixteen or seventeen years old had wired a kid three or four years old with some kind of explosives and sent him into the voting poll where a bunch of people were. And then she set him off. We got all these people in, and it was the first time we had had anything like that. We were all new at it, and I think right then I knew one of the things I was going to have a hard time with were the amputations. It just seemed like every time we turned around after that we were taking a leg off, sometimes an arm, mostly legs. That day we had a woman come in, and we had to amputate one arm and one leg. She was about five months pregnant, and she'd caught a piece of shrapnel right through the uterus and it killed the baby. I had to carry those all out . . . and it was . . . I don't know, I guess from then on that was something that just really bothered me. We put everything in plastic bags and hauled it out, put it in a drum, threw gas on them, and burned them. In the operating room you used what they call lap tapes to soak up the blood. In the States you use them and throw them away. We didn't have that many supplies, and we had to reuse ours. We had three drums, and we'd put the dirty ones in the first one, and all the bits of flesh and fat and everything would kind of come to the top; you'd skim that off, take the tapes up, put them in the second one, wash them a little bit more, and then in the third one. After they are in the third one, they were sent to the laundry and washed. That was a job I didn't care for either.

During that mass casualty there was a little ol' papa-san who had been lying out in the hall on a stretcher for I don't know how long. I hadn't scrubbed that day; I was getting instruments for people and bringing new patients in—putting up new sets and all. One of the anesthesiologists came over and said, "Nick, let's get this guy done, we've got to take his foot off." His left foot was just hanging by a tendon. And he was such a little guy it was easy for me to pick him up. So while the anesthesiologist was fixing his stuff up, I just reached down and picked this guy up to put him on the table. And that foot and tendon wrapped around my wrist . . . All I could do—I knew I was going to pass out—was lie right across him. So I had him up on the table, and I was lying across him, trying to take deep breaths and trying to stay with the program. The anesthesiologist saw what happened, came down, and just very gently unwrapped it and said, "It will be okay now." He said, "Go ahead and take the foot off, and then when one of the surgeons gets loose we'll come in and get it." So I took a pair of scissors and cut the foot off, just cut the tendon was all I had to do. But boy, that one stuck with me for a long time.

There were a lot of good things that happened there at Tuy Hoa too. Chuck Connors came one day. I wanted to see him so badly, and I was scrubbed on a bunch of cases when he came in. Our NCOIC knew how much I wanted to meet him, so he put a cap, a gown, and a mask on him and had him come in, and he autographed the back of my shirt. I was in seventh heaven. And then let's see . . . We had Lana Turner, Sebastian Cabot, and our very favorite— Martha Raye. That lady is something else. I never saw anyone light up the faces and spirits of patients and staff like she did. My good thoughts of Nam always include her and her willingness to give so much to us all.

Another thing we did while we were there is what we called med-cap; the medical civilian-aid program. There were five or six of us that really enjoyed it and went out a lot. I don't know how many klicks or miles it was to the refugee camp, but at first we would take one jeep and one deuce-and-a-half and maybe two of the sergeants would have a rifle with them. They were the only ones that had weapons. I think we had one doctor that always wore his .45, but he was kind of crazy anyhow. We would go up to this refugee camp that had hundreds and hundreds of people in it. There were two civilian Australian nurses there every day, and I don't know how they did it. Because all we ended up doing was giving penicillin shots and cleaning up sores. One time we took a crate of oranges with us and almost got trampled. We were up in the bed of the truck, trying to throw them out, and they just came all over it. It was scary. That's where I was taught to pull teeth. Like I say, I was going with a dentist, and we thought it was a good idea, and I wanted to learn. So he taught me how to numb the areas and how to pull the teeth. Their teeth were terrible. By the last few times we went on med-caps, we were all wearing flak jackets, helmets, and all were armed. It got real hairy around there.

We had only been there three or four weeks, I guess,

and one night the generator went out. We were using an old Quonset hut for an officers' club, and somebody started singing, and before you knew it everybody was coming out of their hooches, and I think every nurse and doctor on the compound was stashed in there singing all the old songs. We built a new club and brought two guys from the engineers over and paid them to put a rock front on the bar. Sent two doctors to Saigon to buy the furniture for it. We had a pretty neat place, but we had flares going off all the time; I don't know how necessary they all were, but they'd close the bar and tell everybody to go to their hooch. We would head for the hooches that were straight out the back door of the club and sit there laughing, talking, and hoping or wishing this wasn't for real. When I look back on it now, it was fairly stupid, because if anybody had ever thrown a rocket or mortar in on us, it would have wiped out the whole operating staff and most of the ward staff too.

The hospital was alone at first. There was a very small engineer unit behind us. There was a Chinook group a few klicks away, and I think eventually they put a landing strip in there for Beavers and another plane that had some kind of infrared stuff, but essentially we were the only ones there. All the security we had was corpsmen guarding you at night. That would just scare the living hell out of you, because some of them aren't too well trained. Just to show you the completely asinine way it was set up—say you start from front to back. There's the water and then the beach. Maybe two hundred yards of beach. Then the nurses' quarters were first, and off to the side of them were the doctors' quarters, or the men's quarters, because we had quite a few male nurses too. Then there was the commander's office and the chaplain and stuff like that. Then the hospital wards, the mess hall, and at the very back, five hundred or six hundred yards away, were all the enlisted men and the weapons. Now, if anything would have happened, they kept telling us it would probably come from the water. I just never understood that. The guys with all the firepower were the farthest away from the beach. And that was why some of us got our own weapons sooner or later. I realize medical people aren't supposed to, but that's a crock too.

The 4th Division moved out as we were moving in, and if we would have needed help in a hurry, the closest people that we trusted were the White Horse Division of the ROK Army. They were a ways from us, but less than ten miles. We always looked to them. We took care of their really bad patients. Something happened one night. We got two or three ROK patients in. They were pretty well shot up, and their CO came over to see them. God, they were good about that. I was taking some supplies into the OR that night and saw this ROK jeep come up and another chopper came in, and they had caught one of the guys that had shot his three men. They put him in the jeep with the officer, and as it was pulling out off the pad and turning left there was just one shot from the jeep.

Then I had an experience a little while after that I'm not sure I've really resolved yet. Joe and Donny and I were coming back from the mess hall one night, walking past triage, when somebody saw us and hollered, "Hey we've got five bad guys. We need help." So we went in, and it was a chopper crew. And there might have been one extra guy with them. There were three bodies, literally stacked, in one corner of triage, and the guys from graves registration were stripping them down, getting their weapons and all their gear and stuff off. They had two guys on the sawhorses. That's how we were set up—they would bring the litters in and set them on sawhorses. We had a wire running across the top that had IVs on it, and you'd just pull them as you needed them. People that worked in there were good. And you had to work fast.

I started working on this one guy with one of our surgeons, and you knew he was dead; he just had the color about him. We couldn't get anything going with CPR, so we cracked his chest, and the arch of the aorta had been shot off. So we, you know, left him and went over to see if we could help with the other guy—he was the pilot . . . and we lost him shortly after that . . . and I hadn't seen that many dead people all at once at any time I was there, except after a napalm raid one night. To see the five of them just kind of lying there . . . You hear "stacked up like cordwood." And they were. They really, really were. . . .

Anyhow. The three of us decided to go back to the OR and get some coffee. A chopper had come in, and somebody hollered, "They got the bastard that shot 'em!" and sure enough, the guys had gotten out of the chopper wreck fine, but as they came out of the chopper a sniper had shot them. And when they brought him to the door I hated him. There were three MPs there; two of them are holding the third one, who's just a young kid, and he's screaming and crying, "Leave me alone, leave me alone with him!" And that's the last thing I remember for about two days. They told me later that I just reached over and got my hands around the VC's neck, and I wasn't about to let go. So they knocked me out. When I came out of it there were two things that were very hard for me to accept. Number one, that I had the capacity to kill a human being—and God, I wanted to so bad. The other was that as a nurse, you know . . . And that just wiped me out.

Well, it was hard to get anything to drink there. The water was atrocious. You couldn't drink beer while you were working. The other thing was, you never knew when you were going to be working. I can't believe the amount of booze we consumed. But never when you were on first or second call—you didn't drink. So I started drinking colas, or pop, any kind of pop I could get my hands on. And even today I'll drink six, eight, ten a day. I've just never gotten over the habit.

I remember one thing that happened, about the second night we were there. We had the three-holers and had to walk about fifty yards to them, and Peggy and I finally got up the nerve to go out to one. We crawled. We were on our hands and knees the whole way, because our chief nurse had scared the hell out of us. She told us, "They know all of your names"—you know, just stuff that we were not prepared for. Anyhow, we're in there doing our thing, and all of a sudden we hear footsteps in the sand, whoosh, whoosh, and then somebody beating on the door. Both of us would have just liked to have died. Well, it was one of our nurse anesthetists who had been in Korea, and she wasn't afraid of anything. She came through that door, and I don't know whether we were ready to crawl down through the hole or jump her. I think I was more scared at that moment than I have ever been in my life! We decided well, we were not going to go walking out to that thing anymore at night, so we got these big tin cans from the mess hall, and everybody was using those at night. Well, that was noisy, so we started putting sand in them. But it all worked itself out, and what was funny—you know, you could be fairly modest when you get there; well, shoot, that didn't last long. No way.

The other thing I remember about Tuy Hoa is the dust. It was unbelievable. It was on everything. I forgot to pull my mosquito net down one day—I'd worked all night, and I was sleeping during the day. When I woke up, my shirt was literally covered with sand. It was like somebody had poured a bucket on me; it was on my face, my nose, eyes, everyplace. Also, it was hard to sleep when it was so hot. We ended up getting some kind of air conditioners in the operating rooms. We had trouble with the lights. If the generator went out, we didn't have any lights. So when we had a bunch of cases, we'd pull the batteries out of the jeeps and hook the lights up to those. We had to do something. Everybody was scared to death somebody was going to drop a flashlight in a belly some day.

I got so proud of the people I was with. There were so many people when they first came in, you thought, "Man, they're never going to make it." Well, in the beginning you didn't know what was going on either. But after the first two or three mass casualties and seeing some of the absolutely horrendous wounds that these people would come in with, it was just amazing how well everybody worked.

A lot of the stuff that I'm saying, I didn't come to realize it or I didn't let myself think about it until later. But the one thing I realized after I'd been there just a fairly short time, was you had to completely turn off when you walked out of that operating room. No matter how bad the stuff was that you had seen, you didn't think about it. You just didn't allow yourself. Because you'd have never been able to come and work on the next chopper load that came in. I think a lot of the problems that I had later were caused by dragging it all up when I came home. It was okay to think about it then because I wasn't going to see it again.

What I think is, most of us when we came home, you know, we got jobs—you've heard the expression "adrenaline junkie," and I know I was that. I went to work at night in the emergency room and soon after that took over as night supervisor of the hospital. This was down in Pittsburg. It was just go, go, go, and I think a lot of it was— yeah, the adrenaline rush was good—the busier you stayed, the less you thought.

This is stuff that I've only started putting together lately. It's funny the way it comes out. I think the saddest part is not being able to talk about it sooner. I finally went and talked to my folks last year after I'd gone through the rap group here. There was stuff that I did and stuff that I saw that I wanted them to know, and I asked them, "Why didn't you ever ask me anything? You never asked me one thing." Their answer—and it was perfectly valid—was, "You never talked about it except when you got mad and tore the paper up or threw something at the television set. We figured you would talk about it when you were ready." I asked my mother if she had noticed any change in me when I returned home. Her answer hit hard because I had not realized much of an outward change. She said, "Yes, you were much quieter except when you got angry, which you did often. You were like a very old woman at times, and your eyes that used to sparkle so much were blank, like they were dead." I'm sure that happened in a lot of families, and nobody knows what to do.

But anyhow, I left Tuy Hoa and went down to Nha Trang, and that was a bigger hospital; we had neurosurgery and some individual operating rooms there. I remember one patient in particular. He was a second lieutenant, West Point graduate. He had been hit by a ton of shrapnel, and one of them had severed his spinal cord, I guess; he was a quad. He was so up mentally it was just unbelievable. When they came in with shrapnel wounds we'd debride them, and then five days later we'd close them—what you call a DPC (delayed primary closure)—because all the wounds were considered dirty. This guy had a lot of them both front and back. And he was on a stryker frame—one of those beds that turn. Well, he had so many wounds that it would take us a year to get him done. He was on his stomach, facedown, and one of the doctors said, "Nick, why don't you get under this stryker, and let's get this guy done." So I was lying flat on my back. They took a sterile towel, and I cut two eye-holes in it—well, we were half joking and half serious—I mean, the guy couldn't get any dirtier. I lay underneath there and was sewing up all of these wounds. Well, he was laughing and we were laughing, and I always remembered that guy. I found out by a strange quirk about four years ago, he came home and was in therapy in the hospital; he married one of the physical therapists there. So that was neat. We only had him a few hours, and we never knew what happened to any of these people, and that was the hardest part.

Skipping ahead just a moment, but it ties right in with this. When Marianne and I went with a couple of the guys back to the dedication of the memorial last year, they had people with the guidebooks, where you could look up the names. And I had seven names to look up. So we went up and were talking to a woman who was a guide, and she said, "Were you ladies nurses there?" and we said, yes. She said, "Oh, my husband is a Vietnam vet. When were you there?" I said, "Well, I was there from February, sixty-seven to February, sixty-eight. Marianne was there in seventy and seventy-one. "Those are the two times he was there, and he was wounded both times!" She asked me what hospital I was at, and I said the 91st Evac at Tuy Hoa, and she said, "That's where he went. He was hit over at some rubber plantation." I said, "Ban Me Thuot?" And she started crying and said, "Yes, Yes." She said, "Where did you work?" I said, "The operating room." And she dropped everything she was holding and threw her arms around me. By then I was crying too, and she just kept saying, "Thank you. Thank you. Thank you." Just over and over . . . Well, that was sort of an indication of what was to come the next five days in Washington, D.C. It was beautiful, it really was. But the corker on the whole thing—she asked Marianne what hospital she was at. And she told her the 24th Evac, on the surgical intensive care ward. She grabbed Marianne. That's where he had been the second time. Talk about a total wipeout. My God! This was a guy—you know, I'm not sure I worked on him, Marianne's not sure if she did, but my God, it's the closest we had come. I know he went through our operating room; he had to because we were the only hospital in the area. So that was really something. Oh, God.

The whole five days we were wearing hats that told where we were in Vietnam, hoping to find other people. The guys would come up and put their arms around us and sometimes give you a kiss and say, "Thank you," and then turn around and walk away. Never knew that anybody cared or knew that much about the nurses being over there. But they just did it one after the other, and they were really something. *Those men made every moment there worth it.*

Back to Nha Trang. I think the thing I remember most about Nha Trang was Tet, the '68 Tet offensive. We spent many a night up on the roofs of the villas watching Puff the Magic Dragon come in and just shoot the hell out of Hon Tray Island, which was out in the bay. We would look back toward the hills with the choppers coming in with their rockets and tracers, and we'd have a case of beer on ice up there; we'd sit and cheer the good guys on. It seems ridiculous sometimes, but that's the way it was.

I have an audio tape of the night that Tet began. There was a motor pool right across the dirt road from where our hooch was, and some small arms fire came across the front of our hooch, which immediately had everybody's attention. Then we heard all this other stuff going off, and at first we thought it was firecrackers and they were just celebrating Tet. Then one of our dogs got out. Milly, who was our psych nurse, and I took out after the dog. On the tape you hear these people hollering, "You assholes, get back in here!" Well, we were going to get the dog, and we brought her back and tied her up inside. Then we got the call to come in because there were casualties, and it's a long crawl from our hooch to the operating room there. But nobody wanted to stand up.

Anyhow, we got to the OR. It was Monday night; it must have been about one or two in the morning. We started getting cases one after the other. We had a big yellow sheet of paper that the doctors used to keep them in some semblance of order. We were getting new casualties in all the time, and they'd have to scratch a name out, and after a while we just used numbers. Just used numbers. Then somebody that was worse off would come in, and you'd have to stick them up at the head. So it kept getting revised. I don't remember the time sequence because we were in there for so long it's hard to remember. . . . All I can do is give you bits and pieces of it. Every time we'd put a patient in a room, they'd bring another one over and lay him outside the door, so there were always people in the halls. By then we had learned that you don't bring somebody right off the plane into the operating room in most cases, which we'd started doing at Tuy Hoa. We learned that if you stabilized them first—got some lines in them, got some blood, ringers, whatever—they had a lot better chance of getting through the surgery. So, unfortunately, war teaches us a lot about techniques we use in civilian medicine.

I started out in the head room, and the neurosurgeon I was working with hated the Army. They had pulled him out of a private practice. He had had a pilonidal cyst or a hemorrhoidectomy done that day. And that guy stood up for five straight days in agony working on those patients. I probably did more neurosurgery in those five days than I've ever done in my life. Geez. Just got some horrid things in. We got the general's driver in; he'd been hit right off the bat, and something had just taken this whole part of his head off, just sliced it. That general sent a major down to sit in the operating room with him. He was there, as far as I know, on the ward until the kid was med-evac'd. And this neurosurgeon—above and beyond the call of duty—he worked well.

That's what it was time and time again. During Tet, I can remember ward nurses coming over, folding our linen for us, learning how to put our trays up. When we'd get out of there for a few minutes, we'd go over and start IVs, big lines and intracaths on people. . . . They were giving us Benzedrine somewhere along the line to keep us awake, because we had to operate. I remember the anesthesiologist had a checklist, and he'd pop one in your mouth and then mark off that you'd had it. The enemy kept coming from the airfield next to us toward the hospital grounds. They wanted the medications and stuff we had in supply. I was taking one patient from the OR to the recovery room, and I saw all these patients in little blue jammies running around with flak jackets, helmets, and rifles; they were working our perimeter. They used anyone that was able to move.

For the first day and a half or two days, I guess, the only food we got they brought in a cardboard box. On one end was half-cooked bacon, in the middle was toast, and on the other end was scrambled eggs. We didn't have any time to eat. As soon as we finished a case, we'd run the instruments back to the workroom, wash those real good, put the set together, wrap it, and get it ready to sterilize. After the first seven or eight cases, we didn't scrub anymore because we were just getting raw; we'd just wash off with some Betadine. Then, if you had the time, you'd run in and grab a piece of bread and throw some eggs on it, put some bacon on top of that, and then another piece of bread; if you were a smoker, it was really bad because you had to hold the sandwich, your coffee, and your cigarette all at once. The one thing I remember about the food was not that it was so bad—anything would have tasted good then—but you'd look down and your hands were all covered with blood. And I didn't care. I just plain didn't care. Somewhere around the third or fourth day, I remember going into the nurses' dressing room to change my scrubs because they were so covered with blood. I got some water to pour on me because my clothes were stuck to me with blood—underwear and everything. I could have pulled it off—I think I did pull some of it off—but I remember pouring water to get it loose. I was probably thinking like when you take a dressing off a patient—if you wet it down it doesn't hurt them as much. But that just seemed so gross.

The thing I think is probably a scene that's in my mind more than anything: I was coming out of the workroom, and the last two rooms in our operating room had tile on the floor, and it sloped a little bit. There were patients outside each room, and I came out of the workroom—and God, I wanted to take a picture so bad, and my camera was in the dressing room—but between the water coming out of the scrub sinks that was splashed down on the floor and the mud from outside and the blood from the people lying there—it was all just running down the hall. It really was. It was mostly water, but it was like something out of a nightmare. And that's a scene that I have flashed on probably thousands of times since then. It's just right there. If I were an artist I could draw an exact picture. Probably even put the color of the hair of the guy that was nearest to me on it. And for me, that just kind of told the whole story. . . . I don't know.

Another thing that happened during Tet—just to show you how stupid things can get. It was probably around the fourth or fifth day, when our supervisor came to me and said, "I want you to take one of the big brooms and go brush all the blood off of the sand outside the OR." I said, "You got to be kidding." She said "No, I'm serious, General so-and-so's coming." I said, "For crying out loud, if he's half a general he doesn't give a damn whether there's blood on the sand or not." We had had stretchers lined up there, and we'd strung a big wire to hang their IVs on. That's where we had some of our patients. She said, "If I have to give you a direct order, I will. Now take the Goddamn broom and go clean the sand." This was about three o'clock in the morning. I had to get out of my scrubs, get back into fatigues, boots, the whole works. I had one of those big industrial brooms, and I had to go up and down the whole front side of the operating room covering up all the blood in the sand. . . . Unreal. Totally unreal! You know, I had patients in there—there were patients still in triage—and I'm getting blood out of the sand. The general probably could have cared less. . . . Here we're in the middle of the Tet offensive, we've done almost seven hundred cases, and some screwball is worried about the blood in the sand.

My DEROS was the twenty-first of February, 1968. The day I was leaving, I was in the OR for a while. We weren't very busy that morning, and as I got ready to walk out, there were about ten or fifteen nurses, surgical techs, and doctors standing around. The double doors from triage opened, and two litter bearers came in, set their litter on the floor, and walked out. The little Vietnamese boy and girl on the litter each had both hands chopped off by the VC. I remember everyone was still just standing there as I walked out. What was there to say? . . .

Coming back home was something. You know, you've heard a lot about the Vietnam vets saying that it was different for them, and all that. Well, at first I didn't quite understand why. Then somebody explained it to me, and it made sense. When the fellows came home from World War II and Korea, they came home by boat. They had that decompression time; they could talk to their buddies. It's a time to get out some of the things that you've been through. Good detox time. I had been working in the middle of Tet and twenty-four hours later was sitting at McChord AFB, and I was just wound up like a ten-day clock.

But one really nice thing happened to me. I had bought a first-class ticket from Tacoma to San Francisco. I bought it while I was in Nha Trang, because I wanted to get on a plane to go home without waiting for this standby bit. I knew I was going to be processed out of the Army at that time, but when we got to the building in Fort Lewis it was six or seven at night. They said, "Well, it's too late; we can't process you out tonight. There's not enough time to figure out all the paperwork." I said, "Well, fine, then I'll get it done down at Oakland, because I'm leaving tonight." I go back down the stairs with my duffel bag and almost to the front door when a second lieuie came out and says, "Captain! Just a minute, we'll have somebody here in a few minutes for you." I said, "Well, don't roust anybody out. I can get out down at Oakland or the Presidio or someplace." "No, ma'am, we'll do it here." So this poor kid comes in and processes me out of the Army. And he said, "Are you going up to SeaTac airport?" I said, yes. He said, "Well, the taxi charges fifteen dollars. I'll take you for ten." I said, "You got it." So he and his buddy took me up to SeaTac.

I went in to the United desk, and there was a young fellow working there, and I told him I wanted to go to San Francisco. I said, "When does your next plane leave?" This must have been about eight-thirty or nine. He said, "Geez, we don't have one until twelve-thirty." Well, I guess my face fell clear down to the desk. He said, "Did you just come in from Vietnam?" and I said, "Yeah." He said, "Wait here," and he ran off down the hall. About two minutes later he comes charging back, grabs my suitcase, pack, and my duffel bag, and says, "Come on! Western's holding the plane for you." And he ran me down. They threw all my stuff right in the main compartment there, and when I got in, he said, "Have a nice trip and welcome home!" I was so tired; I hadn't slept for about two days, and it didn't all hit me right then. Well, the plane took off. We hadn't even gotten it to cruising altitude, and these two flight attendants came up with a bottle of champagne and said, "We'd like you to have this." I said, "Thank you very much, but if I drink anything I'll be flat on my can." She says, "Don't worry, the whole plane will carry you out to the waiting room." And they brought me a salad of some type, and everyone was so nice. Three or four other people sitting in first class came over and said, "Welcome home." So see, my coming home was different from what a lot of people went through. I've never forgotten that guy charging off to get me a seat on a plane and always wished that I hadn't been in such a foggy state that night, so I could have gotten his name and dropped him a line or something.

I wanted to stay in the Army, but my mom had been in a very bad auto accident. So I came home to help my dad take care of her. Then I went back in the Army eighteen months later. I wanted to go back to Vietnam. Well, my parents didn't want me to go, and my sister is the one that really put the screws to the whole thing. When I said I wanted to go back, she said, "You can't go back." I asked her why. She said, "Mom wouldn't answer the front door for the whole year you were gone because she was afraid she'd see somebody in an Army uniform there to tell her that you were dead." And you just can't do that to your family.

I would have loved to have gone back. I remember when the plane took off from Cam Ranh Bay, most of us were crying. This was right after Tet, three or four weeks after Tet, and I was thinking how guilty I felt that I was leaving. There was still so much to do. And I was leaving the best friends that I'd ever had in my life there. Then, when I got home and saw the stuff on the news and read the papers—that was so Godawful, I just couldn't believe it. I wanted to go back right away. It's like they say, "The best year or worst year of your life." But I knew what I could do as a nurse and as a person. I knew that I could stand up to whatever they had to throw at me, and I felt like I was really doing some good.

Chris Noel

ARMED FORCES RADIO,
1966 TO 1970

"Hi, Luv" was the familiar opening phrase of the radio program "A Date with Chris," a fifty-five-minute broadcast that went out on three hundred stations of the Armed Forces Radio Network from 1966 to 1970. Chris Noel was that voice in the headsets and radios of GIs all across Vietnam during those four years. She played top-forty songs, answering their requests, which came by mail; she became their girlfriend, sister, and mother-surrogate from back in "the World."

During Christmas of 1966, Chris made her first trip to Vietnam, where she entertained and visited men in the hospitals and units, and was to return many times during the next four years. During one visit to the 1st Infantry Division, "the Big Red One," she was officially designated an "adopted daughter" by its commanding officer, Maj. Gen. William DePuy.

Since the end of the war, Chris has been an indefatigable worker for the various issues concerning Vietnam veterans and their families.

This interview was conducted in May 1983, after the conclusion of the Vietnam Veterans Fair in San Francisco. The fair's title was "Peace is Alive—A celebration for healing the earth." I attended a panel of women veterans, on which Chris spoke, and the air was charged with emotion. Several of the men in the room were obviously moved at seeing her for the first time, having known her voice so intimately during their year in Vietnam.

LAST NIGHT, AT THE CONCLUSION OF THE VIETNAM Veterans Fair, the vets had a rap group. They asked me to say something, and I wasn't prepared to say anything at all. I tried to talk about the lack of communication my husband and I had developed over Vietnam, and veterans issues, but I never really finished it. What I really wanted to say was . . . "If the man closest to me doesn't understand, how the hell is anybody else going to understand?" . . . I also talked to the vets about the fact that I loved America and I didn't want to run away from America even though I have thought about it in my past. I talked about how the previous night, at the closing of the show, I sang "God Bless America" and asked everybody to join in singing with me—because America is our country, and we are Americans—and very few people sang with me. There were some guys in the back who said they did; there was a guy up front who stood up on his peg legs, took his hat off, put it in front of him, and was standing there as proud as he could be, singing "God Bless America" with tears streaming down his face . . . and Ron Kovic, in a wheelchair, watching with tears running down his face . . . and every-

body sitting there silent . . . The show is over, and it is
still silent. I am baffled; I don't know what the hell is going
on; I can't grasp it. I expressed all of this last night with
this rap group and told them, "You know, in Washington
(at the Vietnam Memorial dedication and salute) the guys
asked me if we could sing "God Bless America." The
Vietnam vets were all standing in this room, singing "God
Bless America" with tears streaming down their faces. But
last night very few of you did want to."

I can remember when I was in Vietnam and I couldn't
say "God bless you." I couldn't do it. . . . Something
happened, and it always disturbed me. . . . I always remember one case that just stands out in my mind. This guy
was dying and I was in the hospital, and they asked me to
come and see him, and the life was going right out of
him. . . . I'm standing there, and I couldn't say "God bless
you." It was like instead I went very numb and sort of in
a mini-shock, just standing there and feeling so stupid with
photographs in my hand, because I had been signing them
to the other guys. . . . And in the seventies, having a real
hard time praying and not understanding how come I
couldn't get a prayer out at night. Looking back and recognizing that I was smoking grass every night so that I
could sleep and I wouldn't dream and have nightmares . . .
and when I woke up in the morning I would be really angry
with myself because I hadn't said a prayer. And that has
really been haunting me.

So at the rap group I sat back and listened to see if I
could find out why nobody wanted to bless America. One
of the guys got up, and with his anger told me how he felt
about it. Another one came over to me afterward and said
that "God Bless America" was originally meant as a
prayer, and if I wanted to sing it as a prayer, he felt it was
okay, but if other people couldn't do it, I should accept it.
Then it dawned on me this morning that if I had had so
much trouble praying, then what was that all about? How
could there be a God that could let this happen? And what
is this about God being so loving, this loving God? There
is so much anger and hostility and hurt and frustration here
among the vets and all these feelings that are going down.

Did I make a mistake by singing "God Bless America"—
so that some of the people are angry with me because I
did, or they don't understand me because I did? I was
happy that I did sing it. There was all this diverse action
going on; it was exactly like the sixties, nothing different.
Not any different than those people who were supporting
their country, doing what was asked of them by their country . . . how some came back disturbed that they did, while
others came back with pride, standing up for who they are
and why they went over there.

I told everyone I have this confusion that I'm sitting
with, and I had this confusion in the sixties: I'm not a
hawk; I'm not a dove; I'm just a person who feels these
needs in talking to the guys all over the free world by radio
and being in Vietnam visiting them. But who am I? Where
do I stand with all of this? There I was: I'm in Hollywood
. . . I'm in Vietnam . . . I'm in glamour . . . I'm in war
. . . I'm hanging out with Dennis Hopper; I'm with the
military . . . torn, torn, torn . . . Where do I fit in this?

So over the last months, I guess I have really been trying
to figure out what I am still doing. I haven't changed. . . .
I'm still in that torn place, and I just want to mend that
gap, get that gap closer together. Being in this strange space
where I'm singing "God Bless America" and thinking, If
we want God to bless us and our friends, then why
shouldn't we want God to bless America? I mean, this is
what we have all been saying at this conference, "Peace,
love, and healing." But nobody wants to bless America.
"America," they are all saying. . . . So I'm standing there
thinking, "What's going on?"—exactly what I was doing
in the sixties. . . . I woke up this morning and realized it's
because most of them don't believe there is a God, so why
should they want God to bless America, when they don't
believe there is a God? Many guys have told me, veterans
from all wars, that when it comes right down to the nitty-
gritty, and someone is hit and dying and lying there in
pain, they scream out for their mothers, "Momma!
Momma!" And they scream out, "God, please let me die"
or "God, please don't let me die." So you see, when it

comes right down to it, they scream out to God and to Momma . . . you see . . .

Some of the things that happened to me in Vietnam involved my reactions to certain situations, and it disturbed me because I felt that I wasn't normal to react the way I did. One time when I was in an open jeep and heading down a road—there were several jeeps, and we were just going along—and I hear all this sniper fire; you could hear the cracks in the air, and I remember these guys said, "Get out! Get out!" And they picked me up and threw me in this ditch and jumped on top of me. There was this little ditch by the side of the road, and I remember I was thinking this is the first time anything like this had ever happened to me, and all I kept thinking was, "What's going on?" And these guys were suffocating me, you know? Then somebody says, "All clear," and my outward reaction was very silent getting back into the jeep, but inwardly it was, "Look what you did to me. Look how dirty I am. Look at me!"

I went down in a helicopter once. I knew we were in trouble, we saw the red lights go and the hydraulic system went out, and you could see the concern in the faces of the chopper pilot and copilot. I mean, I've been in so many helicopters, when something wasn't going right I knew it in a second. But it was like, I was joking, and that is what has always bothered me. I was joking when we were going down—it was like, trying to make light of it while everyone was turning white and getting scared. I was going, "Come on!" you know; I was being this cheerleader as we were going down! But deep inside I didn't think I was going to die; I really didn't think I was going to die, you see. When we went down we hit real hard. We lit right next to a VC village. It was really scary, and I remember the gunner ripped his hand—sliced it right open trying to pull that mounted weapon right off the side of the chopper—and them forming this little perimeter around us, and they were freaking out because they didn't want anything to happen to me.

I've been in a lot of therapy, and I went to this one woman about a year and a half ago in New York. . . . I was having a lot of troubles in New York. I was going through this fear thing. . . . I can't begin to tell you! . . . I was married to a Green Beret that I met in Vietnam, and he killed himself in 1969, right before Christmas. We were married less than a year. I didn't want to go back to Hollywood; I didn't want to stay in Nashville; I wanted to hide out, to be anonymous; I just wanted to be alone. I couldn't stand reading about it in the newspapers; I couldn't handle it. . . . It was just destroying me. What I didn't know—and I can look back now—is that not only was I going through my husband's stress, I was going through my own, and his suicide just devastated me. . . . I needed to talk about it, and I needed therapy. I needed friends and people, but all I could do was just push them away. I knew I wanted to leave New York and go to Texas. I had a country band, and it was pre–urban cowboy and pre–country music, so it wasn't hot in New York at the time. I was doing the clubs and getting skinnier and skinnier, and I was getting very introverted, even though I was performing.

So I was heading for Texas, and right before I left, all these things started going down. One was that I was in the subway and these five black girls came on and put a razor up to my throat. I'm sitting there, and they just walked up and said, "She thinks she is cute." And stuck this razor at my throat. Now what I did is what I always did when things like that happened to me. See, my husband used to put a gun to my head . . . and that was . . . I just sort of learned to not be there. I was there but I wasn't there, and I realize that I did a lot of that in Vietnam. . . . I heard a girl talking yesterday; she kept saying, "I can't watch guys in front of the memorial wall." They were hugging, and a lot of them cried, and a lot of emotions were coming out. She says, "I'm blocking it. I don't want to see it." She didn't want to acknowledge any of it. It was so painful for her to watch their pain. That's a lot of what I have experienced; I experienced it in Vietnam. . . . Some of the pain was so intense, those faces. . . . The faces just haunt me . . . and . . . So, anyhow, on the subway, that's what I did. I just wouldn't let my energy connect with any of their energy at all. It went right through them and past them, so that I became boring to them. They got no reaction from me, none. I guess that was the way I used to save myself when my first husband would flip out. He would just get crazy and pull the weapon out and stick it to my head and want me to do things and want reactions from me, and I learned just not to react at all.

Getting back to the fear thing that was happening to me in New York. I went to see this therapist, talking about this fear. It's not like I was afraid another girl was going to come up and put a razor to my throat, but I felt that something was closing in, that something wasn't right. So I started searching out a therapist and went to a woman who worked with Vietnam veterans. I didn't like her from the moment that I went to see her and never really thought she understood very much about what I was saying. But I went to her anyhow, paying a lot of money, just so I could have someone to talk to. I told her about some of these incidents, like my reaction to going down in the helicopter, and she says, "Don't you realize that was fear?" I looked at her, and I went, "You know, you're right. Not everybody goes to their death with a death mask on. Some people die laughing." . . . And I think that that was one of the things that hit me, that all those reactions were okay. In reality, when we die, we don't put a death mask on. We have this picture. . . . It's like, my dreams and my nightmares for so many years were about distorted bodies, you know, and you couldn't even get them in a casket because the casket couldn't fit the positions the bodies were in. They were all outstretched and stuck up in the air with one foot behind and one foot way up in front of them . . . and you had to have a huge casket to be able to fit the whole body in without cutting something off. You know, people don't die with their hands folded on their chests and their legs out in front of them and are just lying there dead like we see them in caskets in funeral homes; that's not how they die.

What I'm really doing is I'm trying to understand some things myself right now. I'm trying to put some things in perspective because I feel like I'm a tool . . . I do believe in God, and I believe that I've been put here for a reason. I mean, going to Vietnam was the easiest thing that ever happened to me in my life, the easiest. It was just like brushing my teeth—that's how easy it was for me. It came to me: do this—the doors were all open, wheew, there I was. I mean, I was one woman who did what I did; there wasn't any other woman that did what I did. My position was incredibly unique. Sure, I went on auditions; there were all these girls in Hollywood who went on this audition for a radio show—it was another job. I didn't think anything about it. I didn't even know what Armed Forces Radio was, but I got the job. It had nothing to do with who I was, what I looked like, my photographs and résumé. It had to do with my voice and a quality—that's all it was! And everything else just started following. I was just this pretty little sexpot in Hollywood, that's all I was.

I've changed a lot since then. In fact, one of the things that happened to me is that I lost my sexuality, and I didn't know that I had, but I did know that when I was married, the first time in particular, after I had the gun put to my head I was no longer interested in making love to that man . . . and in my second marriage, when I started receiving verbal abuse and constantly was told that he didn't marry me because of my brains, I no longer wanted to make love with that man. Something was very amiss. . . and it came to me. About three years ago, a management team had sent me to see Bernie Wayne, the guy who wrote the song "There She Is, Miss America." I wanted to put together an act; I wanted to start singing; I wanted to start working, making some money, getting visible. I wanted to do the things I knew how to do that I couldn't do anymore—I'd lost it! Anyway, there I was with Bernie Wayne, and I'm singing some songs for him and showing him my act and all this intensity and, I'm sure, the anger was coming out and the suppression and uptightness we get when we are in denial and in pain . . . He looked at me and says, "What happened to your sexuality?" I wanted to hit him over the head . . . but you know what? He was right. I looked at him and said, "I lost it, didn't I?" I started thinking, "What happened to it?" I realized that I lost it along the way somewhere—there was so much pain that I wasn't even sexy anymore. The other night when the Chambers Brothers were playing at the Vietnam Veterans Fair, and these guys were dancing; they were running down the hallways, and they were running back and forth and jumping around and going around in circles, and I'm thinking, "Wow, look at them. Look at these guys." At first I thought maybe some of them were losing it. Jack Mc-Closkey was standing there, and he says, "It's good. Let 'em dance, let 'em dance!" I just watched them, and I wondered how many of them felt they had lost their sexuality or sensuality.

It's so embarrassing for me to catch myself crying when I'm at these vet functions. . . . I go off in a corner and just stand there because I'm so alone. . . . I just stand there facing the wall in a corner, crying. Rather than biting my lip and just saying "I'm not going to let anybody make me feel like this. I'm not going to feel this! I'm not going to feel this!" And you hold it in and you hold it in, and all it does is eat you up. . . . See . . . And this comes from the fact that I've reached a place now where I can talk like this. I could never talk like this because I was so afraid everything I would say would sound stupid.

But drawing from all these life experiences I've had, sometimes I see somebody else doing the same thing that I am doing. Like this guy tells me he wants to leave the country, he doesn't want to live here anymore. I ask him if he's ever heard of the geographical cure. He says, "What are you talking about?" I try to explain to him that it has to do with how people are going from state to state and place to place because they think that things will be better. Just like in Vietnam—thinking when you go home it's going to be better. But when you got home it wasn't better. I mean, it was so bad for some of the guys that they went back to Vietnam! And the ones that stayed here, they left their hometowns because it would be better. Then they left that town because it would be better, and they are still leaving; they think it's going to be better. I told him, "Don't leave, 'cause whatever it is, you are going to have to find it right here. America is a great place. You just don't know it yet because you are not really here; you are still moving around.''

Wow! I'm right here in the Hilton hotel in the middle of one of the most radical cities in the United States, San Francisco—where it all started for the vets—the rejection started right here. This is where they got off the airplane, Travis AFB. This is where they were hit with "Babykiller, pig!" . . . A lot of them never left. They are still here; some of them are exactly where they were when they got here, haven't changed at all. . . . Before I came here, I said, "I wonder what it's going to be like in San Francisco. How many people realize that that's where it all started? How many really realize that this is where they experienced their first rejection, first biggie?" And we come here and talk about peace and love and healing and find a lot of people don't want to do that; they're in such a pained place, so they are just going to run off somewhere else. . . .

I'm really talking about where I've been—that's all I'm talking about. I couldn't talk about these things if I hadn't experienced them. But I see that very much happening. You know, I see vets across the country, and they move around—boy, do they move around—they are the most transient group of people I've ever seen! They will go to rap sessions—they hear something they don't like, they don't go back again. Somebody doesn't treat them the way they want to be treated, and they don't want to know them. It's real hard hanging in there, and it's really hard for me 'cause I get some rejection from the vets. I don't get a whole lot; I can get like, a hundred of neat stuff, good energy popped through right at me, but then one guy will come up with a zinger out of his anger or hurt, and it just totally shakes my rafters. I try to figure, "What does he mean? Is he right?" And I realize that it is his pain; it has nothing to do with me . . . but sometimes I might get it when I'm in a vulnerable time, and that one time overshadows the other one hundred. It's not any different than coming back from Vietnam and having that one in a hundred zap you . . . "Am I a babykiller? Why did they say that to me?"

I went to est training. I was trying to put a lot of pieces

together, so I went to est in New York a little over a year ago. You learn how much control you really have over yourself—like, you are not supposed to take any aspirin or anything. So I wake up with this splitting headache, and I've been dealing with them since at least 1970. I've popped the pills, I've gone to the doctors, I've been on the health kicks, I've fasted, I run every day, meditated, and still get the headaches. So there I am with this headache, and I say, "What do you mean, I can't have an aspirin?" I took two Excedrin and got guilty . . .'cause you make agreements, and they constantly remind you of what your agreement was. What I had heard that day were two words: *responsibility* and *integrity*. So the day I took my Excedrin, I went in, and I'm sitting there listening to all of this stuff, and I'm bored, and I'm pissed, and I don't know why I paid all that money—I'm broke. I'm sitting with these dumb people—I don't even like anybody . . . and finally I decide . . . I don't know, I raised my hand, and the next thing, I had the mike. I started telling everybody how pissed I was at them, I didn't like them, and how I didn't like America, I didn't like the people, and I didn't like the way the Vietnam veterans were treated. And I didn't like the way I was treated. . . . I didn't understand how I could be treated the way I was and Jane Fonda could be a hero. . . . I was angry . . . but I accepted my responsibility for the fact that I bought the trip that was laid on me. I bought the trip that I was crazy, dumb, weird . . . because I went to Vietnam. I heard it so much that I bought it. Nobody had sat down and talked to me about the fact that I have responsibility, I could make choices, I could buy the trip or not buy it. The people who didn't feel like you had to buy the trip were the silent ones; they never said anything. All I ever heard were all those telling me, "Buy the trip, you dumb blond. You're numb! You dumb blond, you're numb! You are stupid—you went to Vietnam!"

The therapist who told me I was experiencing fear in that helicopter was the same person who said she was glad that I showed her a picture of me with the Big Red One, firing a howitzer. Because then she understood that what I was doing in Vietnam was sending men off to their deaths and welcoming them home with maimed bodies. This is what my therapist is telling me, and I am freaking out! I paid her all this money, and she's sitting there coming out with these zingers. . . . She tells me this? It's amazing how a little thing like that can just really zap you.

Getting back to this particular est experience. Being able to stand there and admit out loud to all these people that I take my responsibility and realize that I bought a trip gives me the choice of continuing to buy it or to look at where that trip came from. Who laid it on me? What was their motive behind it? Why do they want to destroy me? What was the motive of that therapist sitting there and telling me I was sending men off to war to die? . . . What was her motive? Who is she?

Last night I heard this guy say, "Wait a minute, you are Americans, but you are not America." So he's coming from another space than where I am coming from. Rather than thinking, "Everybody's wrong, and everybody made me feel like this." When in reality it was a few people that made me feel like this. The majority kept very quiet. They were supporting me, and I didn't know it. When they did say anything, they said it quietly and lovingly, and I didn't hear it 'cause all I heard was the ones with the heavy stuff out there, all the negative stuff. I couldn't let that go and listen to these loving people who were so quiet, who didn't have any animosity toward me whatsoever. The other stuff was so violent and so strong; you look at all the news media of the sixties, and that is all you saw: the war in Vietnam and the violence in the streets and the rage and anger of America . . . citizens out in the streets. Not the ones sitting back home, quiet, going to church . . . waiting patiently for someone they love to come back home. Writing to them, sending them tapes, really supporting them, saying, "Come back, you will be okay. When you come back we will take care of you."

Lily Jean Lee Adams

12TH EVAC. HOSPITAL, CU CHI—OCT. '69 TO OCT. '70

Lily is on the National Board of Directors of Vietnam Veterans of America and chairs its Special Committee on Women Veterans. As a consultant on Vietnam veterans, she counsels, gives lectures, shares resources, referrals, et cetera. "I am hoping to find a research job in the fall; I need more diversity in my life. I'm finding myself consumed in the Vietnam veterans movement and need to break away. I'll always be involved, but not obsessed with it. I want to also utilize my master's degree in psych, which took me eight years after starting from rock bottom.

Lily lives in Atlanta, Georgia. She is married to a Vietnam veteran and has two children.

IT WAS IN MY JUNIOR YEAR OF NURSING SCHOOL WHEN an Army recruiter was invited to give us a little sales pitch on joining the Army. She was dressed in her uniform and showed us this wonderful film on being an Army nurse. She showed us the various hospitals and all the modern equipment (which we were lacking at the nursing school I was going to), so I was very impressed. After the film I asked her, "Do nurses have to go to Vietnam?" And she said, "No. Women volunteer to go to Vietnam. The Army does not send us; we have to volunteer to go." I talked to some of the other girls in my class, and they were saying I was crazy. There were two others that were willing to sign up at any minute, and I thought about it. I wanted to get out of New York City. I was born and raised there, hated it, and I saw this as an opportunity of getting out. I had always wanted to go to San Francisco, always, and figured that would be the quickest way of going. I also wanted to go to Hawaii. I'm Eurasian—half Chinese, half Italian—and had gone through a lot of discrimination in New York. I wanted to go to a place where everybody was like me. I thought, well, the Army sounds adventurous—

I'd be meeting people from all over the country, it would be a very interesting life for me, and it is only two years out of my life.

I was antiwar. I wasn't a protester because I was so involved with nursing school that I wasn't really aware of the political aspect that was going on in the country, but I didn't think it was fair to send young men to Vietnam, and I wanted to do something for them in some way. I felt when they came back from Nam I could take care of them. Then there was Kennedy: "What can you do for your country?" I was part of that era, of that generation, and I thought, "This is perfect. I can serve my country, I can express my feelings about the war, I can get out of New York, and there's a lot of adventure. Plus it pays for my last year of nursing school." So I thought, "What the heck." I signed up.

During officer basic training I started to notice that every class concentrated a lot on Vietnam, so I approached the major who was head of the program and asked, "Why are you always concentrating on Vietnam?" She said, "Well, you will probably go; eventually you will go." I said, "No, I'm not. I'm stateside." She said, "Oh, my dear, no. More than likely you will go to Vietnam." I said, "Look, my recruiter told me that women have to volunteer to go to Vietnam." She said, "Oh my, she must have made a mistake. Maybe she was misinformed." I was fit to be tied. We graduated and I was assigned to Fort Ord, California. I drove from Fort Sam to California, and when I hit Monterey, I thought, "Am I in heaven or what? This is God's country!"

I was assigned to orthopedics and learned that as a lowly second lieutenant I didn't get to work day shifts too often. On evening shift I covered two wards, which was the equivalent of sixty guys, give or take. I had to prep them for surgery and then took care of them post-operatively. I would say 50 percent were from Vietnam that had repeat orthopedic surgery. They were on what was called "medical hold" before they could be discharged to civilian life. The other half were men who were injured during basic, because there was a lot of basic training going on at Fort

Ord. I took care of two patients who had a pact, who didn't want to go to Vietnam. One guy put his leg up on a chair, and the other stomped on it, ruined his knee for life.

The guys who had just come back from Vietnam were the most critical psychologically. You would think they were on speed, they were so high and so hyper. They would sit by my desk and talk the whole night long. At five in the morning the cannon goes off—it's reveille. I'd watch the time for them, because after a while I realized that these guys really freaked out when they heard the cannon—it sounds like a mortar attack. I'd say, ''In five minutes the cannon is going to go off. Now take it easy, it's just a cannon.'' But it didn't matter, they would hit the floor and just shake. Night shift seemed to be the worst shift. I'd hear some screaming and a lot of funny noises in the ward, and it would be the guys having nightmares. I'd sit with them and talk to them, and they'd tell me war stories and how they'd come home and find out their wives were cheating on them, or they'd come home and their family wouldn't want anything to do with them. In the morning when I had to wake them for rounds, I'd have to go to the foot of the bed, grab their big toe, and shake it a little bit, because if you get too close to them or shake them by the shoulders, they would have their hands around your neck within two seconds . . . they were so combat-ready. And it took them a really long time to come down from that.

One afternoon my roommate came in looking really down in the dumps. She said, ''Lily, I have some bad news.'' I said, ''You got orders.'' And she said, *''We* got orders.''' In the beginning I wanted to fight it. I learned you could do what one nurse did—she made believe she had swallowed a bunch of Librium and played the game of being half-crazy and suicidal, and they discharged her. Another one got pregnant. Various women were doing various things so they wouldn't have to go to Nam. . . . I didn't want to do any of that; I didn't feel right doing that. I remember going to work the next day, and the chief nurse, who was a really nice lady, came down and put her arm around me, and we walked down the ward. She said, ''I'm really sorry. We've got a shortage of nurses as it is. They really need nurses in Vietnam, more than they need them here at stateside." I appreciated the fact that she saw me as an individual, she understood how I felt about the war, and she did try to do something. So I accepted it. I went to New York, back home, just to kind of hold on to my roots. Met a couple of people who had gone to Woodstock—I had missed Woodstock by two days—and regretted not being a part of it, but I was very excited because of what was going on in the country. Things were happening, and I was part of the generation, even though I was in the military. This was before the military was a negative concept in the eyes of the country.

So . . . I got to Travis AFB. The flight was at four o'clock in the afternoon—it is amazing how I remember such details—and there was a group of women that I recognized from Fort Sam. There must have been about ten of them. I got very angry because I was thinking, "It's not only me; there are others that are going too." I went down the row, "Did your recruiter tell you that you didn't have to go to Vietnam unless you volunteered?" "Yes." Every single one of them.

We were all getting brave and ready to go when they announced that something was wrong with the plane, they were going to ship us to a motel. So we go into the motel, and there is this one room where everybody is having a big party. We went over thinking that we might as well join the party, had a couple of drinks, and decided we'd better get a good night's sleep. Another woman and I shared one room and were in our pajamas getting ready for bed when this guy walks into our room and sits on the bed. He's talking to me, and I said, "Excuse me for a minute." And we walked out. We went next door, where there were two other women. The four of us against one, you know. After about half an hour of deciding how we are going to do it, we all went back, and the guy was gone. Apparently he got the message that we weren't interested. And that was basically my first introduction to "Well, you are an Army nurse aren't you? I mean, don't you get laid all the time?"

We arrived in Hawaii, the place I had wanted to go since I was a kid—very ironic. Had a cup of coffee, and we all go to the ladies room. I am thinking, "Right now I could walk out. Even though I'm in uniform, I could still do that—I could desert." I learned when I asked the stewardess if she would get me a pillow that she could care less about the women on board. We got the same chicken dinner five times going across the world. Then we look out the window, and there is this beautiful country, Vietnam. It was green and lush, and I couldn't comprehend that there could be a war in such a beautiful place. The plane lands, and I'm one of the first to get out—after seventeen hours I just wanted to get away from the plane. They opened the door, and I could smell this awful smell and feel the high humidity and heat. I backed off! I didn't want to go out there. . . . It was just instinct. So we go down the stairs of the plane, and I heard the roar of a crowd. I looked over and there are all these guys, and they seemed aged. They didn't look like nineteen or twenty; they looked about forty. That is the first thing I noticed. Our plane was their Freedom Bird for home, and that was what had caused the roar.

We got into an area called 90th Replacement. There was Gayle, who was in the same platoon as me at Fort Sam, and Sue, who had this red hair and was engaged to a paraplegic who had been one of her patients. The three of us became kind of chummy, and we were hoping to be assigned to the same area. The guys back at Fort Ord had said, "Ask for Vung Tau. It's on the beach—you'll love it." But it seemed every place I asked for, the chief nurse said they didn't need nurses there. "We need three nurses for Cu Chi." And I had a funny feeling that she was sizing us up, but right away Gayle, Sue, and I say, "Hey, let's go, and we'll stay together." So we volunteered, so to speak, for Cu Chi.

The next day we got on a C-130. Gayle, Sue, myself, and a couple of guys we had met at 90th Replacement. I had become friends with one man who was married with a kid; we had talked a lot, and we were happy to be stationed in the same area. On the way, I asked him what his insignia was. He said, "We are responsible for spraying areas to kill off weeds so that Charlie can't hide in the jungle." I thought, "What an awful assignment. . . . You go to Vietnam to kill weeds?'' All of a sudden I see all the troops on the floor, and I'm going, ''What's going on?'' He says, ''We've just been hit.'' I thought, ''I didn't even know. . . . The Army never taught me how to take care of myself. God, I could be killed so easily without this knowledge.'' I was very angry realizing that these guys on the floor had a better chance of living than I did because I didn't know anything. I'm thinking, ''Yeah, Lily, you are in the war.''

At Cu Chi we were asked by the chief nurse, ''Where do you want to be assigned?'' I said, ''Intensive care'' because I'd had a taste of intensive care at Fort Ord and I just loved it. ICU was a challenge for me. She said, ''It looks like we may be able to send you to ICU, but we are going to put you on orientation. You are going to spend a few days in the emergency room, then we'll send you to recovery room ICU, and then we'll put you in ICU.'' They wanted to give us a feel for what a patient goes through from the minute they land in the ER to when they leave.

So I go to the emergency room and they orient you to where all the equipment is, and it's getting confusing because there is so much to remember. But they don't expect you to do too much, just observe. I hear a chopper land, it becomes very windy, and they bring in a couple of stretchers. One guy I remember has no legs; they are blown off from the thigh down. I'm standing there looking at this, and I'm totally freaked out. I see a lot of blood, I see mud, his green fatigues all soaked, and I'm seeing a lot of action. The doctors and nurses are doing, like, ten thousand things at one time. One is cutting off his uniform, another is starting up an IV, another asking his name, rank, serial number, that business. Blood is going up, and all this is happening at one time. I couldn't even look to see what was going on in the second stretcher because what I was seeing was so horrifying to me that I was, like, in a hysteria. You know, here I am, the nurse and shit—I couldn't even do anything; I was frozen there. I thought, ''The next group that comes in, I'm going to do something. I'm going to prove to them that I'm just as good a nurse as they are, and I'm going to prove to myself that I can get over this shit and do it." Well, they bring in two or three more stretchers, and I'm still in shock—and ready to cry, thinking, "This isn't me. I'm usually the active one." So I'm doing a lot of in-fighting within myself, saying, "What's wrong with you?" And my other half saying, "Jesus Christ, look at this!" All of a sudden I hear a doctor say, "I need someone to hold his head." Everybody's busy, and he repeats, "I need someone to hold his head." I just walked in there—because he defined to me what was needed—and positioned his head while the doctor did manual resuscitation with the bag. After that I was able to finally get in and function. So I felt that I had taken a big step.

I was sent to recovery ICU and reported to the head nurse. She said, "We've got this POW over there. I want you to take care of him. He's got real low blood pressure, has lost a lot of blood." . . . I was angry that they would assign me to someone as low as an NVA. I thought, "I'm not over here to take care of a POW!" I took the vital signs and took over from the nurse that was taking care of him. He was so sick that he had a nurse assigned just to him. I remember that nurse was a male nurse, and he gave me the report. They were using a CVP, which measured the spinal pressure, and that was fairly new to me. The Aramine, which was the medication to regulate the blood pressure, I was familiar with. He told me how much he was dripping, and then he picked up on my anger or uncomfortableness and said, "Do you feel comfortable enough to take care of the patient?" I said, "Yeah, I'm okay as far as the nursing aspects of it, but I didn't come here to take care of gooks." He said to me, "I know how you feel, but just look at it this way: this is a North Vietnamese POW. He's got lots of information, and if you can keep him alive long enough to be able to talk to our interrogators, you're probably saving hundreds of men—there is that possibility. We think that this guy is really important." So I thought, "Well, I can deal with this guy now." I took his blood pressure and I'm working on him for two or three hours, and I start becoming attached to him, like any nurse gets attached to her patient. I'm with him for maybe six or eight hours when Intelligence comes in. I'm thinking, "If they start slapping him around, I'm going to start slapping them around, because I worked my ass off to keep this guy alive." They are interrogating him in Vietnamese, and I'm watching this kid—he is nineteen years old, answering everything. I said to the interrogator, "Oh, come on, he must be lying to you." And he says, "No, this story goes along with that POW over on the other side of the ward. This guy knows that we caught both of them, and if they lie, we will know it." I was listening to all these questions, kind of enjoying learning more about my patient. Then I said to the interrogator, "Would you do me a favor? Would you ask him a question from me?" And he said, "Sure, what is it?" I said, "He doesn't have to answer if he doesn't want to, but I'd like to know how he feels about the war." The interpretation was—and he looked straight at me when he said it—"If I could march in Hanoi, like you are marching in Washington, D.C., I would be doing it."

After orientation they assigned me to the new ward, which was half burn patients and half amputations. Some men had second-degree burns from sunburn. Most of the guys didn't wear shirts, as it was so hot out there, and I remember one guy who got an Article 15 for having a sunburn. We got in guys that had phosphorous burns, which, if you don't neutralize, will go straight through your body. So you have to keep their wounds neutralized, which was really hard to keep up with when you had other patients. The head nurse used to sit on her butt and do nothing. The ward master was in and out, and if you asked him, he would help you move the patient, but the guy was always on his way somewhere, so he was no help. We had a Vietnamese woman who set fire to herself with gasoline when she learned that her GI boyfriend was going home without her after he promised that he would take her with him. Took care of some Vietnamese kids with phosphorous burns, that had urine that was as red as wine. . . .

The other half of the ward was amputations with complications. If you were a clean amputee, you were off to Japan in no time flat, but if you had complications you needed to stay in the evac hospital until you were stable enough to go. One guy had lost one leg, and this night he was in tears. I said, "What's going on? Let's talk about it." He said, "I'm engaged to get married, and I don't know if my girlfriend is going to want to marry me." I was in a dilemma. I didn't know what to say to him. Sue was on duty with me, and I told her about it. She said, "Just tell him that if his girlfriend is as wonderful as he says she is, she will probably go ahead and marry him." I said, "Sue, do me a favor. You talk to him. You are there—you can vouch for her." So she went over and talked to him. He wrote her a letter about a month later, and she said, "Yes, he managed to not only get married, but he walked down the aisle on his prosthesis, without any crutches!"

I remember another GI, with both legs gone, and he'd say, "My legs hurt." And I'd explain to him about the "phantom leg," about the nerve endings. I would lift the sheets and say, "The legs are not there." You have to get them to acknowledge that, because they get psychotic after a while. He would look straight at the TV set and totally ignore me and tell me his legs hurt. He needed a lot of encouragement and love, so I spent a lot of time with him. I'd tell him, "As soon as you get home, they are going to make you do exercises and things with your stumps. You'll get prostheses, and you will be able to walk upright on them. You will be able to do a lot of special things on them, like skiing and parachuting. There is a lot to look forward to." It must have been about two weeks later, not very long, and I get a letter from this guy. He is doing really well; he is thanking me and telling me all of his plans. I realized that even though I wasn't getting any feedback from him at the time, I didn't fail him; I managed to succeed. And that kept me going.

I worked there about four months and found myself getting more and more depressed, because I'd learn that these guys would have a girlfriend at home; I would learn that they were married and had a two-month-old baby at home, that their mother was sick. All this information I was picking up from my patients was getting me down. I decided that I had to get out of there and thought, "emergency room," because you only deal with them a few minutes and out the door they go. But then, Sue had this plan to go to Hawaii, meet her boyfriend and get married, and then ask to get out of Nam. She thought being married would help her to get a transfer. She needed support so I went with her to Hawaii. She got married the next day, and I spent the rest of the week by myself. I sat there two days in a row, just watching people being ordinary people: no rifles, no war, no noises.

I bought a Hawaiian ring that I had seen while I was hanging out at Ala Moana shopping center. I asked the lady, "What do you usually engrave on this kind of ring?" She said, "It's basically a wedding ring, and people put their names on them. You can put anything you want on it." So I said, "Peace and Love." And she said, "Oh, that's very beautiful." She asked why it was so important to me, and I told her about myself. She said, "You must come to dinner. Here is my name and phone number; call me when you have some time." I was very impressed by that, but I never called her because I felt embarrassed that I had poured my troubles out to her. She'd heard enough about Vietnam.

I was at Fort Derussy and a fire engine went by, and I hit the dirt—it sounded like the red alert siren—and then I thought, "Oh shit! How embarrassing." I get up and am brushing myself off, and here are two guys laughing hysterically, and I'm really angry at them. They were laughing because they were enjoying the scene—they had been in Vietnam. So they asked me if I had seen Oahu yet, and they gave me a Cook's tour: "You deserve it." They drove me around the island and then stopped at the Crouching Lion restaurant and said, "We want to treat you to dinner." We had a delicious dinner, and they told me about their time in Nam and how somehow they were lucky enough to get out after four months. They told me how they had had one huge party when they got to Hawaii, dancing in the streets and celebrating, and I was enjoying their joy at being out of the war zone. I told them that I didn't want to go back to Vietnam. They were saying,

"We know it's not the safest place to be, but those guys need you." They were building me up to go back. I was saying, "You know, I could desert." The next day they called and asked if I was still thinking about deserting and promised they would write to me and told me, "just keep the faith." At the airport I'm thinking, "All I have to do is turn around and go to the ticket office and get the hell out of here." And there is a captain who is eyeing me. I'm thinking, "Does he know what I'm thinking? Am I producing a profile?" He kept his eye on me till I got on the plane. I thought, "I wonder if there are people like me that show it right outside that we don't want to go back—that we are thinking twice about it." Sue cried the whole way back. She wrote to her senator and left two months before me—off she went. . . . She was gone.

When I was first in Nam I had met a guy from one of the wards who had an arm in a cast. One day he came in and said, "Come out for a minute." I got out, and before me are about ten guys in jeans and shirts and hats, as if they had just walked off the plane from Woodstock. I was going, "I can't believe my eyes. Who are you?" I learned that they were in a dog scout unit and they lived on the other side of the compound. "You've gotta come over to our place—black lights and day-glo posters, just like home." People are walking down the ramp, medical people, giving a second look, saying, "Where the hell did you come from?" They got that response from everybody and got a little joy out of it. It was like a little bit of home. So this guy says, "When is your next day off?" I say, "In two or three days." He said, "I'll pick you up at seven o'clock, walk you over and back. Don't worry about it— we'll take good care of you." I wanted to take advantage of this opportunity to get out of the hospital area. These guys were sensitive to my feelings; they were saying the right words, and their actions seemed sincere enough to me, so I thought, "Well, why not take a chance?"

He shows up on my day off, and I'm in jeans and T-shirt. He's going, "Wow, you look a hell of a lot better in those clothes." We walked across the compound, about a fifteen-minute walk. I learn he's from New Hampshire and we like the same music, and I'm getting more comfortable. We go into the hooch. There are posters all over the ceilings and walls, and all these guys are dressed in their civilian clothes again. Led Zeppelin is going as loud as it can go—it was party time. Everybody moves over for me to sit down, and I'm just hypnotized looking at all the posters. The guys aren't talking about the war; they are talking about the stupid stuff: harassment, funny things, food, and music. Plus they were talking about home, what was going on—it was wonderful. I was away from the people that talk medicine. I would go there and be very depressed and exhausted, and they would start talking about everything but Vietnam, and within an hour or two I was feeling as good as they were. I continued to go there for four or five months until everybody got short enough that they were all going home. And when they left, I thought I was going to die.

Another part of Vietnam was the chief nurse, "the Virgin Mary," who came around to harass me because I was fraternizing with EMs and I should be dating officers. I told her I was going to date anybody that I damn well please—it was none of her business who I was dating. Then years later, looking back, I realized she could have used that precious time to help me out with the patients. But no, she's got to come around and harass me about who I am dating. She harassed me because my love beads were showing, because I put ribbons in my hair, because I was out of uniform. We knew that our guys appreciated women. To prove a point: you get these guys with their legs blown off and in agony and in fear, and in the middle of all this they stop and look at you and say, "God, you smell so good." And they said it to me all of the time. So I made a point to wear perfume. Or, "God, you look beautiful." And I would think, "Yeah, that is important to them." Here some of these guys were dying, and in the middle of it they'd say, "Oh, you smell good!" A lot of the women went out of their way to look good for their patients, just because they wanted to do that much more for them.

Well, I think I have covered enough about Vietnam. I still haven't decided which was worse: my experience in

Vietnam or my experience coming home. We landed at Travis AFB, and from there we were sent out to the real world through Oakland Army Base. I spent the evening there, and the next day we were processed out. They gave us our pay, and that was it. They didn't provide transportation; they dropped us like a hot potato.

I had a friend in Monterey that I got in contact with, who was expecting me to come home. We decided to spend some time together, and I wanted to do that because Monterey was like home base for me. I took a bus to San Francisco and called my friend in Monterey, who knew some people that could give me a ride down there. So I called them, and we decided to meet at the bus depot. He asked me to describe myself, and I said, "I'm in this green uniform." He said, "You're what?" I said, "Yeah, I just got in from Vietnam." "Oh, shit . . . you're at the bus terminal, right?" "Right." He said, "Why don't you go into the ladies room and change." And I am not understanding it because my thoughts on the flight home were, "Wait until I tell everybody what happened, how we really helped our guys and all the wonderful things that we did as medical people." But then things began to make sense to me. In the bus terminal, people were staring at me and giving me dirty looks. I expected the people to smile, like, "Wow, she was in Vietnam, doing something for her country— wonderful." I felt like I had walked into another country, not my country. So I went into the ladies room and changed.

When I got to Monterey I took the uniform out of my suitcase, threw it to my friend and said, "Burn it." My friend said, "What about your medals? Don't you want to save your medals?" I said, "Fuck my medals." Now I regret it. Not that I want the medals, but it's something, you know, something that I was proud of, and nobody has the right to take that pride away. . . . That's what happened. The attitude took the pride away. I'm changing my feelings about it now; I am proud of having been over there, and I'm not afraid to admit that now—and I'm sorry I don't have that jacket.

I applied for work at the VA hospital. I remember I

wanted to be around Vietnam veterans. The director of nurses was impressed with my résumé, that I was an Army nurse in Vietnam, and I expected her to ask what nursing was like over there. Instead, she wanted to know about the dope addicts, and I'm saying, "What dope addicts?" She said, "Well, we understood there has been a lot of dope addiction in Vietnam—there is heroin, you know, and people are taking it like water." It hadn't hit my brain yet what was going on—that they were making a big deal about dope addicts in Vietnam. They weren't talking about the guys that had their legs blown off, you know, the guys that had their faces blown off—no, they're talking about dope addicts. Dope addicts were, like, a real small percentage. The media made a big deal about it, and the people needed that reason to attack the war even more. I was really angry. I had to have a physical exam before starting work, and the woman who was doing the EKG said to me, "We don't like working here. They are all old men, and it's very depressing. You don't want a job here." And I don't know why this woman said that to me, but I was so lost and confused that I thought, "Well, there must be some reason for this. Okay, I will take her advice." So I didn't take the job.

Instead, I went to another hospital, a large hospital in San Francisco. I was interviewed by the director of nurses, who again was impressed by the résumé, and who again asked me about the dope addicts. I took the job and was in charge of about thirty-five patients. I had one aide, who was not allowed to write in the charts, so I had to do her charts and my charts. Sometimes, if I was lucky, I'd get an LVN, who was allowed to write in the charts and save me some time, but her hands were tied on other things that my corpsmen could have done in Vietnam. I was the type of nurse that, when a patient was going into surgery the next day, I felt it was very important to sit down and talk to them and educate them, as well as alleviate their fears. That was my belief as a nurse. I was always behind in my work, and I said to a nurse after about two months, "This place is overworking me. I'm not getting the cooperation and staff I should be getting, and I'll be damned if I'm going to give poor nursing care.'' So I quit.

I had some money saved from Vietnam and thought I could live off that. Around that time I was starting to hit the bars, looking for Vietnam vets, drinking a lot, and doing things that weren't really me. I was caught up in the bar scene. It was better than sitting home and crying all the time. If you are an attractive woman, you can go into a bar and there will always be somebody to talk to. You can depend on it. And that's what I needed, another human being to talk to.

I had met a GI in Hong Kong when I was on leave, and we became chummy. He came to see me a few times in Vietnam, and it was a nice friendship. Around Christmas-time I sent him a card, 'cause I could remember how it was at Christmas in Vietnam. In fact, even today, Christmas is depressing for me. Our letters became serious, and we agreed to continue our friendship when he came home four months later. Then I thought maybe the full-time job had been too much for me right off the bat, maybe I needed to just take a part-time job. So I went to work at a blood bank, taking plasma. Most of the donors were alcoholics and deadbeats out of the Tenderloin district. I really got attached to the guys, and looking back on it, it was like being around Vietnam vets, 'cause they were guys dealing with a very depressing situation, being very lighthearted and joking around just like the guys did in Vietnam. And when I'd walk through Union Square on my way to work, all the drunks would go, ''Hey, Lily, how are you?'' They were all my guys from the blood bank.

My friend came back from Nam, and we decided we would stick together. We thought the same way, saw the world the same way, and we became very supportive of each other. He went back to the company he worked for before he was drafted, and they said they had no job for him in California, but would he go to Houston, Texas. He asked me, ''How would you like to go to Houston?'' and I said, ''All my life I've wanted to be in San Francisco, and now we're going to Houston?'' But I thought, ''What the hell, I'm killing myself in San Francisco.'' . . . I had

this gut instinct that this guy was going to keep me going.
So we went to Houston. Considering all the crazy things
that were going on, our relationship was very sound, and
we went ahead and got married.

My husband was pretty well settled in his job, and I
decided to work at the Texas Medical Center with Dr.
Cooley, the famous heart surgeon. They were impressed
by my background and put me into the recovery room ICU,
which is similar to Vietnam's recovery ICU. There was a
lot of action; I liked it. But I started to realize that it wasn't
like Vietnam. There was a lot of competition between doctors and nurses, doctors and doctors, et cetera. There would
be a cardiac arrest, and everybody would want to be in on
it. In Nam, if someone was under cardiac arrest, whoever
was there with the patient did it. And whoever was good
at it. . . . For example, there was a sergeant there who
was good at heart massage, and he was so good at it, that
everyone would move out of his way so he could do it. . . .
There wasn't the hierarchy. I was going to classes to learn
more about the EKG monitor, and I wasn't able to retain
anything new. I became very self-conscious of my nursing
skills; I was losing my confidence. I would know this person was going into cardiac arrest and yet not be sure. . . .
In Nam, you know, if I said, "Something's wrong with
this patient—I'm not feeling right about him," the doctor
would work on him until we figured out what it was. A lot
of it was gut feeling, and we all trusted each other's gut
feelings. Yet here, in intensive care, I'd say, "Something's
wrong. I can't pinpoint it, but something is wrong." And
I'd get, "Well, I haven't got time to check this out. If you
can't figure out what it is . . ." This was the attitude that
I couldn't understand.

I'd wake up in the morning and cry. I didn't want to go
to work. My husband would say, "Well, go find another
job." I'd say, "No, I've gotta work at this job until I figure
out why I can't do what I could do in Nam." I thought
maybe I should get out of intensive care and find something
simpler. So I worked for a small hospital as a float nurse,
and I got along fine at that job; it helped my ego. When
people heard that I had lasted for eight months at the other

place, they were saying, "How could you last eight months? The usual rotation is about three." So I started to feel a little bit better.

My husband was transferred back to San Francisco, and I got another job as a float nurse there. I found myself getting bored after a while because I was perfecting each floor: I was dying for a challenge. I was finding that I wasn't happy with nursing anymore; it was different.

I decided to get pregnant, and when I was seven and a half months pregnant, I had toxemia of pregnancy. Went into the hospital, found out I was carrying twins, and one died in uterus. They did an emergency c-section because I was having water in the lungs and my kidneys shut down. I had high blood pressure—something like 280 over 180. They told me the twins died because they had a problem among themselves, that my problem was unrelated to theirs. They did autopsies and found that one twin had some liver damage so . . . we accepted that. I went into a heavy depression. I felt that life was really against me, and for eight months did nothing but sleep twenty-one hours a day. My husband couldn't get me out of it. A neighbor of mine who had had a miscarriage started to bang on the door and made me get out of bed. Then she would come in and dance all around and make me get dressed and drag me outside and tell me that life is really beautiful . . . "Look at the sunshine and the flowers." . . . and she got me out of it.

My husband and I put our heads together, and he encouraged me to go to school. I had the GI Bill. At the same time, we found out that I was pregnant with my daughter Erika. I went to junior college and discovered that I loved it. I loved geology, art, all the subjects that had nothing to do with nursing. I had a lot of fun, got good grades, and decided that psychology might be an interesting subject to get involved in—it appealed to me a lot. I went to San Francisco State University and decided to get my master's in psychology. Got pregnant again with my son, Daniel. He was okay when he was born, but we started having problems with him when we started putting him on solid food at four months. At eight months he had to have a temporary colostomy; 50 percent of his intestines did not have nerve cells. When he was twelve months old, he had 50 percent of his large intestine removed and had what you call a pull-through, with the good intestine pulled down and attached to his rectum. . . . We are still having medical problems with him. His surgeon explained that this condition was familial, but we could not find anyone in either of our families that suffered from this defect. A geneticist friend of mine explained that this condition was genetic. It wasn't until later that I realized the key to this problem could be Agent Orange.

Around that time, my husband had a job change and we were transferred to Hawaii. I thought it was a good omen, because Hawaii would be a real healthy place for Daniel, and I needed a change in geography. And Hawaii has been a healthy place for my son. We moved there during the Iranian crisis, the summer of 1980. Within a few months there were three or four helicopters flying around where we lived, and we didn't live near the military bases. They started to freak me out. I'd run outside, and my kids would run out with me to find out where Mommy was going. I found myself figuring out if it was going to be a good case or a bad case, how to be ready, then realizing after a while that they weren't going to land because I wasn't in Nam. . . . I had seen the ads about the vet center, so I called them, and a guy answered and I felt, "If he rejects me, I don't know what I'm going to do." But this guy said to me, "You're a woman vet—we've been looking for you!" That made me feel really good. So he connects me to a woman, and I said, "Are you a Vietnam vet?" She said, "No, I'm a psychologist and I work here." I said, "I want to talk to a Vietnam vet that knows what I'm talking about." I felt insulted. But then she was saying the right things to me, and I started explaining that we had just moved there and the choppers were getting to me . . . and she had me crying, and I was becoming hysterical on the phone. It was the first time I allowed myself to do that type of thing. She said, "Come down." I said, "Well, I have a child." She said, "You can bring him down, come down." . . . And I said, okay, but I didn't. Then the helicopters would come around, and I'd call and talk to her some more. It took five phone calls before I felt comfortable enough to go down.

Around this time the whole issue of the hostages quieted down, and they were coming home. I remember seeing them getting into cars and seeing all the yellow ribbons and the wonderful reception they got, and I was really happy for them. Then, in the middle of all this, I said, "Wait a minute. What the fuck did they do? They sat around for four hundred and some odd days reading magazines, and I worked my ass off three hundred and sixty-five days saving lives. . . . They are getting this homecoming, and I got beat up, psychologically beat up." I was so angry! I found out that a lot of other vets were flipping out too, and that I was one of many that were going to the vet center on account of the incident.

That is when I got some one-to-one counseling and talked into doing a rap group. They promised that they would make it safe so that the men would understand where I was coming from. The men were very understanding. It's just that when it came time for me to talk about my experiences, they tended to change the subject. I just got the sense that they couldn't deal with it. Because you've got to understand, these guys would see their buddies all messed up in the field, and they'd say good-bye to them on the helicopter and not know what happened to them. I ended up taking care of the end results. . . . And I don't think they wanted to know about that.

It was around the same time—it was a coincidence, or I think that sometimes things are supposed to happen—there was an article in *Ms* magazine. "Please write to Lynda Van Devanter. She is interested in research on women veterans." I didn't have the time to write her a letter, you know, with these two kids running around, and there was so much I had to say, so I did a tape. I told her a little story here and a little story there and basically about what it was like to be a woman in Nam. About a week or so later I got a call, and it was Lynda calling from Washington, D.C. She said, "I got your tape, and I could have done the same exact tape." We talked and talked, and I started to realize that it wasn't me, wasn't my personality, I wasn't getting crazy, it was something that was happening to other people and that it was a reaction to our experience in Nam. I was getting validation that what I had gone through was real heavy shit, no matter what the combat vets said, and my reaction to it was normal. Then she said, "Well, how is your health?" And I said, "Oh, okay, I guess. I had acne and a breast tumor a couple of years after I came back. I had a couple of twins that died, and my son was born with a birth defect." She says, "Have you ever heard about Agent Orange?" I thought, "Oh, my God, that's the answer to all this stuff. Now it makes sense to me."

Then I read in the newspaper how a bill in Texas had been passed to create research in Agent Orange and to provide genetic counseling. I thought, "This is what we need," so I sent the article to the representative of our state. She wrote me this beautiful letter back. She had, in fact, just come back from Texas, had met Representative Shaw, who was the person who had pushed the bill through, and she was very interested in it. She got a powerful senator to introduce the bill. I was introduced to another powerful person, who said, "Do you know what you are doing?" And I said, "No, I don't know what I am doing. . . . Lobby, what is that?" I thought, "Write a letter to your representative, they introduce the bill, and that was it." I didn't know anything. Apparently it was a very important bill to this man too, because he sat with me and told me what to do and who to see. I lobbied people, and he kind of helped out. . . . Apparently I was able to convince a lot of people to support the bill. I had wonderful support from representatives and senators I had lobbied with—not promising me anything, but really looking into things. After hearing my testimony—I talked about the health problems, about my knee joint pains and how I've yet to find a doctor that can help that out: I can't climb stairs, I can't hike or bike, and my family is so used to stopping at the top of a flight of stairs to wait for me, they just automatically do it now. And about how Daniel got adhesions and one third of his small bowel was removed, and he almost died on us—the bill passed.

It was very hard for me. There was a lot of stress, but there were a lot of people that helped me out and kept me going. And my husband supported me the most—he was just wonderful. The governor signed the bill, and I had a chat with him—changed his view about Vietnam vets, and he told me that. I got involved with other vets and coordinated a ceremony at the National Cemetery at Punchbowl on Memorial Day for all those killed or missing in Vietnam. Found myself getting very involved with the issues and feeling good about it. Then the governor's office got in contact with me. They had received a letter about the national salute for Vietnam veterans to be held in November. He asked me to be the state coordinator. I said, "I'd love it, because I'm thinking about going and I don't want to be in that parade by myself."

I remember the first night at the salute in Washington, D.C. The delegation arrived, and I said, "Let's go see the memorial." A couple of guys said, "Yeah, let's go," and this was twelve midnight, but everybody was just so up and excited about being there and having the salute happen to us. We went to the Wall and found two candles burning, reflecting off of it, and it was just beautiful. The next day we went down to Arlington Cemetery, and there were Vietnam vets all over the place. They were all in jeans and fatigues and beards, and it felt wonderful to be there. Jan Scruggs got up, and we were all cheering (this was supposed to be a solemn ceremony). We were getting dirty looks from the World War II vets. Then Weinberger got up and said, "If we have to get into another war, we are going to make sure the country backs its soldiers." And everyone went nuts again. I remember thinking, "It's starting to happen. . . . Good stuff is starting to happen." Then they had the twenty-one-gun salute, and everybody was hitting the bushes, and we were all laughing because part of the humor of it was the fact that everybody else was doing the same thing.

That night at the Wall was interesting for me. I looked at it and thought, "I don't know any of the names except one." It was too dark, and I thought, "I'll never find his name." Then I did a real strange thing. I rubbed my hand along the memorial and ran from one side of it to the other, and by the time I got to the other end I was totally hysterical and crying. I realized I hurt for *all* of them. . . . I felt I took care of *all* of them. I got so much out. It was dark, and nobody could see me. It was the first time I really got the mourning, the grief, out. I bought a big candle and brought it back for my friend that died over there. I found some women's names. I saw people leaving things at the memorial, pictures and what have you. So it was really up and down for me. I did want to meet someone that served with me at the 12th Evac, I wanted that. I wanted to find someone from the dog scout unit, just to say, "If it wasn't for you, I would have gone insane those first few months." And I wanted to run into some patients of mine who were amputees to see how they were doing. And my wishes came true. I was hanging around VVA for a while with Lynda, answering phones. It was totally crazy, and who gets on the phone but this woman that I had known at the 12th Evac, Sharon. I said, "Please come up." And she said, "Well, I was thinking about it, but now that you are there, I'm going to come." I was so happy to see her!

When we had the unit reunions at the hotel, there were Vietnam vets all over the place. Various men would come up to me and say, "Hey, you're a nurse!" They'd give me this big hug and say, "I love what you did for me. It doesn't matter if you were my nurse or not; I loved you!" We were getting all of this positive feedback, meeting people who knew what it was all about, and I was in seventh heaven. Then this guy comes up to me and says, "Where were you at?" I said, "The Twelfth Evac." And he said, "When?" I said, "Sixty-nine and seventy." He said, "I got hit in seventy. I knew that I knew you!" And I said, "I just don't remember you." He said, "I know you, I know you! You took care of me!" I said, "Well, maybe I did." So we talked for a while, and then he put his cane down and said, "Watch this," and he walks down the hallway. I'm looking at him and thinking, "So, he's walking." He turned around and came towards me, and I said,

"Are you a double amp?" He said, "Yes, ma'am." And he told me his story. And I hugged him and said, "You are beautiful!" This whole scene was going on between us like a love scene. Even though I didn't remember him, I thought, "It really doesn't matter. I need this guy, and he needs me. . . . Just enjoy it." He had this half-dead rose in his boonie hat, and he took it off and said, "This is for you." I still have it. It is something one of my patients gave me. A gift back. Then he pulled out an apple and cut some slices off, and I guess it was the best-tasting apple I ever ate. And we didn't want to part. It was wonderful.

Toward the end of the celebration, everybody was going home, and I thought, "I have yet to find a dog scout," and I was a little disappointed. So I went back to the memorial for one last visit. I walked along, then stopped, and there was a picture of a dog scout with his dog, a big color picture. I just sat there and cried. This was the one I wanted. . . . It wasn't a live human being, but it was my connection, and I got that. I knew that this guy was here, and I wrote down the panel number, so that the next time I go there I can pay my respects to him for the way his unit took care of me.

Then I came home, and my husband and my kids met me. My husband said, "Welcome home," which, I found out later on, was a common response. And I said, "Yeah, I'm finally coming home." They each had a lei. My daughter had a red flower lei, my son had a white flower lei, and my husband, a blue one: red, white, and blue leis . . . So I guess that's . . . I want to end on a happy note.

Working round the clock during the Tet Offensive—Cheryl Nicol and fellow nurse take a break.

Above: Cheryl Nicol, newly arrived in Vietnam, at 91st Evac Hospital, Tuy Hoa, 1967. *Below:* Cheryl, the day she left Vietnam, February 1968.

Above: *Chris Noel dances with the troops during a show.* **Below:** *Chris joins a patrol in the jungle.*

Above: WAC Doris Allen checks out a grenade launcher. *Below:* Doris at the "ladies' powder room."

Right: Army nurse Lily Adams "out of uniform," Cu Chi, 1970. *Below:* Triage, 12th Evac Hospital, Cu Chi, 1970. Photo by Lily Adams

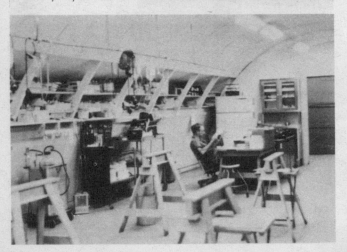

Red Cross worker Penni Evans in the Vietnam mud. **Inset:** *Penni visits tankers of the II Field Force.*

*Penni Evans (**right**) and Margi Ness place a "Donut Dollies" wreath at the Vietnam War Memorial, Washington, D.C., November 1984.*

GLOSSARY

APC: Armored Personnel Carrier
Article 15: nonjudicial punishment for minor offenses
ARVN: Army of the Republic of Vietnam
Bird Dog: light observation aircraft
Boonies: boondocks; field duty
Chinook: medium transport helicopter
CIB: Combat Infantry Badge
Delayed Stress Syndrome: an early term for PTSD
Delta Delta: code for Doughnut Dollies; from NATO phonetic alphabet for letter D
DEROS: Rotation date from overseas station
Doughnut Dolly: Red Cross woman on duty with armed forces
Dustoffs: helicopters for medical evacuation
Grunts: infantrymen in ground combat units of Army and Marine Corps
Hooch: hut or tent used for housing military personnel
Hump: infantrymen's term for carrying pack and armament up and down hills
IG: Inspector General
Kickers: employees of civilian flight companies hired to drop supplies into inaccessible areas; packages were "kicked" out an open aircraft door.
Klick: kilometer
LURPS: Long Range Reconnaissance Patrol members
MACV: Military Assistance Command, Vietnam
Mama-san: older Vietnamese women; derived from English word "mama" and Japanese word "san"
MARS unit: Military Amateur Radio Service; way to communicate to stateside free of charge

Montagnards: aboriginal hill-dwelling people of Indo-China

MOS: Military Occupational Specialty

MUST: Mobile Unit, Self-contained Transportable

NCOIC: Noncommissioned Officer in Charge

NLF: National Liberation Front

NVA: North Vietnamese Regular Army soldiers or units

PTSD: Post Traumatic Stress Disorder

R&R: Rest and Recuperation

ROKs: Republic of Korea army soldiers

Sapper: infiltrator, particularly carrying high explosives

Short-timer: a person with 30 days or less left before DEROS

SRAO: Supplemental Recreational Activities Overseas (American Red Cross). *See* Doughnut Dolly

Stand-downs: Line unit's return to base for short rest period

Steel pot: helmet

Strac: strict adherence to military rules and regulations (from Strategic Army Corps)

Tet: Vietnamese New Year; same as Chinese lunar new year

Tet Offensive: country-wide offensive in early 1968 by Viet Cong and North Vietnamese

Two Shop: Intelligence section; from G-2

VC: Viet Cong

VVA: Vietnam Veterans of America

VVAW: Vietnam Veterans Against the War

XO: Executive Officer

APPENDIX

The intention of this appendix is to illustrate the broad scope of women's experience in Vietnam, thereby recognizing the service of every woman who went there. Although a good deal of effort was made to represent all services, agencies, and companies, the information provided by them was very uneven. The resulting appendix cannot be considered comprehensive in any sense, and I am certain there have, regrettably, been omissions, particularly in the area of civilian organizations.

Special thanks to Mr. Shelby Stanton for sharing his extensive research regarding women in the U.S. Army.

U.S. ARMY
FEMALE PERSONNEL IN VIETNAM

This listing include women in organizations credited with Vietnam service, and thus includes components stationed in Thailand which were eligible for the Vietnam Service and Campaign ribbons for direct support roles.

ORGANIZATION OR UNIT	STATION*	FUNCTIONS
WAC Advisory Element, Republic of Vietnam Women's Armed Forces Corps Training Center	Saigon	Cadre instruction and liasion
WAC Detachment, U.S. Army Vietnam (USARV)	Long Binh	Administrative holding detachment
Headquarters, Military Assistance Command, Vietnam (MACV)	Tan Son Nhut	Personnel, aides, finance, administration
Headquarters, U.S. Army Vietnam (USARV)	Long Binh	Personnel, data processing, supply
U.S. Military Equipment Delivery Team, Cambodia (MEDTV)	Phnom Penh	Clerical, special project (classified)**
U.S. Military Assistance Command, Thailand	Bangkok	Protocol, personnel, aides
U.S. Army Support, Thailand, Special Staff	Bangkok/Sattahip	Secretarial, administrative
U.S. Army Medical and Dental Activity, MACTHAI	Bangkok	Administrative, personnel
133d Medical Group	Korat	Personnel
44th Medical Brigade	Long Binh	Personnel, supply
U. S. Army Medical Command, Vietnam	Long Binh	Personnel, supply
43d Medical Group	Nha Trang	Personnel
55th Medical Group	Qui Nhon	Personnel

ORGANIZATION OR UNIT	STATION*	FUNCTIONS
67th Medical Group	Da Nang	Personnel
68th Medical Group	Long Binh	Personnel
2d Surgical Hospital	Chu Lai	Nursing, personnel
3d Field Hospital	Tan Son Nhut	Nursing, administration
3d Surgical Hospital	Dong Tam	Nursing, clerical
5th Field Hospital	Bangkok	Nursing, personnel, supply
7th Surgical Hospital	Cu Chi	Nursing
8th Field Hospital	An Khe, Nha Trang	Nursing, supply, personnel
9th Field Hospital	Nha Trang	Nursing, supply, personnel
12th Evacuation Hospital	Cu Chi	Nursing, administration
17th Field Hospital	Qui Nhon	Nursing, supply
18th Surgical Hospital	Quang Tri, Pleiku	Nursing, personnel
22d Surgical Hospital	Phu Bai	Nursing, administration
24th Evacuation Hospital	Long Binh	Nursing, administration
27th Sugical Hospital	Chu Lai	Nursing
29th Evacuation Hospital	Can Tho	Nursing, personnel
31st Field Hospital	Korat	Nursing, administration, supply
36th Evacuation Hospital	Vung Tau	Nursing, administration
45th Surgical Hospital	Tay Ninh	Nursing
51st Field Hospital	Tan Son Nhut	Nursing
67th Evacuation Hospital	Qui Nhon	Nursing, personnel
71st Evacuation Hospital	Pleiku	Nursing
74th Field Hospital	Long Binh	Nursing
85th Evacuation Hospital	Phu Bai, Qui Nhon	Nursing, supply
91st Evacuation Hospital	Tuy Hoa, Chu Lai	Nursing

ORGANIZATION OR UNIT	STATION*	FUNCTIONS
93d Evacuation Hospital	Long Binh	Nursing, administration
95th Evacuation Hospital	Da Nang	Nursing, personnel
311th Field Hospital	Phu Thanh	Nursing augmentation
312th Evacuation Hospital	Chu Lai	Nursing augmentation
523d Field Hospital	Nha Trang	Nursing augmentation
1st Logistical Command, Special Services	Long Binh	Club circuit, entertainment, administrative
1st Logistical Command, Headquarters	Long Binh	Protocol, personnel, plans, food service, information, provost marshal security (female)
4th Psychological Operations Group	Tan Son Nhut	Propagandists, film production
Saigon Support Command	Saigon	Personnel, depot administration
Cam Ranh Bay Support Command	Cam Ranh Bay	Personnel, female security search, supply
Qui Nhon Support Command	Qui Nhon	Protocol
46th Special Forces Company Augmentation	Lopburi	Nursing, escort, clerical, aides
525th Military Intelligence Group	Tan Son Nhut	Intelligence analysts, female interrogation

*Typical; hospitals were often mobile

**Manning tables indicates parachutist capability

SOURCE: Shelby L. Stanton, who derived information from National Archives Vietnam Records Group 338, specifically manning and distribution tables of the organizations concerned.

U.S. AIR FORCE

*This organizational listing of C-141 aeromedical evacuation units defines bases from which nurses flew into Vietnam on medevac missions. There is, however, no way to verify that every unit had women assigned as nurses, or as flight attendants.

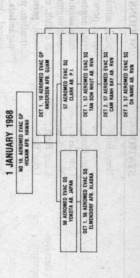

ORGANIZATIONAL DEVELOPMENT OF THE
MAC PACIFIC AEROMEDICAL EVACUATION SYSTEM*
(10th AEROMEDICAL EVACUATION GROUP)
DURING THE PERIOD
1 JANUARY 1968 THROUGH 31 DECEMBER 1969

1 JANUARY 1968

NO 10. AEROMED EVAC GP
HICKAM AFB. HAWAII

DET 1. 10 AEROMED EVAC GP
ANDERSEN AFB. GUAM

57 AEROMED EVAC SQ
CLARK AB 1 P.I.

DET 1. 57 AEROMED EVAC SQ
TAN SON NHUT AB. RVN

DET 2. 57 AEROMED EVAC SQ
CAM RANH BAY AB. RVN

DET 3. 57 AEROMED EVAC SQ
DA NANG AB. RVN

56 AEROMED EVAC SQ
YOKOTA AB. JAPAN

DET 1. 56 AEROMED EVAC SQ
ELMENDORF AFB. ALASKA

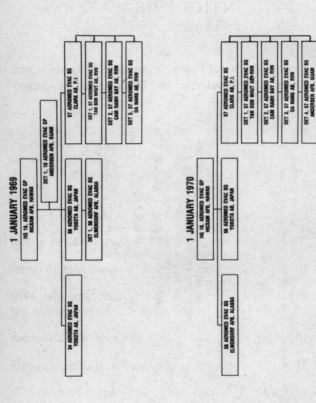

1 JANUARY 1969

HQ 10. AEROMED EVAC GP
HICKAM AFB, HAWAII

- 34 AEROMED EVAC SQ
  YOKOTA AB, JAPAN

- 56 AEROMED EVAC SQ
  YOKOTA AB, JAPAN
  - DET 1, 56 AEROMED EVAC SQ
    ELMENDORF AFB, ALASKA

- DET 1, 10 AEROMED EVAC GP
  ANDERSEN AFB, GUAM
  - 57 AEROMED EVAC SQ
    CLARK AB, P.I.
  - DET 1, 57 AEROMED EVAC SQ
    TAN SON NHUT AB, RVN
  - DET 2, 57 AEROMED EVAC SQ
    CAM RANH BAY AB, RVN
  - DET 3, 57 AEROMED EVAC SQ
    DA NANG AB, RVN

1 JANUARY 1970

HQ 10. AEROMED EVAC GP
HICKAM AFB, HAWAII

- 56 AEROMED EVAC SQ
  ELMENDORF AFB, ALASKA

- 56 AEROMED EVAC SQ
  YOKOTA AB, JAPAN
  - 57 AEROMED EVAC SQ
    CLARK AB, P.I.
  - DET 1, 57 AEROMED EVAC SQ
    TAN SON NHUT AB, RVN
  - DET 2, 57 AEROMED EVAC SQ
    CAM RANH BAY AB, RVN
  - DET 3, 57 AEROMED EVAC SQ
    DA NANG AB, RVN
  - DET 4, 57 AEROMED EVAC SQ
    ANDERSEN AFB, GUAM

Source: USAF Historical Research Center

FEMALE NAVAL PERSONNEL WHO SERVED IN VIETNAM OR CONTIGUOUS WATERS, 1962 to 1973

STAFF OFFICERS:

Commander Naval Forces, Vietnam—Saigon-based staff

Commander Naval Advisory Group, Vietnam—Saigon-based staff

NURSES:

Headquarter Support Activity, Saigon—Saigon Station Hospital:

20 Navy nurses between 1965 and April 1966

Naval Support Activity, Da Nang—Da Nang Station Hospital:

95 Navy nurses between November 1966 and June 1970

Bureau of Medicine and Surgery, Southeast Asia—Vietnamese medical facility at Rach Gia:

7 Navy nurses assigned to AID between 1965 and August 1966; specific locales not identifiable

USS *Repose* (AH-16)—Hospital ship positioned off northern South Vietnam:

145 Navy nurses between December 1965 and May 1970

USS *Sanctuary* (AH-17)—Hospital ship positioned off northern South Vietnam:

141 Navy nurses between October 1966 and December 1973

Military Sea Transportation Service, Pacific—logistic ships off Vietnam:

16 Navy nurses between 1965 and August 1966

Navy records show that there were also civilian nurses serving in Saigon (HQSUPACT) from 1965 and beyond.

SOURCE: Edward Marolda, Vietnam Archivist
Operational Archivist Branch
Naval Historical Center
Washington, D.C. 20374

WOMEN MARINES IN VIETNAM

Women Marines in Vietnam normally numbered 8 or 10 enlisted women and 1 to 2 officers at any one time for a total of about 28 enlisted women and 8 officers between 1967 and 1973.

The first woman Marine in history to be ordered to a combat zone was M/Sgt. Barbara J. Dulinsky, who volunteered for Vietnam duty and reported, as ordered, to the Military Assistance Command in Saigon on March 18, 1967. She was followed by six others that year. Generally, they were to work with the Marine Corps Personnel Section on the staff of the Commander, Naval Forces, Vietnam. The section provided administrative support to Marines assigned as far north as the DMZ. Later, another officer billet was added, with three women serving as historians with the Military History Branch, Secretary Joint Staff, U.S. MACV. For the most part the women Marines worked in Saigon, but on occasion duty took them outside the city and as far north as Da Nang.

At first, the enlisted women were quartered in The Plaza, a hotel-dormitory, two to a room. Women of other services and several hundred men also called the Plaza home. By spring 1968, the enlisted women were moved to the Billings BEQ, located near MACV Headquarters and Tan Son Nhut air base. Generally, the women officers were billeted in Le Qui Don, a hotel-like BOQ. Company grade officers were usually assigned two to a room; WMs and WAVES sometimes billeted together.

Source: "A History of Women Marines 1946–1977" by Col. Mary V. Stremlow, USMCR (Working Draft, March 1979).

Provided by: Reference Section, History and Museums Division
Headquarters, U.S. Marine Corps
Washington, D.C. 20380

USO UNITS IN VIETNAM

During the Vietnam conflict USO maintained centers at the following locations:

Saigon

Da Nang (China Beach, Freedom Hill, Golden Gate, Liberty Center)

Cam Ranh Bay (#1, Aloha, Coffee Bar)

Chu Lai

Di An

Nha Trang

Qui Nhon

Tan Son Nhut

Vung Tau

An Khe

Can Tho

Binh Thuy

During the years 1967–1969 USO's Vietnam operations peaked—17 centers were staffed by hundreds of dedicated employees and volunteers.

Source: Barbara Johnson, Director of Personnel

RED CROSS UNITS IN VIETNAM

Red Cross units were in the following locations. Some units were open a short time; others ran the whole ten years.

Cam Ranh (A.F. and Army)	Phan Rang (A.F. and Army)
Qui Nhon	Cu Chi
Da Nang	An Khe
Nha Trang	Camp Eagle
Phu Bai	Phu Loi
Lai Khe	Dong Ba Thiu
Phuoc Vinh	Binh Luy
Long Binh	Bear Cat
Bien Hoa	Dion
Pleiku	Dong Tam
Saigon	Quang Tri
Chu Lai	Black Horse
Tuy Hoa	Long Gaio
Camp Enari	Xuan Loc

Source: Jeanne M. Christie

AMERICAN FRIENDS SERVICE COMMITTEE

The AFSC carried out two kinds of programs in Vietnam. One, which was called the VISA Program, involved young people—mostly American—working in a variety of institutions in and around Saigon, such as the Buddhist School for Social Services. The other was a service project in Quang Ngai which involved a day-car center for refugee children, and a rehabilitation center providing artificial limbs and braces for amputees and other handicapped civilians. In support of the Quang Ngai program, the AFSC maintained an office in Saigon which also kept in touch with a wide variety of Vietnamese and expatriates about conditions in Vietnam.

Both programs began in 1966. The VISA program ended in 1968. The child day-care program concluded in 1974, while the Rehabilitation Center continued under AFSC auspices until April 1975, when the new PRG government took it over. The AFSC continued to visit and provide material assistance from some years afterward, although the last resident expatriate staff left in October 1975.

About 10 young people were involved in the VISA program and half of them were women. Approximately 50 expatriates worked for some length of time at the Rehabilitation Center, and about half of them were also women. The day-care center staff were all Vietnamese.

Tasks ranged from administrative, through volunteer work with Vietnamese social services agencies, to medicine and physical therapy. Altogether about thirty expatriate women were involved, largely Americans, but including a few British and Japanese.

Source: David Elder
          AFSC
          1501 Cherry Street,
          Philadelphia, PA 19102

427

CIVILIAN CONTRACTORS
EMPLOYING WOMEN
IN VIETNAM

Philco-Ford Facility

Vinnel Corporation

Raymond International

Morrison-Knudson

Brown and Root

Pacific Architects and Engineers

Alaskan Barge and Transport Company

Source: Shelby L. Stanton

ADDITIONAL AGENCIES AND COMPANIES EMPLOYING WOMEN IN VIETNAM

GOVERNMENT AGENCIES:
U.S. State Department
U.S. Information Services
U.S.A.I.D.
C.I.A.
Army Special Services

CIVILIAN AGENCIES:
International Voluntary Services
Catholic Relief Services
Tom Dooley Medical Foundation

AIRLINES (employing women who flew in and out of Vietnam):
Continental
Flying Tigers
Pan American
TIA
World

ABOUT THE AUTHOR

A painter and filmmaker, Keith Walker was a teacher of both subjects for several years. He lives in Oakland, California, and now devotes full time to writing.